Body Language

Body Language

Representation in Action

Mark Rowlands

A Bradford Book
The MIT Press
Cambridge, Massachusetts
London, England

MIT Press books may be purchased at special quantity discounts for business or sales promotional use. For information, please email special_sales@mitpress.mit.edu or write to Special Sales Department, The MIT Press, 55 Hayward Street, Cambridge, MA 02142.

This book was set in Stone Sans and Stone Serif by SPI Publisher Services, and was printed and bound in the United States of America.

Library of Congress Cataloging-in-Publication Data

Rowlands, Mark.
Body language : representation in action / Mark Rowlands.
 p. cm.
"A Bradford book."
Includes bibliographical references and index.
ISBN-10: 0-262-18255-6 (hc : alk. paper)
ISBN-13: 978-0-262-18255-3 (hc : alk. paper)
1. Representation (Philosophy). 2. Externalism (Philosophy of mind). I. Title.

B105.R4R69   2006
128'.4—dc22

2006044903

10 9 8 7 6 5 4 3 2 1

For Emma

'Tis writ, "In the beginning was the Word."
I pause to wonder what is here inferred.
The Word I cannot set supremely high
A new translation I shall try.
I read, if by the spirit I am taught,
This sense: "In the beginning was the Thought."
This opening I need to weigh again,
Or sense may suffer from a hasty pen
Does Thought create, and work, and rule the hour?
'Twere best: "In the beginning was the Power."
Yet, while the pen is urged with willing fingers,
A sense of doubt and hesitancy lingers.
The spirit comes to guide me in my need,
I write with confidence: "In the beginning was the deed."

—Johann Wolfgang von Goethe, *Faust*

Contents

Acknowledgments

This project has spanned life in four countries, Ireland, England, France, and Australia, and so, as you might have gleaned, has been rumbling on for some time. During that time, I have greatly benefited from conversations with: David Chalmers, Andy Clark, Paul Coates, Jerome Dokic, Paul Griffiths, Adrian Haddock, Dan Hutto, Susan Hurley, Richard Menary, Erik Myin, Alva Noë, John O'Regan, Kevin O'Regan, Elizabeth Pascherie, Karola Stotz, Josefa Toribio, Steve Torrance, and Rob Wilson. And thanks to Larry Shapiro who read the entire manuscript for MIT Press, and offered some trenchant and very useful comments.

I owe special thanks to John Sutton, who arranged for me to spend six weeks in Sydney, at exactly the right time of year, where I was able to combine my two great interests: lying on a beach and thinking about philosophy. The two conferences on embodied cognition that John organized at that time provided a valuable opportunity to test the central arguments of this book, and without the excellent feedback I received there, I would no doubt still be scribbling away. My thanks to all involved.

Thanks to the University of Hertfordshire, and to my colleagues there, for providing an excellent environment in which to pursue research. Thanks to Tom Stone at MIT, who supported this project from the word go, and thanks also to Judy Feldmann.

This book was supported by the Arts & Humanities Research Council (AHRC).

Finally, as ever, my greatest thanks are to Emma Rowlands, for her love, support, and, of course, putting up with me while I finished this book.

1 Representation: The Word and the Deed

1 The Word

This book is about the *problem of representation*: how is it possible for one item to represent another? We might equally call it the problem of *content*: how is it possible for an item to possess another as its content? Or the problem of *meaning*: how is it possible for one item to mean another? Or the problem of *intentionality*: how is it possible for one item to take another as its intentional object? Or the problem of *aboutness*: how is it possible for one item to be about another? The central contention of the book is that the problem has been exacerbated, perhaps to the point of insolubility, by a critical, yet largely unnoticed, assimilation: the assimilation of representation to the category of the *word*. Because of this the problem has almost always been understood as one of relating inner to outer—of relating an inner representing item to an item that is *extrinsic* or *exterior* to it in such a way that the former can be about the latter, or have the latter as its content. Understood in this way, representation has seemed deeply problematic, even mysterious. However, I shall argue that it is not this sort of problem at all. Representation has nothing, *essentially*, to do with the relation between a representing item and something extrinsic to it. Accordingly, it has nothing essentially to do with the connection between the inner and the outer. The hope is that divesting the problem of representation of this connection to the inner–outer divide robs it of at least some of its mystery. What was a latent problem becomes a patent problem, and, therefore—maybe, just maybe—not so much of a problem at all.

Words sit on a page. The words that comprise this book are *internal* to the book in the sense of located spatially inside it. Their presence in the book is something that has *genuine duration*: they begin at a reasonably determinate time—when first inscribed—and end at a reasonably determinate time—when they finally fade from the page, or the book is destroyed through misadventure; and, in the meantime, their presence in the book has no intervening lacunas. These words are the bearers of content or meaning, and they are so in virtue of standing in appropriate relations to things *outside* of, or *extrinsic* to, them. Of course, in themselves, they mean nothing at all. To have meaning, they must first be *interpreted*. This interpretation is something in which they have no say—they are *passive* in this regard. Let's look at each of these ideas in a little more detail.

1 Internality The claim that words are *internal* to a book or other document is, of course, a claim about word-tokens, not word-types. It is unclear, to say the least, where word-types are located, and, indeed, they may be located nowhere at all. But word-tokens exist in clearly identifiable regions of space. If in doubt, just look at the previous instantiation of the word "space."

2 Genuine duration Not only do word-tokens occupy identifiable regions of space, they also occupy similarly identifiable regions of *time*. A word token, internally instantiated in a book or on a page, possesses *genuine duration*. That is, the tokening of the word begins at a reasonably precise time, ends at a reasonably precise time, and has no intervening lacunas. To say that the tokening of a word begins at a reasonably precise time is not, necessarily, to say that it begins *at* a time as opposed to *through* time. The inscribing or printing of a word on a page is, of course, something that takes time. So, the beginning of a word-token on a page may be something that occurs through an interval of time rather than at an instant. Of course, one does not have to see things this way. One might claim that the beginning of the word-token does not occur until the inscribing of that token is complete. This issue is, of course, merely stipulative, and we can finesse matters as follows: the claim that the tokening of a word on a page begins at a reasonably precise time is simply the claim that the word-token begins at a time *or* through a period of time, where both of these can be identified with at least reasonable precision. That is not, of course, to say that anyone is in a position to identify this time or this interval. Rather, it is the claim that the time or interval is identifiable in principle, by someone standing in the appropriate epistemic circumstances.

The same is true of the end of the word-token on a page or in a book. If the book is, in Humean fashion, consigned to the flames because it contains neither abstract reasoning concerning quantity or number nor experimental reasoning concerning matters of fact and existence, or, in Hitlerian fashion, because it contains too much of these things, the tokening of a word in a book ends during the period of time in which the flames consume the relevant page. If the book suffers no such misadventure, then the words may slowly fade from the page, and identifying the time during which the existence of the word-token ends is, accordingly, more difficult. But, we can, nevertheless, be certain that there is such a time and we may even be in a position to identify it with reasonable precision.

The issue of intervening lacunas is just as straightforward. If I erase a word from the page, and replace it with a type-identical replica, then what I have done is precisely to replace one word-token with another. Word-tokens, like tokens in general, do not recur. So, the presence of a word-token in a book can have no intervening lacunas. Any such purported lacuna would, in fact, herald the instantiation of a new, distinct, word-token.

The claim that the tokening of a word on a page has a reasonably determinate beginning and end, and no intermittent lacunas, is, as I shall put it, the claim that this word-token has *genuine duration*.

3 Exteriority of content Word-tokens are the bearers of content, or components of the bearers of content. On some views, it is words themselves that bear content. On others, the proper unit of meaning is the sentence, which is, of course, simply a collection of words organized according to appropriate syntactic rules. On either view, this content is extrinsic to the word or collection of words. Words, or collections of words, are about things that are extrinsic to them. This does not mean, necessarily, that what they are about is outside the book or page in or on which the word-tokens are inscribed. Various devices can, of course, direct you to items located in that book or on that page. For example, the imperative, "look at the title of this section," refers you back to page one and the phrase: "the word." It is possible to argue that this phrase-token provides part of the content of the expression. One does not, of course, have to see things this way. One could argue that the content of the expression is provided by whatever it is to which the phrase-token on page one refers. Under very unusual circumstances, we might employ self-referential sentences of the form, "The sentence that you are now reading," which seem to have themselves as their own content. But such sentences are exceptional. Moreover, such cases have no echo in the case of words. Certain unusual sentences may have themselves as their own content, but this is never true of words: when words are *used* to refer it is always to something outside of themselves. And, in the vast majority of cases, the same is true of sentences also. The conjunction of these claims is what I mean by the *exteriority of content*.

4 Interpretation Words (and sentences), in themselves, mean nothing at all. In some circles this fact is known as the "arbitrariness of the sign" and much is made of it. But the claim is, as far as I can see, truistic rather than profound. Words are symbols, and any symbol can, in itself, mean anything at all. Therefore, in itself, it means nothing at all. To have meaning, it needs to be *interpreted*. It is in virtue of such interpretation that word-tokens (or collections of word-tokens) come to stand in appropriate relations to items that are extrinsic to them; and it is these relations that allow word-tokens to be *about* such extrinsic items. In other words, interpretation fixes the semantic relations that a word can bear to what is outside it such that it can possess this extrinsic item as its content.

5 Passivity The role of interpretation in determining the semantic properties of words entails that words are, in a clear sense, *passive* items. Interpretation might, conceivably, take a variety of forms; but in any form, it is a matter of doing things *with* words. On one view, for example, interpretation takes the form of a distinctive mental act. Such a view may or may not be correct, but, either way, it cannot, of course, help us explain the nature of content—such an act will itself possess a content in terms of which it is individuated. Therefore it presupposes content rather than explains how content is possible. A more common option is to suppose that interpretation is a matter of words being *used* in a particular way. It is our use, or *practice*, that provides words with the interpretation they require in order to have content. This idea will be discussed at length in chapter 4. For present purposes, two points are worthy of note. First, as we shall see, it would be a mistake to suppose that this view is immune to the difficulties surrounding the idea of interpretation as a mental act. Doing, at least *prima facie*, seems to be a form of action, and both the status of something as an action and its identity as the particular action it is, are bound up with its connection to intentional states. So, like the corresponding appeal to a distinctive mental act, the appeal to action seems to presuppose, rather than explain, content.

Second, to claim that the interpretation that supplies words with their semantic content is a matter of the way in which those words are used is not to advance a theory of meaning. The claim is, in fact, sufficiently abstract to cover just about any concrete theory of meaning. If, for example, influenced by Kripke (1980), you would like to think of the content of at least some words as determined by causal relations extending back to facts concerning their *baptism* or *deixis*, then you can translate this idea into the claim that some words are used in such a way as to track such causal relations and the deictic facts in which they terminate. If, influenced by Davidson (1984), you would like to think of the meaning of a sentence as consisting in, or perhaps supervenient upon, its truth-conditions, then you can translate this idea into the claim that words are used in such a way as to track the contribution they make to the truth-conditions of the sentences in which they occur. To claim that the meanings of words are determined by the way they are used is not to advance a theory of meaning, for the claim is compatible with any theory of meaning. Instead, it is to deploy a certain pretheoretical picture of the ontological status of words. According to this picture, words don't have meaning because of what they are in themselves but, rather, because of what is done to or with them. Words are entirely passive in the constitution of their content.

2 Representation as Word

To assimilate representations to the category of the *word*, at least as I shall employ this idea, is to assert that they satisfy constraints at least roughly analogous to those identified above. That is:

1 Representations are internal A mental representation consists in an internal configuration of a subject. This is a claim about representation-tokens, not representation-types. It is unclear, to say the least, where, if anywhere, a representation-type is located; such items inherit the fugitive character of all types. But mental representation-tokens possess an identifiable spatial location inside the subject. Representation-tokens might take one of several forms—they might be images, prototypes, proxytypes, syntactically structured symbols, and so on—but in all cases, these representation-tokens are identical with some form of neural configuration in a subject, where this configuration is typically thought of as individuated by way of a subset of its higher-order physical or functional properties. On some models, these higher-order physical or functional properties may be individuation dependent on factors external to that subject: that is, they may be *externally individuated*. However, as Davidson has taught us, external *individuation* of properties does not entail external *location* of items that possess those properties.[1] And the representation-token is located inside its subject even if certain of its properties are individuation dependent on things outside that subject. Representation-tokens, therefore, possess identifiable spatial boundaries, and these are located inside the representing subject.

2 Representation has genuine duration Representation also possesses identifiable temporal boundaries. Indeed, representation, it is typically thought, possesses genuine duration. This is a claim that concerns the process of representation, but it derives from the nature of representation-tokens. A subject represents the world in a given way when the appropriate representation is tokened in it. That is, representation of some state of affairs, *F*, occurs at whatever time the representation of *F* is internally tokened in a subject. This claim may seem to be obviously false with regard to some forms of representation; in particular, those associated with beliefs and other propositional attitudes. After all, I can believe, and bear other propositional attitudes toward, a given state of affairs for many years, and it is no condition of this that the belief continually hovers, occurrently, in the forefront of my consciousness. My belief that Ougadougou is the capital of Burkina Faso is one that I acquired, via Stephen Stich, in the early 1980s (although it has been updated to keep track of more recent political developments). But to have this belief is not to be the subject of any occurrent state. A belief such as this seems to be a *dispositional* rather than occurrent, state. And dispositional states do not, of course, possess genuine duration.

In the face of this obvious point, the genuine duration of representation is typically safeguarded by appeal to the distinction between the *possession* and the *activation* of a representation. Although *a* representation might be possessed by a subject for an indefinite period of time, *representation* of this fact (in that subject) occurs only when the representation is activated— brought on-line in some or other capacity.[2] My belief that Ouagadougou is the capital of Burkina Faso is, for example, typically brought on-line in classroom situations when I am explaining the difference between occurrent and dispositional states. In such situations, my representation is activated and then, and only then, do I *represent* that Ouagadougou is the capital of Burkina Faso. And, it is argued, the activation of a representation-token is something that has genuine duration. It begins and ends at a definite (although perhaps difficult to determine) time, and has no intermittent lacunas. Representation in a subject occurs, then, during this time.

The tokening of words in a book, of course, tends to last longer than that of mental representations in a brain. But this is not a serious disanalogy between the two cases. We might, for example, imagine a book written with vanishing ink. The initiation and rapid fading of activity in a brain is something that begins and ends at definite times, although these may, in practice, be difficult to discern. The activity also has no intervening lacunas. Occurrent state-tokens are, by definition, nonrepeatable. Their temporary cessation is, in fact, their demise and replacement by a distinct occurrent state-token of the same type. If the assimilation of representation to the category of the word is correct, it entails that representation of a state of affairs in a subject has genuine duration in this sense.

3 Exteriority of content   Like words, representation-tokens are the bearers of content, and this content is, typically, extrinsic to them. The content is not, of course, necessarily extrinsic to the *subject* of the representation, since one can have representations about one's internal states. But, in almost all circumstances, this content is exterior to the representation-token itself. This exteriority of representational content has led to a familiar way of understanding the problem of representation. This is the problem of explaining the nature of the relation that one, internal, item bears to another item that is extrinsic to it in virtue of which the former can be about the latter or possess the latter as its content. Once we understand this relation, we will, consequently, understand representation; for the former is in what the latter consists. There are several well-known candidates for this relation, and several well-known problems with each candidate.

4 Representation requires interpretation   Taken in themselves representation-tokens can mean anything at all. This claim is familiar in one context, but less so in another. The claim is a familiar one when we think of representations as the sort of thing revealed by introspection. Suppose, to use the standard example, introspection reveals to us a mental image, and we take this to be a representation of some extrinsic state of affairs. Then, as Wittgenstein has taught us, images can, in themselves mean anything at all. Therefore, in themselves, they can mean nothing at all. To have their meaning constituted, they must have their meaning fixed; and it is interpretation that achieves this.

What is, perhaps, less familiar is that we find a clear analogue of this idea when we think of representations as the sort of thing revealed not by introspection but by empirical investigation of the brain; that is, when we think of representations as neural configurations individuated by way of their higher-order physical or functional properties. Such items can, in themselves mean anything at all. To have meaning, they must be *interpreted*. What supplies the interpretation, in this case, is the way the representation is *used* or deployed: it is interpreted by way of its occupation of a certain functional position in a subject's representational economy. That this is so is obvious for *inferentialist* accounts of representation, according to which the content possessed by a representation-token is determined by the functional or conceptual role of that token, a role that is instantiated in certain systematic networks of causal relations. But it is also, if less obviously, true for many of those theories that understand representational content in terms of informational or teleological relations that stretch from the representation-token to environmental states of affairs.

To see this, consider probably the most influential example of such a view: Millikan's teleosemantic theory of content. We shall discuss Millikan's view in detail later on; here I want to focus on just one aspect of that view. Millikan claims that any mechanism that is to count as representational *must* have the function of controlling some second mechanism in such a way as to ensure that the activity of the second mechanism coincides with a certain condition of the environment (1984: 97–100). That is, any mechanism that is to count as representational must have the function of controlling a second *cooperating* mechanism—either another representational mechanism or an *executive* mechanism that controls behavior directly.

To use a well-worn example (and one that will be even more well worn by the end of this book) consider the prey-detection mechanism of the frog. Millikan's suggestion, in effect, is that we regard this as divisible into a sight mechanism and a strike mechanism. So, when the environment contains small, black, moving things, the sight mechanism fires, and this causes the strike mechanism to fire. Indeed, not only does it in fact cause the strike mechanism to deploy, it has the *function* of causing it to deploy when the environment instantiates a given condition or set of conditions. In doing so, the representational, sight, mechanism serves to *interpret* the behavior of the executive, strike, mechanism. That is, the representational mechanism maps the behavior of the executive on to some condition, or conditions, of the environment. The idea that all content requires an interpreter is, then, reflected in the idea that any vehicle of content or representation-token, requires a co-operator. And, at the root of this idea is the interpretative conception of meaning.

My purpose here is not, of course, to show that the interpretational conception infects all extant accounts of meaning—although I suspect it infects many of them in one way or another. Rather, I have simply tried to show the pull of the idea that representation requires interpretation. It crops up in a variety of theories in a variety of ways; even where, ostensibly, we might least expect it. There is, of course, a certain irony to this. If we think of representations as items revealed by introspection, then the problems with an interpretational conception of representation have been clearly identified for some time. But the conception still exerts a powerful influence over our theorizing about the nature of representation when we think of these as items revealed by empirical investigation of the brain. These issues will be discussed in detail later.

5 Representations are passive Care must be taken unpacking this idea. A word, as we have seen, acquires its meaning because of what is done *to* or *with* it. This idea is not a theory of meaning as such, since it is sufficiently abstract—or vague—to encompass any theory of meaning. Rather, it is a pretheoretical statement of the passivity of words. Words have meaning only because of what is done to or with them, where this provides an interpretation of them. The idea that words are passive, then, is a claim about what makes an interpretation of words possible: interpretation consists in what we do to or with words.

Similarly, both the status of a representation as a representation and the specific semantic properties it bears as a representation are determined by what is done to or with it. Within this general framework, some accounts emphasize the way in which a representation is *produced* (Dretske 1986). In effect, they are based on what, broadly speaking, is done *to* representations—that is, the way in which they are brought about. On such accounts, a mental representation is the terminal point in a neosemantic—causal or informational or informational-cum-teleological—chain originating with the item the representation is a representation of. Representation occurs when, as a result of such a chain being instantiated, a representation is tokened in a subject. To say that a representation is the end point in this sort of chain is not, of course, to say that this representation cannot go on to occur in further chains—ones, for example, involving rational inference or action—but simply to say that it is the fact that it is the culmination of whatever neosemantic chain it is that determines (i) *that* it is a representation, and (ii) *what* it is a representation of. To say that a representation is passive is, therefore, not to say that a subject cannot influence what representations it undergoes by way of its actions, nor is it to deny that representations might play a role in ordering sensations that, following Kant, we might describe in terms of the notion of *spontaneity*—activity, broadly construed. Rather, it is simply to acknowledge that the representational status of item R is the result of an appropriate chain originating from some item X to the subject who tokens the relevant representation. That is, that R is a representation is determined by something that is done *to* it, by its being produced in a certain manner.

Other accounts focus on what is done *with* representations rather than *to* them (in the sense identified above). That is, they emphasize the way in which representations are *consumed* rather than *produced*. Millikan (1984, 1993) has developed a consumerist account, and the basis of this account is that both the status of an item as a representation, and its specific content, are determined by the way in which the representation is employed or *consumed* by representational consumers. The claim that a representation is passive is neutral between producer- and consumer-based accounts. The passivity claim is simply that the status and identity of a representation are determined by what is done to or with it—and whether what is done to or with it consists in its being produced in a certain way or consumed in a certain way is irrelevant.

In the sense deployed in this book, to assimilate mental representation to the category of the word is to think of such representations as satisfying the five conditions identified above. I shall not attempt to argue that this assimilation is incorrect for all cases of representation. The conditions may, indeed, provide an appropriate way of thinking about *some* representations. However, what this book will argue is that they cannot provide an appropriate way of thinking about representation in general. In some cases, representation needs to be understood not in terms of the word but the *deed*.

3   Representation as Deed

To assimilate representation to the category of word is to think of representations as items located in the mind–brain of a subject. To assimilate representation to the category of *deed*, on the other hand, is to think of representations as something that a subject does or achieves.

We can render part of the content—the negative part—of the idea of representation as deed in terms of five counterposed theses to those that constituted the idea of representation as word.

1   Not all representation is internal   Some representations may, indeed, consist in internal configurations of a subject. But representation is not restricted to the formation of these configurations.

2   Not all representation has genuine duration   At least in some cases, representation of a given environmental contingency is not the sort of thing that can occur at a time, nor even through a precisely identifiable period of time. It is not the sort of activity that need always have genuine duration. Representation often has the character of a process rather than a state; and this process need not have temporal boundaries of the reasonably respectable sort implicated in the assimilation of representation to the word.

3   Content is not necessarily exterior to representation   Given the assimilation of representation to the word, the content of a representation is extrinsic to it, in much the same way that the content of a word is extrinsic to it. The problem of representation is, then one of understanding how a representation—or vehicle of content—can reach out to an extrinsic state of affairs in such a way as to possess this state of affairs as its content. The assimilation of representation to the deed, on the other hand, entails that the relation between representational vehicle and content is not always like this. In some cases, representation, does not stop short of that content itself. Content is not, necessarily, exterior to representation. In some cases, representation incorporates the content.

4 Representation does not always require interpretation Some instances of representation involve interpretation, and some instances undoubtedly require it. However, not all representation is like this. Indeed, not all representation *can* be like this. Some cases of representation qualify as such quite independently of the activities of a distinct interpreting agent or mechanism.

5 Not all representation is passive In many cases, representation does not consist in the production or consumption of a representation that sits in the mind of a mental subject. Some forms of representation are essentially active.

Of course, (1*) through (5*) do not take us very far. They simply consist in a denial of the five principal tenets of the assimilation of representation to the word. As such, they merely provide the negative content of the assimilation of representation to the deed, coupled with a few vague gestures toward what form the positive content might take. The remainder of the book, in effect, will be concerned with providing the positive content of this assimilation. It remains in this chapter to provide a few indicators of the shape of things to come.

Consider an activity—the activity of *exploring* the environment, for instance, provides a useful template:

1. It makes no sense, of course, to think of exploration as an *internal* item. Exploring is something we do in the world, and is as external, or as internal, as the world itself (and the world is, of course, both internal and external). 2. Exploring takes time, but it is not the sort of thing that need possess *genuine duration*. In general, there need be no determinate beginning or end point for a process of exploration. When, for example, did Burton and Speke's exploration of the source of the River Nile begin? When they first discussed the project together? When they boarded the train at London?

When they took their first footstep outside Nairobi? Or when they first encountered country that no white person had seen before? It is not that the answers to these questions are difficult to discern; there is no fact of the matter that could be used to decide them. Nor is there any fact of the matter that could be used to identify the termination of this process of exploration. And, clearly, it is not as if their exploration ceased when they sat down to take a rest, or set up camp for the night.

3. In any exploration, what is explored is not *extrinsic* or *exterior* to the process of exploration. On the contrary, the process of exploration and the object of exploration, in an important sense, coincide. If they did not, the process of exploration would necessarily fail, or would not even count as a process of exploration.

4. A process of exploration need not be constituted as such by an act of *interpretation*. Under certain—unusual—circumstances, an act of interpretation might be necessary or sufficient to constitute one's activity as exploring; but this is not generally the case. Many things can explore their environment, most of which are incapable of interpreting their behavior at all, let alone as a process of exploration. Of course, *if* there is a fact of the matter here, that it is a process of exploration, as opposed to something else (foraging, wandering aimlessly, etc.), it must be due to *something*.[3] But this *something* need not be an interpretative act on the part of the explorer.

5. Exploring belongs to the category of *activity*, not passivity; it is something we do, rather than something that happens to us.

To assimilate representation to the category of the deed, then, is to think that *activity*, broadly construed, provides a useful template for thinking about representation. I am going to argue that representing the world consists, partly, in certain sorts of activity in which we engage. Our representing of the world consists, in part, in certain sorts of *deeds* that we perform in that world. The shift from the noun form "representation" to the verb form "representing" is not insignificant. Representations are things. Representing is a process. The assimilation of representation to the category of the deed entails, first and foremost, that representing is primary. Accordingly, it is no part of this book to argue that deeds can be *representations*. Such a claim would not, I think, be inaccurate; but it would be disingenuous. The idea of a representation is, I think, too closely tied to the model of the *word*. Rather, the central claim of this book is that certain sorts of deeds form part of the activity—the *deed*—of representing the world. And, crucially, the part they form of this process *is as genuinely representational as any other part*—the formation of internal configurations included. Deeds can represent the world to no lesser (and no greater) extent than internal representations traditionally construed.

4 Representation All the Way Out!

This, I freely admit, is a strange idea. The central claim of this book is not simply that certain ways of acting on the world can *facilitate* our ability to represent it. Everyone knows that! Or, more accurately, the idea that our ability to represent the world is bound up with our ability to act in it is, by now, a fairly popular idea. The idea underlies a loose coalition of views on the nature of mental processes that, to the extent that they are not hostile to representation *tout court*, allow it an attenuated role in which it fulfills its function only in conjunction with the manipulation, exploitation, and exploration of environmental structures. We shall look at such views in the next chapter. However, I am not simply arguing that the role of representation can be facilitated, supplemented, displaced, or supplanted by abilities to act on—perform deeds in—the world. Rather, I am going to argue that certain ways of acting in the world can *literally* be representational. The vehicles of representation do not stop at the skins of representing organisms. Representing is representational *all the way out!* Representing the world extends out into that world in the form of deeds performed in it. It is not as if these deeds are nonrepresentational facilitators of a genuinely representational core, which consists in relations obtaining between internal items and extrinsic states of affairs. Rather, the deeds are *themselves* representational. And this, I think, *is* a strange idea.

Of course, in one sense the idea is not strange at all. We commonly use stylized behaviors to re-present certain of our emotional states. I might, for example, in a classroom situation employ an extravagant slap of the brow as a mock expression of exasperation. Thus, an action that was originally an *expression* of exasperation can be used, in contexts where the exasperation is not present, as, in effect, a *re-presentation* of exasperation. We all do this sort of thing (and mimes do it for a living). So, the idea that actions can be used as something akin to representations is, in this sense, an entirely quotidian one. However, this is not the sense defended in this book. In the above sort of case, any representational character possessed by the action is inherited from prior representational states of both performer and observer. Thus, in good old Gricean fashion, I intend that my students take this as a playful mock indication of exasperation; they understand that I intend it in this way, and so on. However, what I shall argue is that certain sorts of actions—*deeds*, as I shall call them—can have a representational status quite independently of their connection to prior intentional states. They have this status because of what they are and their relations to the world, but not because of any relations they bear to other intentional states. And *this*, I think, *is* a strange idea.

Indeed, so strange is it that when I first started flirting with it, I had in mind a sort of *explanatory gap* argument for representation. The idea was that it is possible to identify certain items—deeds—that satisfied all the traditional criteria of representation but could not, themselves, be regarded as representations. So, we could not explain representation in terms of its traditional associated criteria. In other words, I was trying to develop a sort of *reductio* of the criteria. And if, after reading the book, you decide that is the best way of construing these arguments, then—believe me—I know where you're coming from.

However, after prolonged wrestling with the problem, I came to appreciate the advantages of allowing that deeds were, in fact, representational items. And these advantages are so crucial to understanding why we should not regard the arguments to follow as a *reductio* that I am going to spend a good proportion of the book developing them. This theme is developed in the chapters 4 and 5, where I develop a certain paradox concerning the role played by action in representation. I shall argue that if we want to introduce action to help us explain the nature of representation, then we must satisfy two competing pressures that pull us in opposite, and apparently irreconcilable, directions. On the one hand, we cannot appeal to a concept of action that presupposes representation; for example, a concept of action that sees actions as individuated by way of their connections to intentional states. This would be to presuppose representation, not explain it. On the other hand, I shall argue, we cannot appeal to a concept of action that does *not* presuppose representation. To do so is to reiterate a certain conception both of the *boundary* between representation and action, and the *role* played by action with respect to representation. The boundary is one that is straddled by merely causal impingements. Across such a boundary, causal pressure can be exerted, but epistemic pressure cannot. And the role played by action consists in merely providing us with new ways of causally impinging on the world. Such a boundary between action and representation, and such a role for action with respect to representation, I shall argue, makes it impossible to use action in an explanation of representation.

Therefore, if we are to employ the concept of action in our attempt to understand representation, this concept must, it seems, both presuppose representation, and not presuppose representation. This paradox is not an opportune eruption designed specifically to fit the purposes of this book. On the contrary, it has a long and respectable history, and to convince you of the scope and importance of the paradox, I shall spend much of chapter 4 looking at this history. Chapter 5 looks at a more recent incarnation of the paradox. The development of what is, in essence, a simple paradox may be overly long for some tastes. I dwell on it because it is precisely the benefits that the view of representation developed in this book yields, vis-à-vis the paradox, that motivates an understanding of the arguments to follow as a *reinterpretation* of the concept of representation, rather than as a *reductio* of the currently accepted criteria of representation.

I shall argue that there is one, and only one, escape from this paradox. This is to employ a concept of action as representational, but where this representational status is not acquired from anything else—for example, from a prior representational state. The concept of action employed must be one according to which such actions are representational but have this status directly; in virtue of what they are in themselves and their relation to the world, and not in virtue of their connection to something that is *already* representational. I shall argue that such a concept exists, and extends over an identifiable category of behaviors that I shall refer to as *deeds*.

The arguments for these claims are developed in chapters 4 and 5. These chapters, then, provide, in a sense to be rendered precise, one motivation for thinking of representation in the way defended in this book. However, the view of representation can be defended independently of this motivation. This will be attempted in chapters 6 through 12. Chapter 6 introduces the notion of a deed. Deeds are conceived of as what I shall call *preintentional* acts. They stand somewhere in between *actions*, traditionally understood, and *subintentional* acts in O'Shaughnessy's (1980) sense. Unlike deeds, they are performed for a reason that the agent does or would endorse. Unlike actions, this reason is not sufficient to individuate them. One consequence of this is that if deeds were to possess representational status, this cannot have been acquired from other representational states. Chapters 7 through 11 then defend the claim that deeds do, in fact, possess representational status.

Chapter 7 argues that deeds can satisfy the first major constraint on representations: the *informational* constraint. That is, deeds can carry information about their environment, or, at least can do so to no lesser extent than internal representations traditionally construed. Chapter 8 argues that deeds can satisfy a *teleological* constraint. That is, deeds not only carry information about their environment, they also have the *function* of tracking environmental features and/or of allowing organisms to achieve specified tasks in virtue of tracking such features. Chapter 9 argues that deeds can satisfy *misrepresentation* and *decouplability* constraints. Deeds can misrepresent the world as well as represent it, and, in appropriate circumstances, can be decoupled from those environmental features it is their function to track. Chapter 10 argues that deeds satisfy a *combinatorial* constraint. Deeds can possess combinatorial structure of the sort required by a genuinely representational system. If the arguments of chapters 7 through 10 are correct, then deeds satisfy all relevant constraints on representation, and so qualify as representational if anything does.

The notion of a "relevant" constraint requires clarification. I am concerned only with those constraints pertaining to the relation between a representational device and its represented object. I am not, and I must emphasize this, concerned with constraints pertaining to the role played by representations in a subject's psychology. The most important of these is a *causal* or *explanatory constraint*: a representation must play a causal role in guiding a subject's behavior, and hence must play a role in explaining the subject's behavior. This constraint, arguably, plays a role in determining what sort of things can count as representations. But I am not arguing that deeds are representations. And I am certainly not arguing that deeds function in precisely the same way in an agent's psychology as internal configurations of a subject. Rather, my claim is that deeds are *representational*, and so I am concerned with the conditions an item must satisfy in order to be *representational*, not to be a *representation*: that is, the sorts of constraints it must satisfy in order to have representational objects. We will return to this issue later.

Chapter 11, the final chapter, puts the ideas and principles delineated in chapters 6 through 10 into practice with an examination of the deeds involved in visual perception. I shall argue that these deeds satisfy combinatorial, informational, teleological, and misrepresentation conditions. The deeds involved in visual representation of the world do not merely facilitate some genuinely representational core, one consisting in a relation between internal and external items. On the contrary, the involved deeds are as representational as any other components of representation.

There is, of course, nothing incompatible with assimilating representation to the category of the word, and assimilating it to the category of the deed—as long as we do not make this assimilation for the same representations! Accordingly, this book does *not* claim that there are no such things as internal representations, traditionally understood. Rather, the claim is that not *all* cases of representation can be explained by way of their assimilation to the category of the word. Some cases of representation take the form of *deeds*. This will be most obviously the case for certain forms of representation rather than others. In particular, the role of deeds in representation is, perhaps, the most obvious in the case of *perceptual* representation. Accordingly, much of the focus of this book will be provided by perceptual representation, and *visual* representation in particular. This is not to say that the role of deeds is negligible in other cases of representation—quite the contrary. But I do think that the role deeds play in these other forms of representation will derive from the way perception can, in such forms, be employed, in an epistemically active way, to help accomplish the cognitive task for which the representation has been produced or activated.

Qualifications aside, if the arguments of this book are correct, the means by which we represent do not stop at the skin. There may well exist vehicles of representation inside the skin of representing subjects. But vehicles of representation do not, in general, stop at the skin. They extend out into the world in the form of deeds. Representing the world is something we do in the world as much as in the head. Representing is representational *all the way out!* This I shall refer to as the thesis of *representation in action*.

2   Content Externalism

1   Weak and Strong Externalism

The idea that action can play at least some role in explaining the nature of representation is one associated with views of the mind that fall under the broad rubric *externalism*. Externalism, however, takes different forms, and these differences are not only important in themselves but also crucial for our purposes. This chapter and the next, therefore, are concerned with distinguishing the relevant forms. This chapter deals with *content* externalism: externalism about the content of mental states. Content externalism is less relevant to the overall purposes of this book than the other major form of externalism—externalism about the *vehicles* of content. For it is in connection with this latter form that the appeal to action, as a way of explaining representation, is likely to be made. Nevertheless, there are certain key distinctions that emerge in connection with content externalism that can be, and often are, reiterated at the level of vehicles. This chapter is concerned with these distinctions.

Content externalism encompasses a spectrum of views, all united by the idea that what is in the mind of a subject is not exhaustively determined by what is in that subject's head. Two distinctions are particularly important for our purposes, and we will have cause to revisit them on several occasions during the course of this book.

1. The distinction between *weak* and *strong* externalism.
2. The distinction between *radical* and *reactionary* externalism.

This section deals with the first distinction; the following section deals with the second.

The appellations *weak* and *strong* have been employed by a variety of people with a variety of meanings. As I shall employ these terms, the distinction corresponds to the difference between externalism understood as a thesis about the *individuation* of mental states, and externalism understood as a thesis about the *constitution* of mental states.

Consider, first, how content externalism can be construed as a thesis about individuation. Following Strawson (1959: 30ff.), via McGinn (1989: 4–6), we can characterize the concept of individuation dependence thus:

*F*s are individuation dependent on *G*s if and only if:
(i) Reference to *F*s requires prior reference to *G*s.
(ii) Knowledge of the properties of *F*s requires prior knowledge of the properties of *G*s.
(iii) It is not possible for *F*s to exist in a world where *G*s do not exist.
(iv) Possession of the concept of an *F* requires prior possession of the concept of a *G*.[1]

We can refer to these conditions as the *linguistic, epistemological, metaphysical,* and *conceptual* conditions respectively. Thus, in the case of a propositional mental state such as a belief, we have:

(i) Reference to beliefs requires reference to appropriate worldly entities.
(ii) We cannot know what someone believes without knowing the nonmental objects and properties his beliefs are about.
(iii) It is not possible for a subject to hold a belief unless her environment contains the appropriate entities.
(iv) It is not possible to master the concept of a belief without having mastered the concepts for the worldly entities beliefs are about.

Understood in this way, content externalism is the thesis that mental content is individuation dependent on things outside the head of the subject. We might put this by saying that externalism is the thesis that the representational content of mental states that have it is *externally individuated,* as long as we are clear that by "external" we mean "outside the head" and not "outside the mind." What I am calling *weak* externalism is content externalism understood as a thesis of external individuation.

There is, however, a quite distinct way of understanding externalism: as a thesis not of how mental content is individuated but of how such content is *constituted.* "Constituted by," in this context, means, very roughly, "containing as a constituent." What I am calling *strong* externalism is content externalism understood as the thesis that mental content has worldly constituents. This is a far stronger claim than that made by weak externalism. Claims concerning individuation do not, in general, entail claims about constitution. Thus, to employ a well-known example originating with Davidson, sunburn is individuation dependent on sunlight in that nothing counts as sunburn that was not produced by solar radiation. However, pretty clearly, this does not entail that sunburn is constituted by solar radiation; it does not contain solar radiation as a constituent (Davidson 1987). So, externalism, as a thesis about the constitution of mental content, makes a far stronger claim than externalism understood as a thesis about the individuation of that content. And traditional arguments for externalism—for example, Putnam's (1975) seminal *Twin Earth* thought experiment—establish only the individuation claim and not the constitution claim.

Nevertheless, various people have defended the constitution claim—notably, but in different ways, John McDowell (1986), Colin McGinn (1989), and Gregory McCullough (1994). McGinn, for example, defends it by arguing that the only reason for not accepting this claim, given prior commitment to the thesis of external individuation, is a residual internalist bias. McGinn points out that hostility to the constitution interpretation of externalism cannot be based on a simple hostility to the idea of mental states having constituents per se. Many internalist theories allow—indeed require—that mental states have constituents: images, bits of cerebral syntax, and so on. But given we accept the claim that mental states possess constituents, and given our antecedent commitment to the principle of external individuation, on what grounds can we insist that these constituents be internal? McGinn argues that there are no legitimate grounds—there is only a tacit commitment to internalism.

Arguments such as this are useful, but, I think, less than compelling. They can be made more convincing by two clarifications. First, as I shall understand it, strong externalism is the claim that mental *content* has worldly constituents, not that mental *states* do. The ubiquitous "state" although perhaps harmless in some contexts is positively misleading in this one. And it is misleading because it is ambiguous between content and vehicle or bearer of content. We shall have cause to revisit this ambiguity later.

However, even when restricted to a claim about mental content, McGinn's argument suffers from certain burden of proof issues. Someone not already wedded to a strong externalist position might argue that the idea that the content of mental states could have worldly constituents is so outlandish that the burden of proof is surely with the person who claims that it does. How, one might ask, as Frege once did of Russell, could Mont Blanc, in all its majestic fifteen thousand feet plus, literally be a constituent of the content of my thought that Mont Blanc is more than fifteen thousand feet high? So the grounds upon which we insist that the constituents are internal are a general hostility to weirdness in the absence of a convincing reason for being weird—or so the argument might go.

The way to get around this objection is to find a way of shifting the burden of proof. The first step in this is to clarify the nature of the constituents of content. Strong externalism need not, in fact, insist that *objects* are the constituents of content. A far more plausible version claims that it is *facts*, rather than objects, that are the constituents of content. If we allow this, then we might argue that, far from being a recherché doctrine, strong externalism is, in fact, an expression of a truism: *when I think that p, that p is what I think.*

Suppose I believe that the cat is on the mat. What is it that I believe? Well, obviously, that the cat is on the mat. The fact that the cat is on the mat is what I believe. This fact is the content of my thought. But the very same fact is also a constituent of the world. So, a constituent of my thought is identical with a constituent of the world. Indeed, if the world, as Wittgenstein once put it, is a world of facts not things, then these facts are identical, it seems, with thinkable content. One does not need to take a stand on any particular model of facts to appreciate this truism. The contents of thoughts are identical with the contents of the world. *Content does not stop short of the world.*

Perhaps this shifts the burden of proof. When I think that *p*, that *p* is what I think. This is a truism. And how, one might think, can a truism be weird?

2   Radical versus Reactionary Externalism

The second pertinent distinction is between what I am going to call *radical* and *reactionary* externalism. Reactionary externalism corresponds to what is typically known as a *dual-component* interpretation of externalism. McGinn captures the general thrust of this interpretation quite nicely:

Our intuitive conception of belief-content combines two separable components, answering to two distinct interests we have in ascriptions of belief. One component consists in a mode of representation of things in the world; the other concerns itself with properly semantic relations between such representations and the things represented. I want to suggest that the former is constitutive of the causal-explanatory role of belief, while the latter is bound up in our taking beliefs as the bearers of truth. We view beliefs *both* as states of the head explanatory of behaviour, and as items possessed of referential truth-conditions. (1982: 210)

This interpretation we might call *reactionary* because it tries to hold on to the general Cartesian division between mind and world, albeit in a somewhat different form. Specifically, the Cartesian idea of the mind as a self-contained interiority is preserved; it is simply that its bounds are redrawn. The bound-aries between inner and outer now correspond to the distinction between, on the one hand, the qualitative/action-guiding/causal-explanatory component of a mental state and, on the other, its representational or semantic compo-nent. And traditional Cartesian theses about the mind—both ontic and epistemic—could now be asserted about the inner component rather than the entire mental state. And so the Cartesian view of the mind persists in rec-ognizable form in the dual-component theory. This theory accepts the force of the externalist arguments against the Cartesian view of the mind, but it attempts to severely limit their consequences.

Of course, if this attempt to safeguard the Cartesian vision is to work, each component must be at least logically separable. Someone who wants to deny the Cartesian vision in any form can accept with equanimity the idea that content supervenes, in part, on various internal items. If the role that these internal items play in constituting content cannot, even logi-cally, be separated from the role played by external factors in constituting such content, then the idea of content as a self-contained Cartesian interi-ority must be abandoned.

This thought provides the basis of a more *radical* interpretation of content externalism. According to this version, we cannot separate the internal qual-itative/action-guiding/causal-explanatory component from the external representational component in the way required by the dual-component model. This radical interpretation might be—indeed, has been—motivated by a variety of considerations—the action-guiding component of mental states does not supervene purely on internal goings on, the qualitative can-not be separated from the representational, and so on. But, whatever its motivation, the general idea behind the radical model is that there are no logically separable components—an inner and an outer—and so there exists no region of reality to which the traditional Cartesian theses about the nature of content might apply.

3   Content Unbound

If we combine the two versions—strong and radical—of content exter-nalism, we find ourselves with a clear vision of content as *unbound*. Let us call the implicated sense of the externalist doctrine *SR-externalism*. According to strong externalism, content, in general, does not stop short of the world: it is identical with worldly facts. According to radical exter-nalism, there is no division or demarcation between content that super-venes on internal processes and content that supervenes on the wider environment. There are not two logically separable types or components of content. This means that we cannot divide content into an external component that is subject to the strong externalist thesis, and an internal component that is not. Thus, according to SR-externalism, not only does content in general not stop short of the world, there is no component of content that does.

According to this view, mental content is not an *internal* item that, when true, somehow corresponds to, or reflects, a worldly counterpart. True mental content is identical with worldly facts; it does not correspond to them. Therefore, *a fortiori*, it is not about something that is *exterior* to it. Worldly facts are not exterior to mental content; they are identical with it.

When we abandon the idea of mental content as an inner item that is about a worldly fact that is exterior to it, we also abandon the *interpretational* conception of content. It is not as if mental content stands in the mind of a subject, and must be linked to its worldly counterparts by way of an act of interpretation. Applied to mental content, the concept of interpretation involves two senses of separation or distance, both of which are denied by SR-externalism. First, there is the idea that an interpretation must be distinct from what it interprets, that the *act* of interpretation must be distinct from the *object* of interpretation. Second, there is the idea that the *object* of interpretation must be distinct from what, via the act of interpretation, that object is *about*. The interpretation relates the object of interpretation to something outside of it, in such a way that it separates those extrinsic items that are in accord with the object of interpretation from those that are not. SR-externalism undermines both senses of separation implicated in the concept of interpretation.

Consider, first, the second sense of separation: the separation of the object of interpretation and those extrinsic items that, via the act of interpretation, it is about. Here, the temptation is, of course, to think in terms of a *correspondence* of some sort. To have the content that it does, the inner item must correspond, in some way, to the item or items it is about. The function of interpretation is, then, to bridge this separation by supplying a function that maps the mental item onto extrinsic state of affairs. The alternative provided by SR-content externalism is clear. The same thing— the fact that p—is a content both of the world and of my thought. At the level of content, there is no separation of world and mind; the contents of one are the contents of the other. The content of a thought is not something that is related to a worldly fact. The content of the thought *is* the worldly fact. The content does not stop short of the world. Content is *unbound*; it is *unconfined*. Therefore, it is not as if we have a gap here, one that needs to be bridged by an act of interpretation. The content of the mental item *consists in* the worldly fact. So, SR-externalism denies the second sense of separation implicated in the concept of interpretation.

Consider, now, the first sense of separation: that between the act and the object of interpretation, between the interpretation and what gets interpreted. Content externalism, in fact, denies this first sense of separation for precisely the same reasons as it denied the second. The need for an interpretation to be supplied from the outside arises only in response to the second sense of separation. It is precisely because we imagined that there exists a gap between the object of interpretation and those extrinsic items that it is about that we need an act of interpretation. The act of interpretation is required to bridge the gap, to map the mental item onto those extrinsic states of affairs it is about. If we deny the gap, then there is no such mapping to be achieved. Therefore, there is no need for an act of interpretation. But if there is no act of interpretation, neither can there be a gap between act of interpretation and object of interpretation. When we deny the second sense of separation implicated in the concept of interpretation, we also, thereby, deny the first.

Moreover, when we reject the idea that mental content is an internal item, linked to the external world by an act of interpretation, we also reject the idea that mental content is essentially *passive*, in that it stands passively in the mind; for that picture only makes sense given the existence of an interpretative act that links it to its worldly counterparts.

Finally, it we think of mental content in the way mandated by SR-externalism, we must abandon the idea that it is the sort of thing that, necessarily, has genuine duration. Indeed, SR-externalism renders problematic all questions of the spatiotemporal location of content. The cat, let us suppose, is on the mat. So, the cat has a determinate spatial location. But where is the *fact* that the cat is on the mat? Similarly, if the cat is on the mat for an hour during its afternoon snooze, then it is there for a determinate period of time. But when is the *fact* that the cat is on the mat for this time? Certainly it is not exhausted by the time at which the cat is on the mat, for it is still a fact long after that time. Facts, unlike objects, are not the sort of things that have determinate spatiotemporal locations. And, if mental content is identical with such facts, neither does mental content.

Therefore, in SR-externalism, we find a rejection, *at the level of mental content*, of the sorts of claims that in the previous chapter I associated with the assimilation of representation to the category of the word. The significance of content externalism, in its strong and radical form, is that it undercuts *any* boundary between content and the world. Externalism is often understood as merely challenging a particular boundary between mind and world—typically, the skin of the subject. But it does not matter where the boundary is. It may be two meters outside the subject's skin. More plausibly, it may be thought to lie somewhere within the brain. The significance of strong content externalism is that it challenges the idea of *any* sort of boundary at all pertinent to content. Mental content is not the sort of thing that has boundaries. Content is, as we might say, *unconfined*. Content is *unbound*. *It does not stop short of the world*. This book, in effect, defends a parallel view of the nature of the *vehicles* of that content.

4   Vehicles Unbound?

If content is unconfined—and I emphasize *if*—then why have we been almost unbreakably attracted to the notion that it is not? And if SR-externalism is a truism, why do we have such a hard time seeing it as such? The answer is that we are *vehicle internalists*: internalists about the vehicles of content.

The distinction between vehicles and contents is one of those peculiar distinctions that are both ostensibly simple and continually flouted. The assimilation of representation to the category of the word nicely reveals its utter simplicity. Word-tokens (or sentence-tokens) are the vehicles of content; they are the things that have or bear content. And the content they bear is their meaning. So, the distinction between content and vehicle of content is simply the distinction between content and what has it. If we assimilate representation to the word, then the distinction is that between a representation-token and the content possessed by that token. But what is a representation-token? According to the assimilation of representation to the word, a representation-token is a concrete, particular, inner config-uration, presumably neural, possessing, and perhaps individuated by, higher-order physical or functional properties. This concrete, particular, internal configuration is the bearer, or vehicle, of content. This character-ization is, admittedly, vague, and I shall do a lot more work tidying up at the beginning of the next chapter. But it suffices for present purposes.

To think about the vehicles of content in this way is to be an internalist about them. The vehicles of mental content are internal configurations of a subject, and the token mental processes undergone by that subject con-sist in interactions between, and transformations of, these internal config-urations. These internal configurations form the nuts and bolts of cognition; the cognitive *architecture* or *hardware* in virtue of which a cog-nizing subject is able to perceive, think, reason, remember, and be the legitimate subject of mental attributions in general. A sufficiently skilled and knowledgeable observer might be able to "read" these configurations: the brain would be to them, as we might say, an *open book*.

Once we think of the vehicles of content in this way, a seemingly irresistible assimilation forces itself upon us. Mental states—at least most of them—are defined by their intentionality; they are about other things, and this *aboutness* forms the basis of their individuation. But token mental states are simply relations to representation-tokens, and representation-tokens are internal configurations of a subject. Therefore, we might think—indeed, typically have thought—these representation-tokens must be about things too. That is, we assimilate the intentionality of mental states to a relation that an internal configuration bears to something extrinsic to it. Typically, this will be an object or, in the case of complex representation-tokens, a state of affairs that is extrinsic to the subject also—an environmental item of some sort. This is not always true; a subject can always instantiate representations that are about other of its internal states. But, the norm is for the represented object or state of affairs to be extrinsic both to the representation-token and the subject of that representation-token. Therefore, we arrive at the idea that the intentionality or representational character of mental states is to be understood in terms of a relation that an internal configuration of a subject bears to an item that is extrinsic to it, and, typically, extrinsic to that subject also. Like words on a page, the internal configurations that constitute representation-tokens might in themselves mean anything at all. They do not bear their semantic evaluation on their face. Rather, they must be *interpreted*. How is this to be done? We must identify their *representational* properties. These are what link them to extrinsic items in such a way that they can be about those items or possess them as their content.

This picture of intentionality sits uncomfortably with the view of content presented by SR-externalism. If the vehicles of content are internal configurations of a subject, then how is the content they bear thus unbound? How can the denial of boundaries at the level of content, a denial implicated in SR-externalism, be squared with the boundaries between inner and outer implicated in vehicle internalism, boundaries around which the relation of intentionality has, precisely, been oriented? How can a content be identical with a worldly fact if what has that content is shut away in its own cranial prison—how can an inner item *possess* a worldly fact as one of its essential, individuative, features?

The unboundedness of content, I think it is fair to say, sits uncomfortably with the boundedness of the vehicles of that content. But this discomfort does not reach the level of an outright incompatibility. But that it should reach this level is neither here nor there. It is no part of this book to argue *from* SR-externalism to a certain conception of vehicle externalism. I am not, that is, going to attempt to deduce the principal conclusions of this book from SR-externalism. There would be little point in such a strategy. Despite my efforts to characterize it as a truism, there is no avoiding the point that SR-externalism is a controversial thesis about the nature of mental content. Indeed, it is difficult to imagine many more controversial theses than SR-externalism. I happen to believe it is true; but many more do not. And, accordingly, it would be pointless to expect SR-externalism to bear any significant argumentative weight.

Moreover, even if SR-externalism were to gain widespread acceptance, the inference from content to vehicles, or from vehicles to content, is one fraught with danger. One might ask, for example, what story about the vehicles of content is required for SR-externalism to be true. And, I think it is overwhelmingly likely that the unboundedness of content is not compatible with just *any* theory about the vehicles of that content. But trying to inject any more precision is logically hazardous, and one is likely to be assailed from all sides by tempting vehicle-content conflations and confusions. Others may be more confident in their abilities to resist such confusions, but it is not a road I particularly want to travel.

Accordingly, the purpose of this chapter has not been to argue for, or defend, the thesis of representation in action. The account of SR-externalism has not been developed with that goal in mind at all. Rather, the project of explicating SR-externalism has been pursued with the aim of delineating the content of the thesis of representation in action, rather than defending that thesis. For, as we shall see, there is a clear sense in which the thesis of representation in action parallels, at the level of vehicles of content, the sort of claims made, at the level of content, by SR-externalism. Why is content unbound? Ultimately, I think, it is because the vehicles of content are unbound—although I shall not try to argue from the former to the latter. The vehicles of content stop short of the world no more than content stops short of that world. And why are the vehicles of content unbound? It is because, I shall argue, these vehicles extend out into the world in the form of certain sorts of actions or *deeds*.

This project of delineating the content of the thesis of representation in action is continued in the next chapter, where we are going to look at what has become known as *vehicle externalism*.

3 Vehicle Externalism

1 Action and Representation

The idea that *action* can play a central role in explaining, or explaining away, our ability to represent the world, is one that has become increasingly popular in recent years. The idea informs much recent work, both in empirical disciplines such as perceptual psychology, developmental psychology, robotics and artificial life, and numerous and variegated recent connectionist attempts at cognitive modeling, and also in philosophical interpretations of the foundations of such disciplines. The latter, in effect, attempt to provide a conceptual framework within which, in the attempt to understand representation, the appeal to action makes sense. This framework goes by a variety of names, including: the *extended mind*, *active externalism*, and *environmentalism*. In this book, I shall refer to the framework by way of the expression *vehicle externalism*.[1]

The difference between explaining representation and explaining it away is, of course, a significant one. Nevertheless, as we shall see, the appeal to action can, at a sufficiently abstract level, be seen to play a similar role in both projects. In this book, the appeal to action in the project of explaining, or explaining away, representation occupies a peculiar, Janus-faced position. On the one hand, I shall defend a version of this claim. Action can, indeed, play an important role in explaining representation. Indeed, the version I shall defend is extremely strong. Certain sorts of action, I argue, can help in the project of explaining representation because these actions, themselves, have representational status. That is, such actions are not merely facilitators of representation; they are *themselves* representational. This, I think, is the strongest possible form of the idea that action can play a role in explaining representation. I shall refer to the idea in this strong form as the thesis of *representation in action*.

On the other hand, as I shall also argue, in its more familiar, and less sanguine, forms, the appeal to action is deeply problematic, and is deserving of serious scrutiny. Indeed, I shall argue that this appeal, in its typical form, yields a serious dilemma: there are two forms of action to which we might appeal in the project of understanding representation, and neither of these, for different reasons, can help us in this project.

These two aspects of the appeal to action are, however, not incompatible. In fact, the second aspect can be used to support the first. That is, the dilemma occasioned by the appeal to action, in its more familiar form, can be avoided if (and I think *only* if) we adopt the thesis of representation in action. This argument is developed in chapters 4 and 5. The remainder of the book then attempts to motivate and defend the thesis on independent grounds. This, however, is the stuff of future chapters. The present one is concerned only with laying out a general framework for thinking about these issues; a framework provided by *vehicle externalism*.

2   Vehicles of Content and Cognition

The distinction between contents and vehicles of cognition is, in essence, a simple one: a distinction between content and what has that content. The most familiar example of the distinction, as we have seen, is to be found in sentences—where we easily distinguish between the sentence form (individuated phonetically if spoken, or syntactically if written) and the meaning that this form bears. In the case of mental content, however, the notion of a vehicle of cognition is not as straightforward. And, indeed, it is common to find the notion of a vehicle used in two distinct ways.

1. The first way of thinking about vehicles follows through on the analogy with sentences, and understands vehicles of content as *bearers* of content. Thus, vehicles of content are mental representations, and what determines whether these are representations will, of course, depend on one's preferred view of representation. Suppose, for example, one endorses some form of teleological account. Then, whether or not something counts as a vehicle of cognition depends on whether it bears the right sort of teleological relations to the stimulus that produces it, or the mechanisms (subpersonal) or organisms (personal) that consume it.[2] Let's work, for simplicity's sake, with a straightforward stimulus-based account. Suppose, for example, that mechanism M, goes into state S, in the presence of environmental feature F. Then, on this account, S will be about F if and only if it is the adapted proper function of M to go into S in the presence of F.

In virtue of this adapted proper function, S has the derived proper function of occurring when and only when F occurs and so represents F.

So, on this view, it is M's being S—the adopting of a certain configuration by a mechanism as its adapted proper function—that is the vehicle of content. The vehicle plays a *token-explanatory* role with respect to the occurrence of the content in question (Hurley 1998: 330–332). This is distinct from the *type-explanatory* role played by the teleological relations themselves. The latter explain why there is content of this type (e.g., "F, there!") at all. The vehicle, on the other hand, explains why content of this type is tokened at this place and time. Note that the vehicle need not, and typically does not, explain why the resulting token mental state has the content that it has. That M is S, for example, does not, by itself, explain content at all—for this you need to invoke type-explanatory factors, such as it being the adapted proper function of M to become S in the presence of F, and so on. So, vehicles, in this sense, are what do the *differentially* token-explanatory work: they are what are left when you subtract the explanation of why content of this type exists at all, from the full explanation of why content of this type is now tokened.

2. The first way of thinking about vehicles is based on the idea that whatever else vehicles are, they are bearers of content. So a vehicle is, in the first instance, a vehicle of content. There is, however, another way of using the term that bears no direct or essential connection to content. The relevant distinction, here, is not between vehicle and content, but between state and process. The above conception of a vehicle sees it as primarily a state—one that has a token-explanatory role in accounting for why a token content, and thus why a token mental state, should obtain. But there is another sense of vehicle that applies primarily to mental *processes* rather than mental *states*. And its most natural application is to a subclass of mental processes: cognitive processes.

There is general consensus on *which* processes are cognitive, but less than general consensus on what makes them cognitive. The divergence is largely because the extension of "cognitive process" is fixed by ostension. Cognitive processes include such processes as perceiving, remembering, thinking, reasoning, and the processes involved in the production and understanding of language. And underlying this ostension is the somewhat vague idea that these are the processes in virtue of which we can accomplish cognitive tasks: perceiving the world, remembering perceived information, reasoning on the basis of remembered information, understanding the information imparted by others, and so on. So, the notion of a cognitive process is defined in terms of the notion of a cognitive task, and this latter notion is defined by ostension.

There are, of course, many processes that are required for the accomplishing of cognitive tasks. Organisms cannot accomplish such tasks if they are dead, for example. But respiration is not, typically, understood as a cognitive process. This is indicative of a further necessary constraint on the concept of a cognitive process: a cognitive process must involve some form of *information processing*—roughly, transformation of information-bearing structures. But this, by itself, is not sufficient. Information is usually understood in terms of relations of conditional probability, or perhaps nomic dependence.[3] But such relations are pretty much ubiquitous. And so it may well turn out that *every* process involves information processing in some sense.

So, a further constraint is needed: to count as cognitive, a process must be of the sort that is capable, perhaps in combination with other processes, of yielding a cognitive *state*. And then we might, though need not, use, for example, the teleological apparatus described above to delineate what is to count as a cognitive state. A cognitive state, S, is a representational state, and its status as representational is determined by its being a state of mechanism, M, whose adapted proper function is to enter S in the presence of certain contingencies. This is not to claim, of course, that all cognitive processes must yield cognitive states to count as cognitive. Rather, the claim is that they be of the sort capable of yielding cognitive states— whether they in fact do so or not. Therefore, as a working definition:

A *cognitive process* is one that: (i) is required for the accomplishing of a cognitive task, (ii) involves information processing, and (iii) is of the sort that is capable of yielding a cognitive state.

As a first approximation, the second concept of a vehicle identifies vehicles with the mechanisms or processes that culminate in the formation of a cognitive state. However, this claim is, clearly, itself ambiguous. The first sense it can take is based on the idea that cognitive processes are implemented in certain subpersonal mechanisms possessed by the cognizing organism. We can refer to these as the cognitive *architecture* of the organism. In this sense, the vehicles of cognition consist in cognitive architecture: the subpersonal mechanisms that allow cognitive processes to be run. However, by extension, the notion of a vehicle can also be extended to the processes themselves—as long as we are clear that these are identified non-intentionally. The vehicles of cognition, in this sense, consist in the information-processing operations that are of a sort capable of culminating in a cognitive state or states, where this state can, alone or in combination with other such states, allow the organism that possesses it to accomplish a cognitive task.

Therefore, the concept of a vehicle is not a unitary one. Henceforth, when I talk about *vehicles of content*, I shall be talking about vehicles as items that bear content—mental representations in some suitably broad sense.[4] When I talk about *vehicles of cognition*, I shall be talking about either (i) the cognitive architecture on which cognitive processes are run or in which they are implemented, or (ii) the cognitive processes themselves, where these are specified nonintentionally (e.g., in terms of their information-processing functions), or (iii) both. Context will usually make clear which sense of vehicle of cognition is being employed. Where it does not, I shall specify.

3   Vehicle Externalism

Armed with this working definition of the various concepts of a vehicle, we can now state the basic principle of what we can call *vehicle externalism*: the vehicles of content and cognition can extend beyond the skin of the cognizing organism.[5] Consider a general theoretical framework underpinning this idea, as laid out in Rowlands 1999.[6] The framework is constituted by the following claims:

(1)   The world is an external store of information relevant to cognitive processes such as perceiving, remembering, reasoning, and so on.

It can be such a store because, in all essentials, information is *ubiquitous*. It is generally accepted that it is in virtue of relations of conditional probability between items, perhaps underwritten by nomic dependencies of either a strict or probabilistic form, that one item can carry information about another.[7] But such relations can be externally instantiated just as much as they can be instantiated in the relation between an internal representation and its external correlate. In virtue of this, information exists in the environment, and there are certain environmental structures that carry information relevant to cognition.

These structures are quite diverse, and the information they embody can, in Grice's sense, be *natural* or *nonnatural*. With regard to visual perception, for example, the optic array—in Gibson's (1966) sense—carries natural information relevant to the solution of certain perceptual tasks. On the other hand, certain forms of visuographic representation—writing being the most familiar example—carry information that is, at least arguably, nonnatural in that it depends on the intentions and understanding of, and conventions devised by, those users. But although the types of external structure involved, and the types of information they embody, can diverge markedly, what unites them, from the perspective of vehicle externalism, is that some of the information they carry can be relevant to the accomplishing of cognitive tasks.

(2)   Cognitive processes are (often) hybrid—they straddle both internal and external forms of information processing.

Cognitive processes are information-processing operations that, since they are the sorts of things that can yield cognitive states (i.e., states defined by their representational content), can be employed to accomplish cognitive tasks. So (2) amounts to the claim that at least some of the information-processing operations in which an organism engages are not purely internal operations. At least some of the information processing that an organism accomplishes, it accomplishes in the world rather than in its head. Information processing straddles both internal operations and external ones.

The external operations typically take the form of *action* on the appropriate environmental structures. These structures carry information relevant to the accomplishing of cognitive tasks, and acting upon them is a way of *processing* information—transforming information *present* in the structures into information *available* in the structures. Thus, the third constitutive principle of vehicle externalism is:

(3)   The external processes involve the manipulation, exploitation, and transformation of environmental structures that carry information relevant to the accomplishing of the cognitive task at hand.

By manipulating, exploiting, and transforming information bearing environmental structures, the cognizing organism is able to make available to itself information that was contained in the structures that, prior to its actions, was unavailable to it. This information will, then, also be available for subsequent cognitive operations.

4   An Example: Visual Perception

To see principles (1) through (3) in action, consider an example: visual perception. One external information-bearing structure relevant to the accomplishing of perceptual tasks is the *optic array*, in Gibson's (1966) sense. Light from the sun fills the air—the terrestrial medium—so that it is in a "steady state" of reverberation. The environment is, in this way, filled with rays of light traveling between the surfaces of objects. At any point, light will converge from all directions. Therefore, at each physical point in the environment, there exists a densely nested set of solid visual angles composed of inhomogeneities in the intensity of light. Thus, we can imagine an observer, at least for the present, as a point surrounded by a sphere that is divided into tiny solid angles. The intensity of light and the mixture of wavelengths vary from one solid angle to another. This spatial pattern of light is the optic array. Light carries information because the structure of the optic array is determined by the nature and position of the surfaces from which it has been reflected.

The optic array is divided into many segments or angles. Each of these contains light reflected from different surfaces, and the light contained in each segment will differ from that in other segments in terms of its average intensity and distribution of wavelengths. The boundaries between these segments of the optic array, since they mark a change in the intensity and distribution of wavelengths, provide information about the three-dimensional structure of the environment. At a finer level of detail, each segment will, in turn, be subdivided in a way determined by the texture of the surface from which the light is reflected. Therefore, at this level also, the optic array can carry information about further properties of objects and terrain.

With this in mind, consider (1). The optic array is an *external information-bearing structure*. It is external in the quite obvious sense that it exists outside the skins of perceiving organisms, and is in no way dependent on such organisms for its existence. It also carries information about the environment. Indeed, according to Gibson, there is enough information contained in the optic array to specify the nature of the environment that shapes it. It carries information because the structure of the optic array depends nomically on the structure of the physical environment that surrounds it. The optic array is, as Gibson puts it, *specific* to the environment. Because of this, an organism whose perceptual system detects optical structure in the array is, Gibson argues, thereby aware of what this structure specifies. Thus, the perceiving organism is aware of the environment and not the array and, more significantly, is in a position to utilize the information about the environment embodied in the array.

We can derive an important methodological corollary from this. Suppose we are trying to understand the perceptual processing involved in accomplishing a given type of perceptual task. If we accept the concept of the optic array, we have to allow that at least some of the information relevant to this task will be located in the array. Perhaps, as Gibson sometimes seems to suggest, this information will be sufficient for the accomplishing of the task. Perhaps it is not—in which case we might find it necessary to postulate some form of internal-processing operations that somehow supplement or embellish the information contained in the array. Even if this is so, however, one thing is clear. We cannot begin to estimate what internal processing an organism needs to accomplish unless we already understand how much information is available to that organism in its optic array. The more information available to the organism in its optic array, the less internal processing the organism needs to perform. An understanding of the internal processes involved in visual perception is logically and methodologically secondary to understanding the information available to the perceiving organism in its environment.

Consider now (2) and (3). The key idea here is that by acting on the optic array, and thus transforming it, the perceiving organism is able to make available to itself information that was, prior to this action, present—at least conditionally—but not immediately available. When an observer moves, the entire optic array is transformed, and such transformations contain information about the layout, shapes, and orientations of objects in the world. The transformation of the array makes available to the organism information that was, prior to the action, there in only a conditional or dispositional form. More specifically, by effecting transformations in the ambient optic array—by transforming one array into another systematically related array—perceiving organisms can identify and appropriate what Gibson calls the *invariant* information contained in the optic array. This is information contained not in any one static optic array as such, but in the transformation of one optic array into another. Invariant information, therefore, takes the form of higher-order variables that can be identified only when one optic array is transformed into another. In the absence of such transformations, invariant information is present, but only in conditional form: conditional on certain types of transformation being systematically related to certain changes in sensory input.

What is crucial here is that (i) the optic array, a structure external to the perceiving organism, is a locus of information for suitably equipped creatures, and that (ii) a creature can appropriate or make this information available to itself through acting upon the array, and thus effecting transformations in it. What the perceiving organism does, in effect, is *manipulate* a structure external to it—the optic array—to make available to itself information that it can then use to navigate its environment. If information relevant to perception is contained in the array, then manipulating the array to make this information available is, in effect, a form of information processing.

The key to this account is the idea of effecting transformations in an information-bearing structure in such a way as to make available to the perceiving organism information that was, prior to this, present (at least conditionally) but unavailable. But this idea seems to be precisely what information processing is. To see this, let's switch focus to a traditional internalist approach to perception. Such an approach is likely to be organized around the following tripartite distinction:

Sensation   This consists in all processes leading up to the formation of the retinal image (typically made up of around 120 million pointwise measurements of light intensity). This image, in itself, contains very little visual information. Indeed, the poverty of information is typically thought to render the retinal image cognitively useless.

Perception   The retinal image is gradually transformed along the visual pathways, by processes that essentially serve to structure, embroider, and embellish the information contained in it. The construction of edges, boundaries, shapes, colors, and so on, provide structures that are more suitable for subsequent processing by nonperceptual mechanisms.

Cognition   All subsequent processes fall under the category of cognition. Such processes are typically taken to include postsensory operations concerned with the recognition and categorization of objects and also purely semantic operations aimed at incorporating the resulting representations into the subject's psychological economy.

First of all, consider what this tripartite distinction reveals about the purpose of perception. The purpose is to make something available to the perceiving organism—an item to which postsensory, properly cognitive, processes can be applied. Or, if you don't like that way of putting it, the purpose is to produce an information-bearing item that is available to postperceptual processing. Either way, the notion of *availability* runs to the core of the concept of information processing. Information-processing operations are ones that involve the production of an information-bearing item that is then available for further operations.[8]

Switching focus to the perceptual processing itself (rather than the relation between perceptual and other forms of processing), we are likely to find theories organized around the following framework:

1. Perception begins with stimulation of the retina by light energy impinging on it.
2. This results in a retinal image, characterized in terms of intensity values distributed over a large array of different locations.

3. Retinal images carry relatively little information, certainly not enough to add up to genuine visual perception.

4. For perception to occur, the information contained in the retinal image has to be supplemented and embellished (i.e., processed) by various information-processing operations.

5. These information-processing operations occur inside the skin of the perceiving organism.

This sort of framework is clearly evident in the well-known model developed by David Marr (1982). For Marr, visual perception begins with the formation of an informationally impoverished retinal image. The function of properly perceptual processes is to transform this retinal image into, successively, the raw primal sketch, the full primal sketch, and then the 2½D sketch—the culmination of properly perceptual processing. At each stage in the operation, one information-bearing structure is transformed into another. The retinal image, reputedly, contains very little information, but it does contain some. The retinal image is made up of a distribution of light-intensity values across the retina. Since the distribution of intensity values is nomically dependent on the way in which light is reflected by the physical structures that the organism is viewing, the image carries some information about these structures. Then this information-bearing structure is transformed into the raw primal sketch. In the raw primal sketch, information about the edges and textures of objects has been added. The application of various grouping principles (e.g., proximity, similarity, common fate, good continuation, closure, and so on) to the raw primal sketch results in the identification of larger structures, boundaries, and regions. This more refined representation is the full primal sketch.

Abstracting from the details, a very definite picture emerges of what constitutes information processing in the case of visual perception. Information processing consists in the transformation of information-bearing structures with the aim of rendering available information that was previously unavailable. This is achieved by way of the production of an information-bearing item that is available to be accessed by subsequent processes. But the transformation of information-bearing structures with the aim of rendering available information, embodied in a new structure—that was previously unavailable—is precisely what is going on in the case of the transformation of the optic array. Through action, one information-bearing optic array can be transformed into another. And in this transformation, information is made available to the organism—information that can now be accessed by other cognitive systems possessed by that organism—information that was previously unavailable. So, if we are happy with the idea that the sorts of internal operations employed in traditional models of perception are examples of information processing, then we have no reason for denying that the same is true of the operations involved when an organism acts on the structure of light around it.

So, in the case of visual perception at least, not all the information processing that is going on occurs inside the perceiving organism. Information is something that the organism does in its world as well as in its head. But, as we have also seen, information processing is a core component of the concept of a cognitive process. Cognitive processes are information-processing operations that occur as a means of accomplishing a cognitive task. If we think that the information processing that a perceiving organism achieves extends, in part, outside its skin, then, it seems, we have little reason for denying that its cognitive processes extend in the same way and for the same reasons.

One could, of course, always *stipulate* that the concept of information processing is to be restricted to processes occurring inside the skins of organisms. One can stipulate anything one likes. However, given that information is embodied in structures external to organisms, and given that an organism can effect transformations in these structures to make information available to itself—information that can then be used in subsequent processing—it is difficult to see the point of this restriction. In other words, there seems to be no great theoretical divide between manipulating *internal* information-bearing structures and manipulating *external* information-bearing structures to make available to oneself, or to one's cognitive operations, the information that results. To claim that only the former constitutes genuine information processing seems little more than an internalist prejudice.

I, and a number of other people, have argued elsewhere that substantially the same sort of account can be told for many other cognitive operations also, including remembering, reasoning, and the processes involved in language production and understanding.[9] This book is not the place to rehearse these arguments further. In chapter 5, I shall examine a recent form of vehicle externalism tailored specifically to visual perception. And this may be taken as providing additional arguments for being a vehicle externalist. But, my primary interest in this book is not in establishing the truth of vehicle externalism, but rather in developing a certain conception of representation that coheres with vehicle-externalist principles. However, one does not have to be a vehicle externalist to accept this account of representation—although, admittedly, it helps. And if one is a

vehicle externalist, one does not have to accept this view of representation—
although again, I think it helps, as I shall argue. The arguments developed
in the following chapters can be endorsed quite independently of vehicle
externalism.

5   Vehicle Externalism and Representation

One claim that unites all forms of vehicle externalism is that the role traditionally assigned to representations can, at least to some extent, be taken
over by suitable action on the part of the representing organism. The first
fault line in vehicle externalism is determined by the way one answers the
following question: can *all* of the role traditionally assigned to representations be played by suitable action on the part of the representing organism? If you answer "yes" to this question; then you combine vehicle
externalism with a form of *eliminativism* about representation. I shall discuss eliminativism about representation in the next section.

Suppose, however, that you answer "no" to the question. Then you
have a choice to make. How, precisely, does one understand the connection between representation and action? There are at least two distinct
possibilities.

The first possibility, in essence, is a form of *dual-component* interpretation, where this label is (obviously) intended to draw attention to parallels
with the corresponding interpretation of content externalism identified in
the previous chapter. As we saw there, this interpretation we might justifi-
ably regard as a *reactionary* interpretation of content externalism because it
tries to hold on to the general Cartesian division between mind and world,
albeit in a somewhat different form. Specifically, the Cartesian idea of the
mind as a self-contained interiority is preserved: it's simply that its bounds
are redrawn. The boundaries between inner and outer now correspond to
the distinction between, on the one hand, the qualitative/action-guiding/
causal-explanatory component of a mental state and, on the other, its
representational component. And traditional Cartesian theses about the
mind—both ontic and epistemic—can now be asserted about the inner
component rather than the entire mental state. Thus the Cartesian view of
the mind persists in recognizable form in the dual-component theory. This
theory accepts the force of the arguments against the Cartesian view of the
mind, but it attempts to severely limit their consequences.

Of course, as we saw in the previous chapter, if this attempt to safeguard
the Cartesian vision is to work, each component must be at least logically
separable. Someone who wants to deny the Cartesian vision in any form

can accept with equanimity the idea that content supervenes, *in part*, on various internal items. If the role that these internal items play in constituting content cannot, even logically, be separated from the role played by external factors in constituting such content, then the idea of content as a self-contained Cartesian interiority must be abandoned. And, as we also saw earlier, this thought provides the basis of a more *radical* interpretation of content externalism, according to which internal and external components could not be separated in the way required by the dual-component interpretation. If there are no logically separable components, then there exists no region of reality to which the traditional Cartesian theses about the nature of mental content might apply.

Vehicle externalism also admits of a dual-component interpretation, one that parallels the interpretation of mental content. A case of representation can, on this interpretation, be factored into two components; one that is genuinely representational, one that is not. What is involved in being a genuinely representational component of representation is something that can be cashed out in terms of one's preferred account of the representational relation—informational and teleological accounts, or some combination being popular candidates. This genuinely representational component, on the dual-component interpretation of the extended model, functions in tandem with suitable acts of environmental action—worldly manipulation, exploitation, and transformation, for example.

The relation between these two components can be extremely intimate. It may be, for example, that the genuinely representational component of at least some representations has been *designed* to function in tandem with acts of environmental activity, so that the former cannot fulfill its function in the absence of the latter. However, what is crucial to the dual-component interpretation is the claim that the action-based component is (i) logically distinct from the representational component, and (ii) is, therefore, not itself genuinely representational. The action-based component allows or facilitates the genuinely representational component, sometimes perhaps essentially, but it does not itself represent anything.

Like the corresponding interpretation of content externalism, the dual-component interpretation of the relation between representation and action is, I think, essentially a defensive, even reactionary, response. The response acknowledges the force of the arguments for vehicle externalism, and the consequent intimacy of the relation between representation and action, but seeks to limit their significance. In particular, the dual-component interpretation retains the essential core of the orthodox conception: the idea that representation is a relation obtaining between two distinct states, one internal and one extrinsic. Of course this relation, by itself, is not claimed to exhaust representation: to properly understand representation as a whole, we must factor in another component, an action-based component. Nevertheless, at the core of the genuinely representational component of representation, we find the same traditional structure. Tradition is in no way undermined by the dual-component interpretation. On the contrary, it is retained and merely supplemented.

However, as with content externalism, there exists the possibility of a more radical interpretation of vehicle externalism. A radicalized version of vehicle externalism will be based on the idea that, in any case of representation, we cannot separate action guiding from the genuinely representational component in the manner presupposed by the dual-component interpretation. There are, in fact, no two logically separable components. However, one way of developing this idea would deliver us straight back into the hands of eliminativism. This would occur if we tried to reduce the representational component to the action-based component. There is a fine line between reducing one item to another, and eliminating the former in favor of the latter. What I have in mind, however, is quite different.

The idea I shall defend is that the role action—the *deed*—plays in representation is *itself* representational. The action-, or activity-, based component of representation is not, as we might put it, externally related to representation. This component does not, as the dual-component interpretation alleges, play the merely facilitatory or supporting role of allowing the genuinely representational component to do its genuinely representational work. Rather, the action-based component of representation is *itself genuinely representational*. That is actions, of the sort involved in the manipulating, exploiting, transforming, and exploring of environmental structures, can *themselves* be representational. It is not as if we have a genuinely representational core at the heart of representation, a core that corresponds, in all its essentials, to the contours of the traditional conception. In representation, we cannot, in fact, distinguish a genuinely representational core component from an action-based component. Rather, the action-based component is itself representational. Representation is representational *all the way out.*

6   Eliminating Representation?

Certain strains of vehicle externalism go hand in hand with a general antipathy toward the idea of representation. For example, many *dynamicist* approaches staunchly reject the idea that the concept of a representation will play any genuine role in accounting for cognition. Thus, for example, Thelen and Smith, pioneers of the dynamicist approach toward cognitive development, write:

Explanations in terms of structures in the head—beliefs, rules, concepts and schemata, are not acceptable. . . . Our theory has new concepts at the centre—nonlinearity, re-entrance, coupling heterochronicity, attractors, momentum, state spaces, intrinsic dynamics, forces. These concepts are not reducible to the old ones. (1994: 339)

We posit that development happens because of the time-locked pattern of activity across heterogeneous components. We are not building representations of the world by connecting temporally contingent ideas. We are not building representations at all. Mind is activity in time . . . the real time of real physical causes. (Ibid.: 338)

Similar sentiments have been expressed, at one time or another, by Maturana and Varela (1980), Skarda and Freeman (1987), Smithers (1994), Wheeler (1994), and van Gelder (1995). Nor are these sentiments restricted to narrowly dynamicist approaches. Although occupying a somewhat different theoretical position, we find the roboticist Webb arguing against a representational interpretation of her robot cricket. Webb's cricket is able to locate and orient itself toward the direction of a cricket's song even though it possesses no general mechanism for identifying the direction of sounds, nor any mechanism for discriminating the song of its own species from other songs. In short, the robot cricket does not build a rich model of its environment and then apply some deductive inference mechanism to generate action plans. Webb comments:

It is not necessary to use this symbolic interpretation to explain how the system functions: the variables serve a mechanical function in connecting sensors to motors, a role epistemologically comparable to the function of the gears connecting the motors to the wheels. (1994: 53)

It is, of course, plausible to suppose that the general framework for thinking about cognition advocated by dynamicist approaches is that which, in fact, inspires much recent work in robotics, so that Webb's claims and those of Thelen and Smith are two sides of the same coin. Nevertheless, similar sentiments are also expressed by those whose theoretical orientation is quite different. Thus, in connection with visual perception of the environment, O'Regan and Noë claim:

Indeed, there is no "re-presentation" of the world inside the brain: the only pictorial or 3D version required is the real outside version. What *is* required however are methods for probing the outside world—and visual perception constitutes one mode via which it can be probed. The experience of seeing occurs when the outside world is being probed according to the visual mode. . . . (2001: 946)

And this certainly seems to be an expression of the idea that we can eliminate representations, traditionally construed, in favor of action of an appropriate sort.

Underlying the diverse expressions of this sentiment is a single, but important, thought. The ability of an organism to perceive and cognize is intimately bound up with its ability to engage in on-line, feedback-modulated, adjustments with respect to relevant structures in its environment. Cognition occurs when inner and outer are caught up in a complex and dynamic dance, a web of interdependencies and interrelations, and, consequently, there does not exist the separation of inside from outside necessary for what is on the inside to qualify as representational.

Consider, for example, van Gelder's well-known discussion of the Watt governor (1995: 347–350). A *governor* is a device that regulates the speed of a flywheel that is driven by a steam engine and that itself drives further machinery. The problem arises because there will be constant fluctuations in the steam pressure delivered by the engine, and in the workload of the flywheel (i.e., the number of machines being driven). Because of this, the speed of the flywheel will also fluctuate. To keep the rotation of the flywheel uniform, the amount of steam entering the pistons (which drive the flywheel) is controlled by a throttle valve. The more steam there is, the greater the speed. At one time these corrections were made by a human engineer, who manually controlled the amount of steam entering the pistons. The question is: how might these adjustments be automated?

One strategy, that, according to van Gelder, is essentially computational in character, would involve a series of steps and measurements. A computational solution to the governing problem might, for example, be based on the following series of rules:

1. Measure the speed of the flywheel.
2. Compare the actual speed, v, against the desired speed, u.
3. If $v = u$, return to step 1. Otherwise:
a. measure the current steam pressure, Pa.
b. calculate the desired steam pressure Pd.
c. Measure the difference between Pd and Pa.
d. calculate the necessary throttle valve adjustment to make $Pa = Pd$.
4. Make the necessary throttle valve adjustment.
5. Return to step 1. (van Gelder 1995: 348)

According to van Gelder, this qualifies as a computational procedure because it exhibits a set of familiar features, ones that differentiate computational from noncomputational procedures.

First, the procedure essentially involves the notion of *representation*. The device measures the speed of the flywheel, and creates a token that stands for this speed. It then performs numerous comparisons of this token with other tokens—for example, the token that stands for the desired or ideal speed. This eventually results in the production of an output representation: a specification of the alteration to be made in the throttle valve. Second, these operations are discrete and occur in a precise sequence, determined by the algorithm specified in 1 through 5. This sequence involves a cycle of environmental measurement (i.e., the speed of the flywheel) and a calculation of the appropriate change in throttle-valve adjustment, followed by the production of an output representation that produces this change. This procedure is computational, therefore, because it literally computes the desired change in throttle-valve adjustment by manipulating symbols according to a series of rules.

The actual solution to the governor problem was, however, not of this sort. The solution consisted in the development, by James Watt, of the centrifugal governor, or Watt governor, as it is now often known. A vertical spindle is attached to the flywheel, with two hinged arms attached to this spindle. Attached to the end of each arm is a metal ball. The arms are then linked to the throttle valve so that the higher the arms swing out, the less steam is allowed through. As the spindle turns, centrifugal force causes the arms to swing out, and the faster it turns, the higher the arms fly out. However, this now reduces steam flow, causing the engine to slow down and the arms to fall. This in turn opens the valve and allows more steam to flow. With suitable calibration, the governor can be set up so as to maintain uniform engine speed in the face of significant variations in pressure and workload (van Gelder 1995: 347–350).

The Watt governor, van Gelder claims, constitutes a fundamentally different type of control system from the computational alternative described earlier. In particular, the Watt governor is, van Gelder argues, noncomputational. And it is noncomputational precisely because it is nonrepresentational (ibid.: 353). His argument for this runs as follows.

He begins with what he takes to be an uncontroversial account of what makes something a representation. A representation, according to van Gelder, is a state of some system that, "by virtue of some general representational scheme, stands in for some further state of affairs, thereby enabling the system to behave appropriately with respect to that state of affairs" (ibid.: 351). Then, van Gelder argues that states of the engine-flywheel-governor system fail to qualify as representations in this sense.

We might be tempted to suppose, for example, that the angle at which the arms are swinging represents the speed of the engine. What makes this supposition a natural one is the fact that there is an intimate and interesting relation between the speed of the engine and the angle of the arms. However, this relation is not, van Gelder argues, a representational one. The reason for this is that there does not exist the degree of independence of arm angle and engine speed that would allow the relation to qualify as representational. Crucially, the angle at which the arms are swinging is not only determined by the speed of the engine, it also determines the speed of the engine. Since the arms are directly linked to the throttle valve, the angle of the arms determines the amount of steam entering the piston, and hence the speed at which the engine is running. Thus, arm angle and engine speed are, at all times, mutually determining. Therefore, there does not exist the degree of independence that would allow us to talk of the arm angle "standing in for" engine speed, as would be required if the former was a genuine representation of the latter. There is nothing mysterious about this relation of codependence: it is perfectly amenable to mathematical analysis. The point urged by van Gelder, however, is that the concept of representation— of something standing in for some other thing—is too simple to account for the interaction between governor and engine (1995: 353).

One straightforward response to a dynamicist-inspired attempt to eliminate representation acknowledges that dynamicist models may have interesting things to say about *some* instances of cognition, but denies that such models are capable of accommodating *all* cases of cognition. Of particular importance, here, is whether dynamicist models have the resources to handle what Clark and Toribio (1994) call *representation-hungry* problems and problem domains. The standard cases of behavior dealt with by dynamicist models concern behavior that is continuously driven and modified by the environment. However, not all cognition occurs in these sorts of circumstances. And the postulation of internal representations seems at its strongest when it occurs in connection with behavior that is disconnected or *decoupled* from immediate environmental modulation and feedback. Such behavior will include (i) the coordination of activity and choice with states of affairs that are distal or counterfactual, and (ii) the coordination of activity and choice with states of affairs that are complex and untidy.

Examples of the first sort will include activities such as planning to visit one's brother in Australia, working out the consequences of some course of action that you might or might not follow later in the day, working out what would have happened if only you had done X instead of Y, and using mental imagery to count the number of windows in one's house while sitting at one's desk in one's office. All these cases are characterized by some form of physical disconnection or decoupling from the states of affairs that are the objects of one's cognitive states—either because those states of affairs are distant in space or time, or because they are not actual but counterfactual in character.

The case for mental representations seems particularly powerful in these sorts of contexts. In the case of distal or counterfactual states of affairs, there simply is no environmental feature present that could provide for the sort of environmental modulation and adjustment that plays such a central role in dynamicist approaches.

Examples of the second sort involve, primarily, states of affairs that are *nonnomic*.[10] A property is nomic if it falls directly under a physical law of nature. Having a certain velocity, for example, would be an example of a nomic property, since it falls directly under natural laws such as Newton's laws of motion. Most of the properties that we selectively respond to, however, are nonnomic ones. The property of clashing with a shirt is one that might be possessed by a tie, but it is not the sort of property that falls directly under a law of nature.

Our ability to selectively respond to nonnomic features—by, for example, picking one tie out of the wardrobe rather than another—means that we are responding to more than straightforward physical features of the environment. This ability provides one of the most important motivations for the postulation of representations. To track a property such as *being a matching tie* we seem to use an indirect route—we track this property by first tracking more basic features of the world—color, shape, and so on—and their instantiation in shirt and tie. Once we have detected the presence of features such as these, we then *infer* the presence of a matching tie. But this seems to involve the use of a representation in the form of a hypothesis about what makes something a matching tie (e.g., relative to shirt X, something, Y, is a matching tie iff . . .).

One problem for dynamicist approaches, then, consists in the suspicion that although they might provide appropriate models for certain kinds of cognitive activity, they do not do so for all forms of cognition. Dynamicist approaches may be suitable for handling cases of cognition that receive constant environmental feedback and adjustment. However, they are less promising for the kinds of cognition that involve some form of disconnection with the physical environment—either because the environment is distal or counterfactual, or because the cognizing subject is responding to (nonnomic) features that are, physically, extremely complex or unruly.

This dispute is ongoing.[11] However, the argument I am going to develop does not depend on how this dispute is ultimately concluded. The eliminativist interpretation, in any of its forms, involves appeal to the ability of an organism to continuously modify and modulate its behavior on the basis of environmental contingencies and associated information. The ability to do this is the ability to engage in *activity* with respect to the world. The argument I am going to develop in the next chapter takes this activity as its starting point. I shall argue that the eliminativist, in effect, faces a dilemma. Either the conception of activity to which the eliminativist appeals presupposes representation, and therefore cannot explain it away, or, the conception of activity is wholly inappropriate for either explaining representation or explaining it away. Moreover, once developed, this argument will have far wider application than merely undermining eliminativist proclivities vis-à-vis representation. It will cast doubt on the validity of any appeal to action in the explanation of representation, whether this explanation is performed with eliminativist intent or not.

7   The Dual-Component Interpretation: Unnatural Couplings

At the other end of the spectrum is another type of mistake that some vehicle externalists—including, alas, I—have tended to make. This mistake is most clearly embodied in the dual-component interpretation of vehicle externalism, since this wants to hang onto the traditional idea of a genuinely representational core that is merely facilitated in its activity by an action-based component. Whereas eliminativist approaches want to jettison the concept of representation altogether, this alternative mistake is to grip far too tightly to an entrenched and conservative view of what representation is, and then suppose that it is possible to graft this onto a vehicle-externalist account of cognitive processes. The result, in effect, is a schizophrenic divorce of cognitive processes from the products of those processes.

Suppose we accept the general vehicle-externalist premise that cognitive processes, and the architectures in which such processes are implemented, are extended out into, or distributed onto, the world. But then we try to hang onto a traditional account of representation according to which it is essentially a relation between an inner representing item and an extrinsic, and typically outer, represented one. The result is that we will be committed to the idea that although cognitive processes are, in part, extended into the world, the products of those processes, representational vehicles, are inner items. In effect, in terms of the distinction introduced at the beginning of this chapter, this is to divorce, and, I think, *unacceptably* divorce, externalism about the vehicles of *cognition* from externalism about the vehicles of *content.*

A moment's thought reveals just how strange this coupling is. If cognitive processes can be distributed onto the world, why *should* representation be thought of exclusively as a relation between inner and extrinsic (and typically outer) items? Why *can't* representation be distributed onto the world in much the same way as cognitive processes? If the vehicles of *cognition* are distributed onto the world, what reason can there be for maintaining that the vehicles of *content* are limited to what obtains inside the skin of organisms? What the vehicle externalist needs, I now think, is a revision of the concept of representation along externalist lines. Representation is not *essentially* a relation between inner representing item and outer represented item. Representation exists out in the world as much as in the head—or, to put the same point another way, there is no principled way of separating action from representation. This is not because, as the eliminativist urges, representation is less than real. Rather, it is because representation is very real indeed, and it is to be found in more places than we had initially supposed.

Representations, I shall argue, do not stop at the skin anymore than cognition does. The products of cognitive processes are bound by the skin no more than are the processes themselves. Representation is not simply what guides behavior. Rather, it *extends into* the behavior. Representing is representational *all the way out.*

4 The Myths of the Giving

1 The Myths of the Giving

As we saw in the previous chapter, the appeal to action, in some form, is essential to the vehicle-externalist account of cognition. On this account, part of the burden of representing the world can be offloaded onto appropriate forms of action: the manipulation, exploitation, and transformation of information-bearing structures in the environment. There is disagreement as to how much of this burden can be thus offloaded. Eliminativist interpretations of vehicle externalism think that the entire function of representations, traditionally construed, can be taken over by appropriate forms of action. Other, less sanguine, interpretations think that some, but not necessarily all of this role can be thus taken over.

In this chapter and the next, I shall argue that the appeal to action—either to explain representation or to explain it away—is deeply problematic. In particular, there are three types of mistakes that the appeal is in danger of making; or, as I shall put it, three types of *myths* to which the appeal is in danger of falling victim. Following Susan Hurley, I shall refer to these, for reasons that will become clear, as the *myths of the giving*. I shall argue, in this chapter and the next, that the cumulative effect of these myths is to make the appeal to action—as a way of explaining or explaining away representation—subject to a *dilemma*; a dilemma from which there is only one escape. To begin, however, it is necessary to introduce and distinguish the myths. The first version of the myth is, perhaps, best introduced in connection with Wittgenstein's well-known arguments concerning the nature of rule following.

2 The Rule-Following Paradox

The meaning of a sign is *normative*. The precise way in which this is so will, of course, vary from one type of sign to another. Some signs are used to apply to items extrinsic to them. For such signs, there is a correct and incorrect way of applying them. That is, a given sign of this form *should* be, or is supposed to be, applied to certain things and not to others. Other signs—the logical connectives provide an obvious example—can function by contributing to the sense of a larger sign-complex of which they form a part. But in this case too, there is a legitimate and illegitimate way of employing the sign. The meaning of a sign is normative, then, because there is a correct and an incorrect way of using the sign.

According to Wittgenstein, the fundamental problem of representation is accounting for this normative aspect of signs. What, precisely, constitutes the way a sign is supposed to be used? A natural thought is that we might circumscribe the use of a sign by way of a *rule*—one that specifies how the sign is to be used. Wittgenstein undermined this idea by showing that it leads to a certain type of paradox. This is sometimes referred to as a *skeptical* paradox. This expression is unfortunate since it suggests the problem is primarily an epistemological one; and, for Wittgenstein, it is not. A more accurate name would be the *rule-following paradox*.

Suppose someone begins a mathematical sequence as follows: 2, 4, 6, 8, 10, 12, 14 . . . 996, 998, 1000. . . . However, when they get to 1000, they continue as follows: 1004, 1008, 1012, 1016. . . . It is overwhelmingly natural to suppose that, upon reaching 1,000, they made a mistake. The natural response is that they were following a certain rule: the "$x+n$" rule. Their behavior after reaching 1,000 is a contravention of this rule since they now, apparently, started to follow the "$x+2n$" rule. The sheen of simplicity, however, is only apparent.

Perhaps, for example, they were, all along, following not the "$x+n$" rule but the more complex rule: "$x+n$ iff $x \leq 1000$, if not $x+2n$." So the question is, what constitutes the person following the "$x+n$" rule (and subsequently making a mistake) and the "$x+2n$ iff $x \leq 1000$, if not $x+2n$" rule (and subsequently carrying on correctly)? To capture the normative character of signs, we must be able to distinguish what a person *should* do with a sign from what they *in fact* do with it. The suggestion is that we can do this by appeal to a rule that specifies how the sign is to be used. If this is to work, we need to identify what constitutes following one rule rather than another. And to do this we need to be able to distinguish between following one rule incorrectly and following a distinct rule correctly.

One response we cannot make, of course, is that after reaching 1000 they made a mistake because they were supposed to go on doing *the same thing*. This is because, what counts as *the same thing* can only be defined relative to the rule they in fact adopt. If they adopted the more complex rule then, after reaching 1000, they did in fact go on doing the *same thing*—for this is precisely what the rule they were following all along told them they should do when they reached 1000.

Perhaps, then, when a person understands how to follow a mathematical rule, the rule must somehow pass before their mind. But how would this occur? Is it that the picture of the rule "*x+n*" appears before their mind's eye? However, then the problem is that the picture is, logically, just another symbol. So, for it to determine how we continue the mathematical progression, we would first have to interpret the formula "*x+n*." Perhaps, for example, "+" is used in a way such that it means "+*n* iff *x* ≤ 1000, +2*n* otherwise." In which case, when the person reaches 1000, they, in fact, continue to correctly follow the rule. The presence of a mathematical formula before one's conscious gaze cannot provide an interpretation of what one is supposed to do, for it is itself subject to a variety of interpretations.

Perhaps, one might think, that following the rule consists in the fact that the person consciously thinks to themselves, "when I reach 1000, I will continue adding 2 and no other number." But this merely pushes the problem back a step to the interpretation of terms such as "adding" and "number." Perhaps, for example, "number" is being used in such a way that for any *x*, *x* is a number iff *x* ≤ 1000, and if *x* ≥ 1000, then *x* is a "schnumber" rather than a number.[1] And, of course, any appeal to the idea that the rule is "when I reach 1000, I will continue adding 2 and not 1, 3, 4, 5, . . . *n*" would entail that whenever a person correctly followed a mathematical rule, they must simultaneously be thinking an infinite number of thoughts.

To capture the normative character of signs, we need to be able to distinguish what a person *should* do with a sign from what they *in fact* do with it. However, the appeal to rules in drawing this distinction is useless because any rule *hangs in the air* along with what it interprets: a rule is, logically, just another symbol, and thus, to specify how a sign is to be interpreted, it must first have *its* interpretation fixed.

The problem persists if we switch our focus from mental to behavioral facts. A person's behavior at any given time is compatible with their following an indefinite number of rules. A person continuing a series 2, 4, 6, 8, 10, 12 . . . is, in fact, compatible with his following an infinite number of algebraic formulae ("*x+n* iff *x* ≤ 16, if not *x+2n*," etc.). Indeed, since numbers are infinite, the person's behavior will, necessarily, always be compatible with his following an infinite number of algebraic formulae.

So, there does not seem to be any fact—whether mental or behavioral—about an individual person at a given time that determines that they are following one rule rather than another. Thus, Wittgenstein argues, we arrive at a paradox:

This was our paradox: no course of action could be determined by a rule, because every course of action can be made out to accord with the rule. The answer was: if everything can be made out to accord with the rule, then it can also be made out to conflict with it. And so there would be neither accord nor conflict here. (1953: §201)

This paradox is not primarily an epistemological one. The central problem is not how we can know, or find out, what rule someone is following. The core problem is metaphysical: what *constitutes* a person's following one rule rather than another? There is, it seems, no fact of the matter that constitutes a person's following the "$x+n$" rule, rather than the "$x+n$ iff $x \leq$ 1000, otherwise x+2n rule". But if there is nothing that constitutes their following one rule rather than another, there is also nothing that constitutes the difference between their following a rule correctly and their making a mistake. The difference between the correct and incorrect following of a rule is not a difference that can be drawn at the level of an individual at a time. And, if this is true, we can draw no distinction, at this level, between the correct and incorrect following of a rule; nor does it make sense to talk of the *correct* application of a rule.

3   The Myth of the Giving 1(a)

I am not concerned with defending Wittgenstein's development of the paradox. Rather, my concern is with his response to it. This response seems to involve, in some capacity or other, an appeal to the concept of a *practice*:

And hence also "obeying a rule" is a practice. And to think one is obeying a rule is not to obey a rule. Hence it is not possible to obey a rule "privately": otherwise thinking one was obeying a rule would be the same thing as obeying it. (1953: §202)

This response turns on a distinction between thinking that one is obeying a rule and obeying it. This distinction is logically dependent on the distinction between the correct and incorrect application of a rule. In the absence of the latter distinction, there can be no former distinction. And, to draw this latter distinction, Wittgenstein claims, we need to understand that obeying a rule is a *practice*.

Concerning Wittgenstein's concept of a practice, there are notorious problems of interpretation. Is a practice something that can be constituted by or through the actions of a single person? An affirmative answer yields the *individual* interpretation of the concept of a practice; a negative one yields the *community* interpretation. On the former interpretation, the required distinction between correct and incorrect use lies in the contrast between an individual's use of a sign on one occasion and her use of that sign on repeated occasions. On the latter interpretation, the distinction between correct and incorrect use lies in the contrast between an individual's use of a sign and the use of that sign employed by the community as a whole.

However, whichever interpretation we adopt, the appeal to practice is a deeply puzzling one. It is difficult to see how it could make any impact at all on the rule-following paradox. The worry is, of course, that the appeal to practice presupposes content, hence cannot explain it. Appeal to a practice is appeal to *what we do*. However, on the most familiar construal, doing is a form of acting and, as such, is essentially connected to intentional states. The precise nature of the connection will depend on one's preferred view of action. It may be that what we do is simply a bodily movement caused by suitable intentional states. Or it may be that what we do is a successful trying—one individuated by reference to the bodily movements it causes. There are various possibilities—but all of these strongly link the idea of what we do to the concept of intentional states—whether intentions, volitions, tryings, belief-desire couplings, and so on. In particular, on *any* theory of action, both the *status* of an item as an action, and its *identity* as the particular action it is, depends on its standing in some or other appropriate relation to intentional states.[2] However, intentional states are individuated by their content. But the rule-following paradox is a problem about how content is possible. The appeal to practice presupposes the existence of states that are individuated by way of their content and which, thus, bear their content essentially. Thus, far from providing the basis of content, practice presupposes content.

We can generalize this problem. Any attempt to explain the possibility of meaning, content, or representation by appeal to practice—to what we *do* broadly construed—is guilty of what Susan Hurley (1998) has called *the myth of the giving*. Hurley introduces this myth as a counterpart to a more famous one: the myth of the *given*. The latter pertains to a certain mistaken conception of *perception*: it is the mistake of understanding perception as pure *input* from the world, unadulterated by the synthesizing activities of the subject. The myth of the *giving*, on the other hand, pertains to a mistaken conception of *action*: the mistake of understanding action as pure output to the world. The myth of the giving plays a prominent role in this book. However, I shall argue that the myth can, in fact, take three distinct forms, forms not properly distinguished by Hurley. The other two forms will be identified in the following sections.

The first version of the myth, then, is the idea that we can take the content of *action* as an unproblematic given, and then use this to explain the possibility of content. The problem, of course, is that any such appeal to action is circular. There is—to pick up on a point that will prove important in later chapters—a salutary lesson here for anyone who thinks that an appeal to action is a straightforward panacea to the problems involved in achieving a satisfactory understanding of representation. To appeal to a subject's action in an account of how that subject is able to represent the world is to presuppose the possibility of representation, not explain it. We shall look at how this problem specifically applies to vehicle externalism in the next chapter.

I am not, it is important to realize, accusing Wittgenstein of this mistake. The mistake is made by those commentators on, or supporters of, Wittgenstein who understand his appeal to practice as an attempt to identify a ground or *foundation* of content. But it is not, I think, a mistake made by Wittgenstein. In other words, the correct response to the paradox, and indeed Wittgenstein's response, is not a constructive one. The response should not be to show how, *pace* the paradox, meaning is possible—by, for example, identifying the fact that makes it possible for individuals to mean or understand something by a sign. That is, the correct response—and this is what the appeal to practice is, in fact, intended to highlight—is not to attempt to identify a foundation of content. Rather, the response involves challenging the assumptions that led us to the paradox in the first place. We shall look at this issue later in the chapter.

4   The Myth of the Giving 1(b)

The first form of the myth of the giving, then, consists in (the mistake of) taking action as an unproblematic given that can be used in an explanation of representation. There is a slightly different, and somewhat more familiar, form that the first version of the myth of the giving can take. Action need not just mean bodily action, it can also mean *activity* more broadly construed—and so incorporate mental as well as bodily activity. If we think of action as mental activity, then the myth of the giving consists in a relatively familiar, and largely discredited, *interpretational* conception of meaning—a conception that was, indeed, one of the targets of Wittgenstein's ruminations on rule following.

The key to the rule-following paradox is, I think, to be found in the somewhat puzzling remarks that appear just after the statement of the paradox, and the appeal to practice is to be understood firmly in the context of these remarks:

What this shows is that there is a way of grasping a rule which is *not an interpretation*, but which is exhibited in what we call "obeying the rule" and "going against it" in actual cases. (1953: §201)

If following a rule is to be possible at all, then there must be a way of following a rule that does not consist in an interpretation of that rule, where "[w]e ought to restrict the term 'interpretation' to the substitution of one expression of the rule for another" (ibid.). Instead, the following of the rule must, somehow, be exhibited in what we call obeying the rule or contravening it. The appeal to practice, then, is intended to highlight this alternative mode of following a rule—a mode untainted by the interpretational conception of this ability. Understanding this difficult point is the key to grasping Wittgenstein's view.

As a beginning, consider Kripke's well-known reading of Wittgenstein. According to Kripke, the key to the rule-following paradox lies in the idea that, "no matter what is in my mind at a given time, I am free in the future to interpret it in different ways" (1984: 207). Embodied in this idea is, in essence, a *two-factor* model of how mental items relate to the world. Intentional mental states, as we have seen, make a normative claim on the world. A belief is something with which only certain states of affairs would accord. If a certain belief is entertained, then the world ought to be a certain way if the belief is to be true. Similarly, an expectation is something with which only certain future states of affairs would accord. And an intention is something with which only acting in a specific way would accord. Kripke, in effect, advances a two-factor account of this normative status. On the one hand there are the items standing in the mind of the subject, on the other there are the interpretations that the subject places on those items. It is the interpretation, and *only* the interpretation, that links the items in the mind to their intentional objects in such a way that the former can be about the latter. In other words, interpretation supplies *content* to mental items. Interpretation maps mental item onto worldly fact; it supplies a mapping function that relates the mental item to the world in such a way that it can sort extramental facts into those that are in accord with it and those that are not. In short, mental items stand in the mind of the subject. They are linked to the world in virtue of their content. And this content is supplied by interpretation.

Seen in this light, the paradox rests on an eminently questionable assumption: the idea that mental items are semantically inert items whose content is fixed by an act of interpretation. Why *must* we think of mental items like this? A certain picture, once again, holds us captive. It is the assimilation of mental items to the category of the *word*. Mental items stand in the mind like words stand on a page. A word can mean anything, and so, in itself, means nothing. To have meaning, it needs to be interpreted. A mental item, likewise, is in itself semantically inert; to mean anything—to sort extramental items into those that are in accord with it and those that are not—it must be interpreted.

However, an act of interpretation is, of course, an intentional act, and as such possesses, and is individuated by, its content. So, the act of interpretation cannot explain how content is possible. To suppose that it can is to fall victim to the second form of the first version of the myth of the giving—the *myth of the giving 1(b)*, as I shall call it. Once again, action is taken as an unproblematic given; it's just that in this case the action in question is *mental* action—interpretative activity—rather than the more visible, bodily, correlate allegedly involved in the concept of a practice. Seen in this way, the mistake involved in the appeal to practice is, in effect, to retreat from one form of the myth of the giving to another: from taking the content of mental activity as an unproblematic given to taking that of action as such a given.

The conclusion we should draw, of course, is not that content is impossible, but that the assumptions on which the rule-following paradox has been erected should be rejected. In particular, we should reject the conception of mental items as, in themselves, semantically inert. In endorsing this assumption, we immediately set up a *boundary* between mental items and the world—a boundary that it is the function of interpretation, and the resulting content, to bridge. And the rule-following paradox works precisely to the extent that we have antecedently accepted this boundary. Once we do this, the boundary becomes seemingly impossible to bridge and we find ourselves with a serious worry about the possibility of content. The answer is not to try to bridge the boundary, but to disallow it. How do we do this?

The key lies in understanding how, as Wittgenstein puts it, there can be a way of following a rule that is not an interpretation. We need a conception of content that is not predicated on a picture of a, in itself, semantically inert item that becomes coupled with a logically separable act of interpretation. The first step is to look more closely at the concept of interpretation.

As we saw in chapter 2, built into the concept of interpretation is the idea of *separation* or *distance*—but in two significantly different ways. First, there is the idea that an interpretation must be distinct from what it interprets; that the act of interpretation must be distinct from the object of interpretation. On the one hand, there is the interpretation; on the other, there is that which it interprets. The interpretation of an item can only come from outside of that item. It is this first sense of separation that is ultimately responsible for the "regress of interpretations" problem that destroys interpretational conceptions of meaning. Second, there is the idea that the object of interpretation must be distinct from what, via the act of interpretation, that object is about. The interpretation relates the object of interpretation—the vehicle of content—to something outside of it, in such a way that it separates those extrinsic items that are in accord with the object of interpretation from those that are not. It is this, second, sense of separation that is responsible for the "exteriority of content" constraint that is, partly, constitutive of the assimilation of representations to the category of the word.

The concept of interpretation involves both senses of separation or distance. And in attempting to reject the interpretational conception of content, one must be careful to reject both of these, and not merely one. The key to excision lies in what seems to be a truism: *when I think that p, that p is what I think*. And, as we saw in chapter 2, this apparent truism is an expression of something far more controversial: *SR-content externalism*. In other words, SR-externalism provides us with the means of rejecting the assumption that leads to the rule-following paradox. And this thought provides the basis of contextualist responses to the paradox associated with Baker and Hacker (1984) and McDowell (1993). If mental content is, indeed, unconfined in the sense specified by SR-externalism, then such content is identical with worldly facts. This undermines the picture of content as a necessary bridge between a semantically inert mental item and the world, and so undercuts the need for interpretation as the supplier of that bridge.

On this interpretation of Wittgenstein's arguments, the appeal to practice serves a quite different function. Far from being a programmatic gesture toward a positive account of how content is possible, the appeal, as McDowell puts it, "is to remind us that the natural phenomenon that is normal human life is itself already shaped by meaning and understanding" (1998: 277). Or, as Wittgenstein himself puts it: "Commanding, questioning, recounting, chatting, are as much part of our natural history as walking, eating, drinking, playing" (1953: §25). This is a claim with which this book wholeheartedly concurs, as long as we are clear that when we talk of human forms of life being "shaped" by meaning and understanding, we must firmly resist the picture of this as a phenomenon occurring from the inside out—as if the meaning and understanding that shape our

forms of life has an inner source that is somehow imposed on what is outside it. Wittgenstein's later thought is so important precisely because it
resists, indeed is defined in opposition to, this picture.

5   The Myth of the Giving 2

The second form of the myth of the giving is the one that most closely parallels its more famous sister myth: the myth of the *given*, and, accordingly,
is best understood in relation to the latter. In its most familiar form, the
myth of the given is the mistake of supposing perceptual experience to be
a matter of "pure input from the world to mind with no active contribution from the receiver" (Hurley 1998: 14). If this conception of experience
were correct, then the world could play no *normative* role in the formation
of one's experiences. Perceptual experiences are normative in this sense: if
a perceptual experience with the content *that p* occurs, then the world
should be *p*. The myth of the given robs experience of this normative
dimension: the experience is the result of purely causal impingements on
the senses, impingements that do not fall within the *space of reasons*. The
myth of the given, in effect, establishes a particular type of boundary
between experience and the world, a boundary that can be straddled by
causal impingements. It is a boundary across which causal pressure may be
exerted, but epistemic pressure may not. As a consequence, we may, as
McDowell (1994) famously puts it, have *exculpations* for our experiences,
but we do not have *justifications*.

   In parallel, the myth of the giving is the mistake of supposing action to
be a matter of "pure output from mind to world" (Hurley 1998: 15). The
myth involves an analogous boundary between action and intention, volition, or trying. A straightforward—and now largely discredited—causal
theory of action provides the most obvious example of this version of the
myth. A causal theory of action identifies actions with bodily movements.
A bodily movement counts as an action in virtue of its causal antecedents
such as intentions, volitions, or tryings. There is nothing intrinsic to an
action that makes it an action. It is its extrinsic relations that constitute it
as such. Causal theories of action, of this simple sort, are not currently popular, and for good reason. The standard objection is that they make actions
contingently actions. Since the same bodily movement can occur with or
without the prior trying, and since actions are identical with bodily movements, the same action can exist as a nonaction. The problem, however, is
that actions are necessarily things you do, but mere movements are not
things you do at all. Thus an action cannot be identical with a movement.

It is not my purpose here to evaluate this type of attack. I am concerned with what the attack is generally taken to show—that an adequate account of actions needs to bring the inner intention, volition, or trying into more intimate relation with the action. Central to the causal theory is a boundary between actions and intentional states that can be bridged by causal impingements alone. But we need more than a merely causal relation between trying and action. We need the boundary between trying and action to be more *permeable*. That is, we need to allow the *content* of the trying to flow *into* the action—to become an intrinsic part of the action, to *inform* the action (in a roughly Aristotelian sense). And to do this is to reject the myth of the giving. In effect, I think, much of the current antipathy toward causal theories of action can be traced to a desire to avoid this version of the myth of the giving.

We need to avoid this myth because actions make normative claims just as much as experiences do. The latter make normative claims in this sense: if an experience with the content *that p* occurs, then the world *should* be *p*. Similarly, actions make normative claims on tryings: if an action of the type ϕ-ing occurs, then this *should* be preceded by an intentional state of the sort we would characterize as *trying to* ϕ. The identity of an action depends on what *should* cause it, not on what merely *does* cause it. In asserting a merely causal connection between actions and intentional states, the causal theory fails to accommodate this normative dimension of action, and in its failure falls victim to the myth of the giving 2.

The myth of the *given*, therefore, is predicated on a conception of the boundary between perceptual experience and the world as one that is straddled by merely causal impingements. Correlatively, the myth of the giving, in this second form, is predicated on a conception of the boundary between intention, volition, or trying, and action as a boundary that is straddled by merely causal impingements. The former fails to accommodate the normativity of perception. The latter, for precisely parallel reasons, fails to accommodate the normativity of action.

6   The Myth of the Giving 3

There is a yet further distinguishable form that the myth of the giving might take. This consists in (the mistake of) supposing that when action plays a role in representation this role is restricted to that of providing additional means for an agent to causally impinge on the world. The role that action plays in representation is purely causal. This is distinct from the second form of the myth. The second form concerned the nature of the *boundary* between action and representation; the third form of the myth, however, concerns the nature of action itself.

This third form of the myth is as regrettable as the other two. To see this, remember that the goal we are pursuing is understanding—that is, explaining or explaining away—representation. The assumption we are making is that action, broadly construed, can help us, to a greater or lesser extent, with this goal. But representation, we have seen, is a normative phenomenon. This may be its most enduring, and most perplexing, feature; and as we have seen, for Wittgenstein, the central problem of representation lies in its normativity. Given this assumption, suppose that we now conceive of the role played by action in representing the world in purely causal terms. Action gives us additional ways of causally impinging on the world. These ways may, at some level, be extremely *useful* in helping us represent the world. They may play a very important role in *facilitating* our ability to represent the world. However, we are supposing that this facilitatory role is restricted to causal impingements: it allows us to causally impact on the world in new and apparently expedient ways, but it has no *normative* dimension. This idea of course, is an expression of what, in the previous chapter, we identified as a *dual-component* interpretation of vehicle externalism.

This interpretation entails that the action-based component of representation, the causal facilitator of the genuinely representational core, can play no role in explaining the normative dimension of experience. But this dimension of representation derives from its content—it is because representations possess content that they make claims about the way the world *should* be. This means that if the action-based component of representation plays a purely causal, facilitatory, role, then it can play no role in explaining representational content. To do so, it would have to be possible to factor off content into normative and nonnormative components. But normativity is an essential feature of content; anything that is to count as content *must* be normative. Therefore, it is not possible to factor off content in this way. And therefore, any purely causal component of representation could play no role in explaining representational content.

Given one further assumption, however, this failure of a purely causal action-based component to play a role in explaining representational content leads to serious trouble for the dual-component theory. The assumption is this: *the normatively constrained content of a representation exceeds that which can be provided by the internal, genuinely representational, component alone.* As we shall see in the next chapter, vehicle externalism is committed to this claim. Moreover, there are, as we shall also see, excellent reasons for thinking this claim is true.

The dual-component interpretation of vehicle externalism, then, is an embodiment of the third form of the myth of the giving. What this myth does is factor the vehicles whereby we represent the world into normative and nonnormative components. This will work only if the normatively constrained dimension of representation does not exceed that which can be provided by the internal, genuinely, representational core. If this were so, then there would be no need for the action-based component to play a role in explaining the normativity of representation. However, if the normatively constrained dimension of representation exceeds that which can be provided by the internal, genuinely representational, core, then the action-based component would be required to do work in explaining the normativity of representation. And, as a purely causal component, this is precisely what it cannot do.

No addition of nonnormative material can ever provide us with an understanding of a phenomenon that is *essentially* normative. No number of exculpations can ever add up to a justification. This is not to deny, of course, that the action-based dimension of representation *does* provide us with additional means of causally impacting on the world. There is a causal story to tell here. But if the normative dimension of representation exceeds that which can be provided by the internal, genuinely representational, component alone, and if action is to play a role in representation, there must be more than a causal story to tell about this role. In such circumstances, action must be *infused* with normativity if it is to play any role in helping us understand representation.[3] The action-based dimension must itself be normative; it must be part of the space of reasons.

7   The Power of Myth

We are now in a position to appreciate the problematic nature of an appeal to action in our attempt to understand—explain or explain away— representation. In the traditional sense of action, both the *status* of an item as an action, and its *identity* as the particular action it is, derives from its connection to antecedent intentional, hence representational, states.[4] Therefore, to appeal to action in this sense is to presuppose representation rather than explain it. The appeal, therefore, falls victim to the first form of the myth of the giving. Essentially, this is the same mistake as that made by those who think that the appeal to practice is a *solution* to the rule-following paradox. Or, it is the same mistake as that made by those who think content can be explained by way of interpretation—to presuppose content rather than understand it.

Therefore, if we are to avoid the first form of the myth of the giving, we cannot appeal to a conception of action whose status and identity as action derives from antecedent representational states. Such actions would have an intentional or representational status that is *inherited*, and to appeal to these actions would be to presuppose representation rather than explain it. It should also be evident that essentially the same problem would arise if we were to appeal to a concept of action that inherits not full intentional status from antecedent representational states, but merely some of the necessary features of representation. For example, if the actions to which we appeal were to possess a *normative* status that they have inherited from the normative character of antecedent intentional states, we would be presupposing one of the defining features of representation, rather than explaining it. And, of course, in the project of understanding representation, this would be a Pyrrhic victory at best. To understand representation, we need to understand how the normative status of representations comes to be, and not merely import this status from elsewhere.

Therefore, without further argument, in our attempt to understand representation, the appeal to a normatively constrained concept of action is immediately suspect, at least if this normativity is imported from other normative states: the danger is that we are presupposing precisely what we need to explain. This, however, is unfortunate, because if we are to avoid the second and third forms of the myth of the giving, then, in our attempt to understand representation, we cannot appeal to a concept of action that is *not* normative. That is, we cannot understand action as merely providing us with additional means of causally impinging or impacting on the world. And we cannot understand action as separated from intentions, or other representational states, by way of a boundary traversable only by causal impingements. If we do so then we lose any help that action might provide us with in our goal of understanding representation. Representation is essentially normative, and I shall argue the normatively constrained dimension of representation exceeds that which can be provided by some internal, genuinely representational core. Therefore, if the action-based component of representation is not normative, it can play no role in helping us understand representation. The addition of no amount of material into the space of causes can ever reposition that material into the space of reasons. No number of exculpations can ever add up to a justification.

Therefore, the appeal to action as a way of helping us understand representation faces a dilemma. If representation is an essentially normative phenomenon, and this normative dimension exceeds that which can be provided by an internal, genuinely representational core, then appeal to a nonnormative conception of action can, in no way, help us understand representation. If, on the other hand, we appeal to a concept of action that acquires its normative status from antecedent intentional—hence normative—states, then we have simply presupposed the most perplexing feature of representation and not explained it. So, it seems that the concept of action to which we appeal in our goal of understanding representation must both be, and yet cannot be, a normatively constrained concept.

There is a way out of this dilemma. The appeal to a representational, hence normative, concept of action will beg the question only if the action acquires its representational and/or normative status from prior intentional states. If it does, then we shall, of course, be assuming representation to explain representation. And we shall be assuming a normatively constrained item in our attempt to understand how representation can be normatively constrained. But suppose, however, that the representational and/or normative status of the action is not derived from anything else. Suppose the action is representational because of what it is in itself, and its relations to the world, and not because of its relation to a prior, or distinct, representational state. And suppose its normative character were to be similarly original and not derived. Then, the appeal to this type of action would not beg the question. We would, thus, avoid the *first* form of the myth of the giving.

Moreover, in employing this conception of action in understanding representation, we would not be reiterating the sort of boundary between representation and action that is implicated in the *second* form of the myth of the giving. There is no boundary between representational and action-based components of representation: both are representational. Therefore, there is no worry about whether this boundary is the sort of thing that can be bridged only by causal impingements.

Finally, in employing this concept of action, we would not be reiterating a purely causal, nonnormative, conception of the role played by action in representation. Both representational and action-based components would be representational, hence normative. Therefore, the fact that the normative dimension of representation exceeds that which could be provided by an internal, genuinely representational core need not trouble us. The additional normativity could, in these circumstances, be provided by the action-based component. We would, thus, avoid the *third* form of the myth of the giving.

Does the requisite concept of action exist? Are there such things as actions that possesses representational and normative status but do not acquire this status from any other representational or normative states? In the second half of this book, I shall argue that there are. These are not actions in the traditional sense. They are what I shall call *deeds*.

8 A Note on the Current Dialectical Situation

The current dialectical situation is complex (and is not going to get much simpler in the foreseeable future). So, it is well to distinguish various strands, strains, and themes in the position as it has been developed so far, and as it will be developed in the pages to come.

The function of chapters 2 and 3 was to delineate the content of the thesis of representation in action. To this end, chapter 2 exploited certain parallels between this thesis—a thesis concerning the *vehicles* of content—and what I referred to as SR-externalism, a controversial thesis concerning the nature of *content*. Chapter 3 carried on this project, discussing the nature of vehicle externalism and identifying the possible stances this form of externalism could adopt with regard to the nature of representation. The purpose of *neither* chapter was to provide an *argument* for the thesis of representation in action. The discussion served the purpose of explaining or illustrating the thesis to be defended in this book; but it does not seek to *defend* this position.

The function of the arguments developed in this chapter, culminating in the previous section have been, in effect, to show why it would be a *good thing* if we could identify a subspecies of action that is representational and is so independently of its connection to other representational items. The claim that there exist such items is what I have referred to as the thesis of *representation in action*. So, the arguments developed in this chapter have been intended to show why it would be a good thing if the thesis of representation in action were true. This project will be continued and consolidated in the next chapter, where I shall attempt to concretize the somewhat abstract discussion presented so far with a specific case of vehicle externalism: the *sensorimotor* or *enactive* approach developed by O'Regan and Noë, among others.

Perhaps the first rule of philosophical inquiry, however, is (or should be): *wishing doesn't make it so!* It might be a good thing if the thesis of representation in action were true. But the facts may just not, ultimately, play ball. So, in the second half of the book, I am going to motivate and defend the thesis of representation in action on entirely independent grounds. The strategy developed there is to try and show that a certain subclass of actions—deeds—can possess representational status *independently* of, but for *precisely parallel reasons* as, representations traditionally construed. That is, the sorts of factors that are thought to confer representational status on classical representations also confer such status on deeds. So deeds count as representational if anything does. A defense of this idea begins in chapter 6 and extends right through to the end of the book.

5 Enacting Representation

1 A Paradox and a Myth

This chapter examines an influential recent version of vehicle externalism: O'Regan and Noë's *enactive* or *sensorimotor* account of visual perception. This is not simply because the account is important in itself, but also because I want to use the account as a means for developing the paradox, identified in the previous chapter, concerning the role played by action in an explanation of representation. The paradox is that we both *need* and *cannot use* a representational conception of action. We require what we are disqualified from having. On pain of begging the question, of assuming an undischarged concept of representation, we cannot use such a conception in our explanation of representation. Nor, for the same reason, can we employ a conception of action that involves an undischarged appeal to essential features of representation, such as normativity. But, on the other hand, a nonrepresentational, nonnormative, conception of action will not accomplish what we need it to. Both problems turn on what, following Susan Hurley, I have called the *myth of the giving*, but each turns on significantly different versions of this myth. The only way to avoid the resulting paradox, I shall argue, is to embrace the idea that some forms of action—*deeds*—are both normative and representational because of what they are in themselves and not because of their relation to other representational or normative states. And this is the thesis of representation in action. The remainder of the book, then, will clarify this thesis, and defend it on *independent* grounds.

2 The Vehicles of Vision: The Traditional View

According to tradition, the vehicles of visual perception are internal representations. When such representations are activated, we have a visual experience of the visual world. This experience reveals the world to us as a rich, detailed, complex arrangement of objects and properties. Accordingly, the representation, in virtue of which the world is experientially revealed to us in this way, must be similarly rich, detailed, and complex.

Cortical maps are, perhaps, the most plausible candidates for these visual representations. A cortical map is a region of the cortex where information about the visual world is retinotopically organized, and, in virtue of such organization, cortical maps can correctly be thought to carry information about the visual world.

Suppose you are looking at a scene in front of you, say a bowl of fruit. Then, according to tradition, corresponding to each feature of your visual experience—the greenness of the apple and its shape, the yellowness of the lemon and its shape, the shiny whiteness of the ceramic bowl, and so on—there will be a corresponding feature of the visual representation currently activated in your brain.

This is not to say that the activated visual representation is in any way similar to the experience—it is not, for example, as if the representation must be partly green and roughly spherical just because the apple is. We all know what is wrong with that view. What it does mean, however, is that if you have a visual experience as of a green and roughly spherical apple, then part of the corresponding visual representation must *represent* greenness, and a component of that representation must *represent* rough sphericality. Nor does this view require that the representation be spatially structured like the scene in front of you. What is essential to the view is the existence of *some* sort of mapping function from features of the representation to features of the experienced scene. This existence of such a function is precisely what makes the representation a representation of the scene.

Given the existence of an appropriate mapping function, a representation will be a *true* or *veridical* one if every feature of the representation maps onto a feature of the represented scene. It will, in addition, be *complete* if for every feature of the represented scene there is a corresponding feature of the representation where the latter maps onto the former. Conversely, a representation will be *false* if there are features of the representation that do not map, via the appropriate mapping function, onto any feature of the represented scene. And the representation will be *incomplete* if there are features of the represented scene that do not map onto any feature of the representation.

This view, presented in admittedly very broad outline, is still much the orthodoxy. Visually experiencing the world consists in the production of internal representations, and these, ideally, will be true and complete. When this is the case, the richness, complexity, and detail of the experi-

enced world is mirrored in the richness, complexity, and detail of the associated representation.

3   Change Blindness

Recent experimental work casts significant doubt on this orthodox view of
visual experience. Most important and striking in this regard are the experiments on what is known as *change blindness*, conducted by O'Regan (1992),
Blackmore et al. (1995), O'Regan et al. (1996), and Rensink et al. (1997).

The classic form of a change-blindness experiment is something like this.
Observers are shown displays of natural scenes and are asked to detect
cyclically repeated changes—a large object shifting, changing color, or
appearing and disappearing. Under normal circumstances, changes of this
magnitude would be easily noticed. And this is because such changes
would create a transient signal in the visual apparatus that would be
detected by low-level visual mechanisms. This transient automatically
attracts attention to the location of the change, and the change would
therefore be immediately seen.

There are, however, ways of nullifying the role of the visual transient,
and this is precisely what is done in the change-blindness experiments.
One method involves superimposing a very brief global flicker over the
whole visual field at the moment of the change. A similar effect can be
achieved by making the change coincide with an eye saccade, an eye blink,
or a cut in a film sequence. In each of these cases, a brief global disturbance
swamps the local transient and thus prevents it from playing its normal
attention-grabbing role. Another method involves creating a number of
simultaneous local disturbances—which appear something like mud
splashes on the scene—that act as decoys and so minimize the effect of the
local transient.

The experiments showed that under these sorts of conditions, observers
have great difficulty seeing changes, even though they are very large and
occur in full view. Indeed, measurements of the observer's eyes indicated
that they could be looking directly at the change at the moment it occurs,
and still not see it (O'Regan et al. 2000).

The idea that visual perception consists in the activation of an internal
visual representation of a portion of the visual world, it is argued, renders
these results mysterious. For, on this orthodox representational model, all
that would be required to notice a change in such a scene would be to compare one's current visual impressions with the activated representation;
when and how the discrepancies between the former and the latter arose

would be irrelevant. Thus, it is argued, the change-blindness results support the claim that there is at least no complex and detailed internal representation. We do not notice even significant changes in a scene because we have no internal template against which to measure or compare them.

It might be thought that the peculiarity of these experimental results might derive, at least in part, from the artificial nature of the experimental situation. However, as Simons and Levin (1997) have shown, the same sorts of results can be obtained when one switches from computer screens to real-world situations. One striking experiment turned on a slapstick scenario—of which Simons and Levin are the undisputed heavyweight world champions—in which an experimenter, pretending to be lost on the Cornell campus, would approach an unsuspecting passerby to ask for directions. Once the passerby started to reply, two people carrying a large door would walk between the inquirer and the passerby. During the walk through, however, the original inquirer is replaced by a different person. Only 50 percent of the direction givers noticed the change. Yet the two experimenters were of different heights, wore different clothes, had different voices, and so on. Moreover, those who did notice the change were students of roughly the same age and demographics as the two experimenters. In a follow-up study, the students failed to spot the change when the experimenters appeared as construction workers, placing them in a different social group. The conclusion that Simons and Levin (1997: 266) draw is that our failures to detect change arise because "we lack a precise representation of our visual world from one view to the next." We encode only a "rough gist" of the current scene—just enough to support a broad sense of what's going on insofar as it matters to us, and to guide further intelligent information retrieval as and when needed.

4   Inattentional Blindness

Closely related to the phenomenon of change blindness is what is known as *inattentional blindness*. Change blindness is a diachronic phenomenon: the subject is blind to changes that occur through time. Inattentional blindness, on the other hand, is a synchronic phenomenon: the subject is blind to certain aspects either of a static scene, or of a persisting phenomenon that occurs throughout a changing scene (cf. Rensink 2000).

As an example of the first sort of inattentional blindness, consider a series of experiments devised by Mack and Rock (1998). The experiments were concerned to determine what is consciously perceived in the absence of visual attention. To this end, the focus of the experiments was on determining whether an object unexpectedly present in the visual field would be consciously noticed.

Consider one example. Subjects were visually presented with a cross on a computer screen, and asked to report which of the arms was longer. The difference was small, so the task required some concentration. The cross was presented briefly (approx. 200ms), followed by a masking stimulus— an unrelated visually presented pattern. Following the masking stimulus, the subjects were required to make their reports. On the third or fourth trial, however, a "critical stimulus" was also shown on the screen with the cross. This might take the form of a colored square, a moving bar, and so on. Subjects were not expecting this. The question was: would it be consciously noticed?

The experiment was run in two main forms. In the first, the cross was presented centrally (at the point of fixation), and the critical stimulus was presented parafoveally. In the second, the cross was presented parafoveally, and the critical stimulus occurred just behind the fixation point. When the critical stimulus was presented parafoveally, 25 percent of subjects failed to spot it. This is already a surprising result. But when presented near fixation, this figure jumped to a massive 75 percent of subjects who failed to report the stimulus. The difference might stem from the fact that the need to focus visual attention away from the normal central point—when the cross was presented parafoveally—demanded increased visual effort and attention. In addition, it may have been necessary for subjects to actively inhibit information from the point of fixation.

From this Mack and Rock draw an unambiguous conclusion. There is, they claim, "no conscious perception at all in the absence of attention." This may seem trivial—and it would be if attention were defined in terms of conscious awareness. But what Mack and Rock really mean is that there is no conscious perception of an item in the absence of expectations and intentions directed at that item. And this claim is far from trivial.

The importance of attention—expectation and intention—is highlighted by some rather striking findings observed by Haines (1991), and Fisher, Haines, and Price (1980), who had professional pilots land an aircraft in a flight simulator under conditions of poor visibility using a head-up display (or HUD)—that is, a display that superimposes flight guidance and control information on the windshield. On various occasions during the pilot's landing approach, they were presented with an unexpected critical stimulus in the form of a large aircraft located directly ahead of them on the runway. Although the aircraft was perfectly visible despite the head-up display, two of the eight experienced commercial pilots simply did not see the obstacle on the two occasions they were confronted with it, and simply landed their aircraft through the obstacle. This failure, it is argued, results from the extreme improbability of such an occurrence, and because the pilots were concentrating on either the HUD or the landing maneuver.

The importance of attention and expectation is nowhere more apparent than in another famous experiment (Neisser 1979; Simons and Chabris 1999; Simons 2000) in which subjects watch a video of two teams, one in white and one in black, passing basketballs (one per team). The viewer must count the number of successful passes made by the white team. Afterward, subjects are asked whether they saw anything else, anything unusual. A short time into the film (about 45 seconds) an intruder will make an appearance—walking through the middle of the players. The intruder may be the semitransparent figure of a woman holding an umbrella or a semitransparent man in a gorilla suit. On some trials, the woman or man in gorilla suit were presented in fully opaque form. In the semitransparent condition, 73 percent of subjects failed to see the gorilla, and even in the opaque condition 35 percent of subjects failed to see it (Simons 2000: 152). Simons concludes, "We do not realize the degree to which we are blind to unattended and unexpected stimuli, and we mistakenly believe that important events will automatically draw our attention away from our current task or goals" (ibid.: 154).

5   The Filling-In Hypothesis

The results garnered from the various experiments on change and inattentional blindness are not in question. But what is very much in question is what these results show. One tempting response is to suppose that the phenomena can be explained in terms of the idea of *filling in*. If it seems to us as if we see a rich, detailed, and stable world, but this richness, detail, and stability is nowhere mirrored in features of our internal visual representations, this must be because the brain, somewhere along the line, *fills in* the missing information.

The concept of *filling in* has its most familiar application to alleged gaps in our visual experience deriving from the *blind spot*. In each eye, there is a region where the optic nerve leaves the retina. In this region there are no photoreceptors, with the result that it can receive no visual information. In ordinary perceptual situations, we are never aware of the blind spot; since the blind spots of the two eyes do not overlap, an item that falls on the blind spot of one retina will fall outside that of the other. Even under monocular viewing, the blind spot is not easily revealed. Close your right eye and fixate on the midpoint between two dots on a uniformly colored piece of paper. There is no experience of a gap or discontinuity in the visual field. Now move the paper slowly toward your face. At some point, the left dot disappears as it enters the blind spot. What is noticeable, however, is that one continues to perceive a uniform expanse of brightness and color. This is an example of what is known as *perceptual completion*: the color and brightness surrounding the area corresponding to the blind spot are used to complete the blind area, so that one has an experience as of a uniform expanse.

Perceptual completion is a phenomenon that characterizes the *content* of visual experiences: it describes the way things seem to the subject in the having of that experience. In this case, the world appears continuous rather than discontinuous. Filling in, on the other hand, characterizes operations that occur at the level of the *vehicles* of that content. The idea that the brain fills in missing information is a hypothesis that attempts to explain how perceptual completion is achieved. One cannot, therefore, infer the existence of filling-in operations simply from the phenomenon of perceptual completion—to do so would be to confuse vehicles and contents.

The filling-in hypothesis is, in fact, a controversial one. Dennett (1991) famously attacks the notion of filling in—the basis of his case being provided by the (ingenious) idea that the same phenomenon of perceptual completion at the level of experiential content can be achieved by the brain following, in effect, a "same-again" algorithm at the level of vehicles. In the case of the blind spot, for example, the same perceptual-completion phenomenon will be evident if the brain simply ignores the ("expected") absence of information, rather than filling in this absent information.

The issue here is, in part, an empirical one. But it is not entirely divorced from conceptual considerations—and, in particular, ones concerning the nature of visual phenomenology. And, although there is some empirical evidence for the existence of filling-in operations,[1] the idea that the brain, *in general*, performs operations whose function is to fill in absent information rests on a naive account of that phenomenology.

To see this, consider another of Dennett's examples (1991: 354–355). Suppose you walk into a room and notice that the wallpaper is a regular array of hundreds of identical Marilyn Monroes (à la Andy Warhol). To identify a picture as one of Marilyn Monroe, you must foveate it, since your parafoveal vision does not have good resolution—not good enough to discriminate between Marilyns and colored shapes. You are, however, able to foveate only two, perhaps three, of the pictures at any one time.

Nevertheless, if you were to enter the room, you would instantly see that the wall was covered with identical Marilyns. Thus, the richness and detail that seems to be present in our experience is not mirrored in the richness and detail of the visual representations that, we might suppose, are responsible for this experience. And, according to the filling-in hypothesis, this gap between visual representation and visual content is closed by the brain's filling in this information—supplementing and embellishing what is contained in the basic visual representation.

This explanation, however, seems to rest on a mistaken conception of visual experience (Noë 2002b). If you foveate on the wall of Marilyns, it will indeed seem to you as if there is a wall of Marilyns in front of you. But this is not to say that it seems to you as if you experience the whole of the wall's surface. On the contrary, the phenomenology of your experience is quite different. It does indeed seem to you as if the whole of the wall is there at once. But it does not seem to you as if *every* part of the wall's surface is represented in your consciousness at once. In other words, the sense of the phenomenological presence of the wall does not translate into the consciousness, at any given time, of every feature of the wall. Rather, Noë argues, "you experience the wall as present and you experience yourself as having access to the wall by looking here, or there, attending here, or there. It is no part of ordinary phenomenology that we experience the whole wall, every bit of it, in consciousness all at once" (2002b: 4). And, if this is correct, it cannot be the function of filling in to perceptually complete visual fields in this sense—to produce a visual experience that presents the wall to you as if every part of the wall's surface is represented in your consciousness at once.

6   The Grand-Illusion Hypothesis

There is another interpretation of the experimental results that has become known as the *grand-illusion* hypothesis. According to this hypothesis, our experience about the world embodies a systematic and pervasive mistake. The mistake is not one—as in traditional epistemological concerns—about the nature of the world. It is not that our experience reveals the world to us in systematically misleading ways. Rather, the mistake concerns our experience of the world. In having experience, we are not systematically mistaken about the nature of the world; we are systematically mistaken about the nature of our *experience*!

O'Regan, who at one time endorsed a version of the grand-illusion hypothesis, expresses the view as follows:

Despite the poor quality of the visual apparatus, we have the subjective impression of great richness and "presence" of the visual world. But this richness and presence is actually an illusion. . . . (1992: 484)

And, in the same vein, Susan Blackmore and her colleagues write:

We believe that we see a complete, dynamic picture of a stable, uniformly detailed and colourful world, but [o]ur stable visual world may be constructed out of a brief retinal image and a very sketchy, higher-level representation along with a pop-out mechanism to redirect attention. The richness of our visual world is, to this extent, an illusion. (1995: 1075)

Underpinning the grand-illusion hypothesis, then, is the claim that (i) it seems to us as if we see a rich, detailed, and stable world, when, in fact, (ii) we see no such thing. The conclusion that the grand-illusion hypothesis wishes us to endorse is that we are systematically mistaken about the way our experience seems to us.

The grand-illusion hypothesis, I think, cannot be sustained. In particular, it rests on three, complementary, confusions. Consider Blackmore's statement. Embodied in this, is, *first*, the mistaken account of visual phenomenology examined above. Visual experience does not, in a single fixation, present the world to us as if every part of it is represented in our consciousness at once. That is, it does not, in a single fixation, present the world to us in the form of a "complete, dynamic picture of a stable, uniformly detailed and colourful world."

The second confusion is between, on the one hand, the way an *experience* seems, and, on the other, the way the *world* seems in the having of an experience. We do not, of course, contra Blackmore, see a "*picture* of a stable . . . world." We don't see pictures at all. Maybe we see the world *in virtue of* having pictures (representations) of it—although, as we shall see, the change- and inattentional-blindness experiments cast serious doubt on this, at least if we think of such pictures as sufficient for seeing the world. But we obviously do not see the pictures. Most philosophers would now recognize that the idea of seeing visual representations is a nonstarter. But this is only a symptom of a deeper confusion—one that is still not consistently recognized *as* a confusion. This is the idea that the phenomenology characteristic of vision derives from our being aware of certain features of our experience—ones that collectively constitute what it is like to have that experience. To put the same point another way, it is the idea that experiences can *seem* a certain way to their subject. I have argued elsewhere (2001) that experiences do not seem or feel a certain way to their subjects—they are not the sort of thing that can sustain the attribution of *seeming* or *feeling*. Rather, in the case of straightforward visual experience, it is not visual experiences that seem a certain way. In the having of a visual experience, the *world* seems a certain way. In looking at the blue ocean in front of me, it is not my experience that seems blue. Rather, in the having of this—and presumably *in virtue of the having of* this—visual experience, the ocean in front of me seems blue. Matters may be a little more complicated if we shift our attention to introspective experiences (although, in my 2001 I have argued that the same general principles apply). However, in the case of ordinary visual experience, it is not the experience itself that seems a certain way but, rather, that the world seems a certain way in the having of the experience. Therefore, when the defender of the grand-illusion hypothesis claims that it seems to us as if we see a rich, detailed, and stable world, we can accept this claim, but simply need to append the clarificatory rider that this means that the world—and not the experience—seems to us as if it is rich, detailed, and stable.

Suppose, however, we fail to spot this ambiguity, and persist in thinking of the experience as presenting itself to us as rich, detailed, and stable. Then, given one further confusion, we will immediately be landed with the grand-illusion hypothesis. This third confusion is, in effect, one of *vehicle* and *content*. In this instance, the confusion turns on running together the *experiences* in virtue of which the world seems a certain way and the *mechanisms* or *representations* in virtue of which the world can seem this way. The second confusion gave us the idea that visual experiences seem a certain way. Our third confusion yields the idea that the way an experience seems must be grounded in features of the internal visual representation in virtue of which, allegedly, the experience seems this way. The details of the way a visual experience seems must be matched and grounded, on some or other mapping function, in features of the visual representation. And the richness, detail, and stability that exist in the way the experience seems must be matched in similar richness, detail, and stability of the visual representation that, allegedly, underwrites it.

The upshot is that when we conduct change- and inattentional-blindness experiments of the sort described above, we conclude from them that visual representations do not possess the sort of richness, detail, and stability that we have come to think of as being possessed by our visual experiences. Then we are tempted, via confusion 3 (the vehicle–content confusion), to conclude from this that, therefore, our visual experiences cannot really possess the sort of richness, stability, and detail that we naively take them to have. And we are further tempted to conclude from this, via confusion 2 (the experience–world confusion) that although it seems to us as if we see a rich, detailed, and stable world, we, in fact, see no such thing. And this is the grand-illusion hypothesis.

7 The Sensorimotor or Enactive Approach

The most interesting and plausible response to the problems of change- and inattentional-blindness is, I think, what has become known as the *sensorimotor* or *enactive* approach (O'Regan and Noë 2001, 2002; Noë 2004). The underlying idea is nicely presented by Mackay (1967). Suppose you are a blind person holding a bottle. You have the feeling of holding a bottle. But what tactile sensations do you in fact have? Without the slight rubbing of the skin, tactile information is considerably reduced, and information pertaining to temperature will soon disappear through the adaptation of receptors, and so on. Nonetheless, despite the poverty of sensory stimulation, you have the feeling of having a bottle in your hand. Broadly speaking, there are two general approaches to explaining how this can be.

According to the traditional, representational, approach, the brain supplements, extends, and embellishes the impoverished information contained in sensory stimulation with what are, essentially, various forms of inferential process. The result is the construction of an internal representation of the bottle.

Mackay's answer, however, is quite different, and provides a useful illustration of the enactive approach. According to Mackay, information is present in the environment over and above that contained in sensory stimulation, and this information is sufficient to specify that you are holding a bottle. In what does this information consist? According to Mackay, it is in this: your brain is tuned to certain *potentialities*. For example, it is tuned to the fact that if you were to slide your hand very slightly, a change would come about in the incoming sensory signals that is typical of the change associated with the smooth, cool surface of glass. Furthermore, your brain is tuned to the fact that if you were to move your hand upward, the size of what you are encompassing with your hand would diminish (because you are moving to the bottle's neck), and so on.

What does this talk of "tuning" mean? Basically, your brain has extracted various laws of what O'Regan and Noë (2001, 2002) call *sensorimotor contingency*. Roughly, your brain has extracted, and has now activated, certain laws pertaining to the way motor action will be accompanied by changes in sensory input; it has, that is, extracted a certain mapping function from motor activity to sensory input. This provides the additional information lacking in sensory stimulation, information that specifies that you are holding a bottle.

According to Mackay, seeing a bottle is an analogous state of affairs. You have the impression of seeing a bottle if your brain has extracted knowledge concerning a certain web of contingencies. For example, you have knowledge of the fact that that if you move your eyes upward toward the neck of the bottle, the sensory stimulation will change in a way typical of what happens when a narrower region of the bottle comes into foveal vision. You have knowledge of the fact that if you move your eyes downward, the sensory stimulation will change in a way typical of what happens when the label is fixated by foveal vision.

As O'Regan and Noë have shown, visual perception, just like haptic perception, obeys its own rules of sensorimotor contingency. In fact, these sensorimotor contingencies can be divided into two sorts: (i) apparatus-related contingencies, and (ii) object-related contingencies. Contingencies of the former sort are related to the structure of the visual apparatus. Here is a trivial example: in the contingency that the eyes close, the visual stimulation becomes uniform (i.e., blank). Here's a less trivial one (O'Regan and Noë 2001: 941). As the eyes rotate, the sensory stimulation on the retina shifts and distorts in a very particular way, determined by the size of the eye movement. In particular, as the eye moves, contours shift, and the curvature of lines change. For example, if you are looking at the midpoint of a horizontal line, the line will trace out an arc on the inside of your eyeball. If you now fixate upward, the curvature of the line will change — represented on a flattened-out retina, the line would now be curved. In general, straight lines on the retina distort dramatically as the eyes move, somewhat like an image in a distorting mirror. Since contingencies deriving from the structure of the visual apparatus characterize all vision, they constitute, O'Regan and Noë claim, the defining characteristics of visual sensation, and they are what distinguish visual sensation from sensation in other modalities.

Object-related contingencies, on the other hand, derive from the structure of the various objects of perception. We have already encountered these. As I slide my eyes up the bottle, from the label to the neck, the change in sensory stimulation typical of what happens when a narrower region of the bottle comes into foveal vision, is a sensorimotor contingency that derives from the structure of the bottle.

Each form of perception has its own contingency rules, and, according to O'Regan and Noë, what differentiates visual perception from other forms is the structure of the rules governing the sensory changes produced by various motor actions. The sensorimotor contingencies within each sensory modality are subject to different invariance properties, and so the structure of the rules that govern the perception in these modalities will be, in each case, different. To learn to perceive visually is to learn the rules of sensorimotor contingency governing the relation between changes in the orientation of the visual apparatus and the resulting changes in the character of the perceived world.

If the sensorimotor approach is correct, there is little need to explain the haptic perception of the bottle in terms of the production or activation of an internal representation. The work of such a representation can be performed by the bottle itself. The bottle is an external structure that carries information over and above that present in any sensory stimulation the bottle is currently inducing in the hand. How does it carry such information? By providing a stable structure that can be probed or explored at will by the haptic modality. Mackay's suggestion is that the same is true of visual perception. The bottle also provides a stable structure that can be explored at will by the visual modality. Thus we arrive back at the general framework for vehicle externalism outlined in chapter 3. Visual perception is essentially hybrid, made up of internal processes (the extraction and activation of the laws of sensorimotor contingency) plus external processes (the probing or exploration of information-bearing structures in the environment). Visually perceiving is a process whereby the world—understood as an external store of information—is probed or explored by acts of perception, and the results of this exploration are mediated through the laws of sensorimotor contingency.

We now have an explanation of the sense of phenomenological presence we encountered in the previous sections. We have a sense of seeing the whole of the wall of Marilyns—the wall seems phenomenologically present to us in its entirety—even though phenomenological reflection on our experience reveals only a small number of clearly presented Marilyns. The explanation the sensorimotor model gives of this sense of phenomenological presence is simple and elegant.

First, the impression we have of seeing everything derives from the fact that the slightest flick of the eye allows any part of the wall to be processed at will. This gives us the impression that the whole wall is immediately available. Suppose you try to ascertain whether you are in fact seeing everything there is to see in a scene. How could you check this? Only, it seems, by casting your attention on each element of the scene, and verifying that you have the impression of constantly seeing it. But, obviously, as soon as you do cast your attention on something, you see it. Therefore, you will always have the impression of constantly seeing everything (O'Regan and Noë 2001: 946). Is this impression erroneous? It would be erroneous only if seeing consisted in the production of an internal representation isomorphic with the part of the world seen. If, on the other hand, we accept that seeing consists in combining the results of environmental probing with a knowledge of the laws of sensorimotor contingency, we are indeed seeing the whole scene, for probing the world, and a knowledge of these laws, is precisely what we do and have as we cast our attention from one aspect to the next.

Second, in addition to our ability to direct our attention, at will, to the visual world, the visual system is particularly sensitive to *visual transients*. When a visual transient occurs, a low-level attention-grabbing mechanism appears to automatically direct processing to the location of the transient. This means that should anything happen in the environment, we will generally consciously see it, since processing will be directed toward it. This gives us the impression of having tabs on everything that might change, and so of consciously seeing everything. And if seeing consists in explor atory activity combined with knowledge of sensorimotor contingencies accompanying such exploration, then this impression is not erroneous. We do, indeed, see everything. The suspicion that we do not derives from a residual attachment to the idea that seeing consists in the production of an internal representation that maps onto the outside world.

8 Imagery, Dreams, Hallucinations

According to the enactive approach, our sense of phenomenological presence—of seeing a complex, rich, and detailed visual world—derives from our ability to direct our attention at will to any aspect or area of a complex, rich, and detailed world. Complexity, richness, and detail are all out there in the world, and our sense of phenomenological access to them stems from our ability to direct our attention at any time to them. Thus, central to the enactive approach is our ability to act on, exploit, and manipulate, a complex, rich, and detailed physical world.

This being so, the fact that there is something that it is like to undergo nonperceptual experiences is going to provide the most obvious source of objections to the enactive approach. There is something that it is like, for example, to form a mental image of a scene, there is something that it is like to have dreams, hallucinations, and so on. The sense of phenomenological presence we have when confronting the physical world can also, it might be thought, similarly be exhibited in a dream or hallucination.

As an objection to the enactive approach, what underlies the appeal to imaginings, dreams, and hallucinations, it might be argued, is the idea that the quasi-visual phenomenal character of these items is so close to the phenomenal character that exists in visually perceiving the world that both cry out for the same, unified, explanation or, at least, a fundamentally similar explanation. Therefore, since we cannot give an enactive account of quasi-visual phenomenal character, it might be thought, this casts significant doubt on the enactive account of visual phenomenal character.

This thought, of course, has a long and distinguished philosophical history, and is what underwrites both sense-datum and representationalist accounts of perception. The enactive account, employing so prominently the idea of the exploration of environmental structures, should entail that the phenomenal character of visual experience differs in fundamental ways from the experience of visually imagining, dreaming, or hallucinating. Thus, it might be thought, the enactive account cannot account for the logical possibility of imaginings, dreams, and hallucinations being phenomenally indistinguishable from genuine visual perception.

If this is the basis of the appeal to quasi-visual phenomenal character, then we can turn the sense of dissatisfaction that underlies it on its head. Indeed, the appeal can be used to *support* the enactive account. The existence of quasi-visual phenomenal character attaching to acts of imagining, dreaming, and hallucinating would pose a threat to the enactive account of visual phenomenal character only if the former were indeed indistinguishable from, or at least very similar to, the latter. But let us suppose the converse were true: suppose visual phenomenal character not only differed from its quasi-visual cousin, but did so *in ways predicted or entailed by the enactive account* of the former. Then, this would not only undercut the force of the appeal to quasi-visual phenomenal character if used as an objection to the enactive account of visual phenomenal character, it would moreover mean that the appeal to the former would support the enactive account of the latter.

One entailment of the enactive model of visual phenomenal character is that the stability of the perceived visual field is a function of the stability of the visual world—the world toward which the exploratory perceptual activity is directed. Without the stable world to hold our perceptual activity together, we should predict that any quasi-perceptual activity that is not directed toward a similarly stable world should lack the consistency, coherency, and stability of genuine perception. And this, of course, is precisely what we get in the case of dreams and hallucinations.

The enactive account of visual phenomenal character accords a central role to our ability to direct our attention at will to any part of the visual world. It is this that underlies the sense of complexity and detail that typically attends genuine visual phenomenology. We can direct our attention in this way only because the world provides a stable and enduring structure that supports such exploratory activity. Thus, another prediction that the enactive model makes is that it should be much more difficult, if not impossible, to direct one's attention in mental imaginings, dreams, and hallucinations. What empirical work has been done on this issue bears out this prediction.

Consider, for example, Chambers and Reisberg's study of perceptual versus imaginative flipping of ambiguous images (Chambers and Reisberg 1985). Subjects were asked to observe and recall a drawing. The drawing would be ambiguous, of the duck–rabbit, faces–vase, old lady–young lady sort. The subjects, who did not know the duck–rabbit picture, were trained on related cases to ensure they were familiar with the phenomenon of ambiguity. Having been briefly shown the duck–rabbit picture, they were asked to form a mental image of it, attend to this image, and seek an alternative interpretation of it. Despite the inclusion in the test group of several high-vividness imagers (as measured by the Slee elaboration scale), none of the fifteen subjects was able to find an alternative construal of their image. However, when subjects were later asked to draw the imaged duck–rabbit, all fifteen were then able to find the alternative interpretation. The significance of this is that the ability to reinterpret the external drawing depends on slight changes in foveation: the external structure is subtly probed by the visual modality. The inability of subjects to discover the alternative construal of their image suggests that this sort of probing cannot be performed in the case of mental images. The directing of attention within mental images is, at the very least, much more difficult than within the perceived visual world. And this is precisely what we should expect if the enactive model of visual phenomenal character were true.

Finally, visual phenomenology differs from that which attends acts of imagining, dreaming, and hallucinating in one final way. Many of the rules of sensorimotor contingency evident in visual perception simply do not operate in the latter sorts of experiential acts. To take just one example, even if it were possible to focus one's attention in, say, particularly vivid dreams or hallucinations, such focusing is not attended by the sensorimotor contingencies that characterize visual perception. For example, in dreams, straight lines do not become curved as they move from the center of foveation (or whatever passes for foveation in dreams).

In short, the appeal to quasi-visual phenomenal character provides the objector with a two-edged sword. Far from undermining the enactive account of visual phenomenal character, the most reasonable construal of the evidence, I think, suggests that it in fact supports that account.

9   The Myth of the Giving 1: The Eliminativist Interpretation

The enactive or sensorimotor account is, I think, best understood as a specific version of vehicle externalism. According to the enactive model, the vehicles of visual perception are not confined to the heads, or skins, of perceiving organisms, but extend into the world in the form of exploratory activities of relevant, information-bearing, structures. Seeing fundamentally involves the ability of a perceiving organism to keep track of the systematic connections between what it does and what it experiences. The organism's sensory input is systematically dependent on its actions, and having visual experience is a matter of identifying these dependencies. Therefore, the role traditionally assigned to internal representations can, to a considerable extent, be played by a combination of:

1. The ability to act on the world—i.e., to probe and explore environmental structures by way of the visual modality.
2. Knowledge of the *sensorimotor contingencies* that relate such activity to changes in visual input.

It is possible for the myth of the giving, in its first form, to arise in connection with both the appeal to action and knowledge. This is precisely what we should expect given that, as we saw in the previous chapter, the relevant notion of *activity*, in terms of which the myth of the given can arise, is sufficiently broad to incorporate both bodily *and* mental activity—in this case represented by *action* and *knowledge* respectively.

Before proceeding, I should emphasize that I am not accusing O'Regan and Noë of falling victim to the myth of the giving. Their goal is not to explain the possibility of representation *tout court*, but to explain how *visual* perception is possible. And given this project, they are perfectly entitled to appeal to other forms of representation if they so choose. My point here, however, is that it is going to be very difficult to cash out the enactive model without appeal to representation in some form. So, any temptation to think that the enactive approach gives general succor to eliminativist approaches toward representation should be resisted. That is, one cannot infer eliminativism about representation from enactive principles without falling victim to the first form of the myth of the giving—taking activity, broadly construed, as an unproblematic given.

According to the eliminativist interpretation, the enactive approach would essentially obviate the need to postulate visual representations in any form. The role of representations has been entirely usurped by the possibility of acting on the world. Some suggestions of this sort of interpretation can be found in the writing of O'Regan and Noë. For example, as cited earlier.

Indeed, there is no "re-presentation" of the world inside the brain: the only pictorial or 3D version required is the real outside version. What *is* required however are methods for probing the outside world—and visual perception constitutes one mode via which it can be probed. The experience of seeing occurs when the outside world is being probed according to the visual mode. . . . (2001: 946)

But, whether or not O'Regan and Noë are committed to it, the wholesale rejection of internal representations seems implausible. The primary worry, here, is that any attempt to eliminate representation in this way, in fact, involves a tacit appeal to representational states. Representation, is, so to speak, reintroduced through the back door. The "back door" in this case can take two forms: the *knowledge* of sensorimotor contingencies, or the *action* of probing, exploring, and exploiting the environment.

Consider, first, the idea of *knowledge* of sensorimotor contingencies. O'Regan and Noë's official position is that knowledge of sensorimotor contingencies is a form of "practical knowledge":

Visual experience is a mode of activity involving practical knowledge about currently possible behaviors and associated sensory consequences. Visual experience rests on know-how, the possession of skills. (2001: 946)

On this view, then, knowledge of sensorimotor contingencies is a form of *knowing how*. And, indeed, O'Regan and Noë reinforce the practical character of this knowledge by their frequent use of concepts such as *mastery*:

Visual perception can now be understood as the activity of exploring the environment in ways mediated by knowledge of the relevant sensorimotor contingencies. And to be a visual perceiver is, thus, to be capable of exercising mastery of vision-related rules of sensorimotor contingency. (2001: 943)

To see is to explore one's environment in a way that is mediated by one's mastery of sensorimotor contingencies, and to be making use of this mastery in one's planning, reasoning, and speech behavior. (2001: 944)

We shall say that perceivers have the sensations in a particular sense modality, *when they exercise their mastery of the sensorimotor laws* that govern the relation between possible actions and the resulting changes in incoming information in that sense modality. (2002: 84, emphasis theirs)

The sensation of red is the exercise of our mastery of the way red behaves as we do things. (2002: 85)

The suggestion seems to be that knowing the laws of sensorimotor contingency is like the exercise of a skill one has mastered—as one might have mastered the art of riding a bicycle, or of driving a car. Indeed, driving a car is one of the examples they employ to explain their general position.

What is the "feel" of driving a Porsche as compared to other cars? To answer this question you would probably say: the feel of Porsche driving comes from the particular way the Porsche handles, that is the way it responds to your actions. When you press on the gas, the car accelerates particularly fast. When you turn the wheel, the car responds in a way typical of Porsches. (2002: 82)

Driving a Porsche, one might suppose takes, as we might say, a *little getting used to*. But when you are used to it, you have mastered the art of driving a Porsche.[2]

So far, then, the idea seems to be that knowledge of sensorimotor contingencies amounts to a type of practical knowledge significantly akin to knowing how to drive a car. However, this interpretation does not seem to square with other claims O'Regan and Noë make. Many of their explanations of the character of visual experience appeal to a form of knowing *that* rather than knowing *how*. Thus, in explaining the character of our experience of red, they write:

In what does your focusing on the red hue of the wall consist? It consists in the (implicit) knowledge associated with seeing redness: the knowledge *that* if you were to move your eyes, there would be changes in the incoming information that are typical of sampling with the eye; typical of the nonhomogeneous way the retina samples color; knowledge *that* if you were to move your eyes around, there might be changes in the incoming information typical of what happens when the illumination is uneven, and so on. (2001: 961, emphases mine)

This exercise [of our mastery of sensorimotor contingencies] consists in our *practical understanding that* if we were to move our eyes or bodies or blink, the resulting changes would be those that are typical of red, and not of green patches of light. (2002: 85, emphasis mine)

In the first passage, there is a shift to talk of knowing *that*, rather than knowing how. In the second passage there is a curious running together of *practical knowledge* with *knowing that*, and this strongly suggests that whatever they mean by practical knowledge, it cannot be knowing *how* in the traditional sense. Moreover, in explaining the character of the haptic perception of a knife, they write:

You know *that* if you move your fingers upwards, you will encounter the ring attached to one end of the knife, and if you move it the other way, you will encounter the smoothness of the plastic surface, and the roughness of the corkscrew. It is this knowledge that constitutes the haptic perception of the object. (2002: 88, emphasis mine)

And, indeed, knowing *that* fits far more closely with every explanation they give of the exercise of one's mastery of sensorimotor contingencies. Thus, for example, they cite with approval Mackay's account of the haptic and visual perception of a bottle, which seems to clearly involve knowledge that, rather than knowledge how. That is, as you slide your eyes up the bottle, you anticipate *that* the sensory stimulation reaching you will change in a manner consistent with the narrowing of the bottle neck. Indeed; you don't even need to slide your eyes up the bottle, you just need to know *that if* you were to slide your eyes up the bottle, *then* your incoming sensory stimulation would change in a manner consistent with the narrowing of the bottle's neck, and so on.

The vacillation between knowing how and knowing that is, I think, exacerbated by O'Regan and Noë's tendency to frequently shift from talk of mastery of sensorimotor contingencies to knowledge of the *laws* of sensorimotor contingency. It is not entirely clear what these laws are. At one point, for example, they write:

> We shall say that the missile guidance system has mastery of the sensorimotor contingencies of airplane tracking if it "knows" the laws that govern what happens when it does all the things it can do when it is tracking the airplanes. (2002: 83)

So, knowledge of laws, in this sense, is knowledge of what happens to your visual input when you do certain things. At other points, the laws involved seem quite different. Thus:

> As a result of such differences, lawful changes in the neural influx occur as a function of the eyes' position. The laws underlying these changes, that is, the sensorimotor contingencies, are indicative of the fact that the patch is being sampled by the visual apparatus, and not via, say the olfactory or tactile modalities. (2002: 84)

Here, the suggestion seems to be that the relevant laws are the ones governing neural influx—which seem, on the face of it, to be very different from the laws governing the way one's experience changes contingent upon one's actions. In any event, whatever the form of the laws appealed to, the result is an unfortunate masking of the appeal to knowledge that. One speaks of knowledge *of* laws, and this may give one the impression that knowledge of laws is not a form of knowing that—but, of course, it really is. Knowledge of laws is knowledge of certain facts—roughly, facts that take the form of universally quantified conditional or biconditional statements that support subjunctive counterfactuals, and so forth. And, in another of their variations, O'Regan and Noë do employ the idea of knowledge of facts when explaining the idea of mastery of sensorimotor contingencies:

Yet so long as the missile guidance system is, for example, tuned to the *fact that* it can turn to bring the airplane back into the camera's sights, we would still say that the missile guidance system is currently visually tracking the airplane. (2002: 83, emphasis mine)

Knowledge of facts is knowledge *that*. So, although O'Regan and Noë's official position is that knowledge of sensorimotor contingencies is a form of practical knowledge, what this knowledge in fact turns out to be is, I think, a form of knowing *that*. And this matters—deeply.

Knowing that is, of course, a representational state. So, if our theory makes essential use of the concept of knowing that, we can hardly claim that the theory has eliminated the need for representation. We have simply tacitly reintroduced the concept of representation by way of the appeal to knowledge. Combining the enactive account's appeal to knowledge of sensorimotor contingencies with a general eliminativism about representation is, I suspect, a nonstarter.

There is another way in which the enactive approach might presuppose representation rather than eliminate it. This turns on the role played, in the approach, by *action*. For, on its usual construal, action, itself, presupposes representational concepts. Both the *status* of an event as an action, and its *identity* as the particular action it is, depends on its connection to prior intentional states. The precise nature of this connection will depend on which theory of action you endorse, but that there is *some* appropriate connection is asserted by all theories. For example, suppose you are patting your head while rubbing your stomach. Consider, first, what makes this an action. On any traditional philosophical account of action, its status as an action depends on its standing in some appropriate connection to intentional, hence representational, states. The term "appropriate" is defined only *within* a theory. On a causal theory of action, for example, "appropriate" is explained in terms of certain sorts of causal relations—the movement constitutes an action because it is caused by some prior intentional state—an intention, volition, belief-desire complex, and so forth. Other theories give different accounts of what an "appropriate" relation is but all assert that bearing *some* relation to other intentional states is essentially involved in being an action.

Second, let's shift focus from the question of the status of an action to that of its identity. How many actions do we have here? Is patting your head while rubbing your stomach one action, or two, or many? Again, on traditional accounts, the individuation of actions is essentially bound up with the individuation of other intentional states. Returning to the causal theory, for example, the idea would be that if my intention or volition is a single state, then the action counts as one rather than many. Thus, if my intention is to pat my head while rubbing my stomach—a single intention—then the action counts as one action. If, on the other hand, I am the subject of two distinct intentions—to pat my head, and rub my stomach—which just happen to be contemporaneously activated, then the action counts as two, rather than one.

In this way, traditional accounts of action make both the *status* of an event as an action, and its *identity* as the particular action it is, essentially dependent on its relation to other intentional states. But intentional states are individuated by their content. And content arises through representation. So, the appeal to action presupposes representation and therefore cannot explain it. And, *a fortiori*, it cannot eliminate it. Once again, the attempt to view the enactive approach as licensing a general eliminativism about representation cannot be sustained.

However, the importance of this point is more general than simply providing grounds for rejecting enactive-inspired eliminativism. If the appeal to action is to play *any* role in helping us understand representation, we cannot appeal to a concept of action that presupposes representation. The typical, philosophical, sense of action is thereby precluded. We need another concept of action, a type of action that does not inherit its status and identity from its connection to intentional states. Actions of this sort, I shall call *deeds*, and will characterize them properly in the next chapter. Deeds are, of course, available to O'Regan and Noë in their development of the enactive approach. The argument of this section has not been directed against that approach as such. On the contrary—I think that the approach is fundamentally correct. Rather, I have, in effect, been advancing a case for why the enactive approach needs the concept of a deed.

Any account of representation that invokes the concept of activity—both bodily and mental activity—at least as traditionally understood, is invoking a representational concept. To suppose otherwise—to take activity as unproblematically available for one's account of representation—is to fall victim to the first form of the myth of the giving.

10 The Dual-Component Interpretation

To attempt to explain representation by appealing to a concept of action that is representational is to fall victim to the first form of the myth of the giving. As we have seen, however, there are two further, logically distinct, forms that this myth might take. In its second form, the myth concerns a certain conception of the boundary between representational states and activity: it is the mistake of supposing that this boundary is the sort of thing that can be straddled by causal impingements alone. In its third form, the myth concerns the nature of the activity itself: it is the mistake of supposing that this activity consists merely in providing us with additional ways to causally impinge on the world. In both cases—with respect to the boundary between representation and activity, and with respect to the activity itself—there is, no doubt, a causal story to be told. The boundary is such that it can be straddled by causal impingements, and the activity does provide us with additional ways of causally impinging on the world. However, if we are to avoid the myth of the giving in the latter two forms, there must also be more than a causal story to tell concerning both the boundary and the activity.

To avoid these latter forms of the myth of the giving, we must reject a *dual-component* interpretation of the enactive approach; for, as with vehicle externalism in general, this interpretation makes the enactive approach susceptible to the third (and indeed second) form of the myth of the giving. Applied to the enactive model, the dual-component interpretation consists in the idea that visual perception is composed of two components. Internal representations of the worlds exist, but they are not the rich, complex, and detailed maps that orthodoxy has taken them to be. Instead, they are rough, partial, and incomplete—providing their possessors with only the general gist of the visually presented world. These protorepresentations have been designed to function only in conjunction with environmental probing and exploration by way of the visual mode and knowledge of the relevant sensorimotor contingencies.

The dual-component interpretation can accept that the connection between internal and external components may be extremely tight. Typically, the rough, partial, and incomplete internal representations may have been *designed* to function only in tandem with the probing, exploring, and exploiting of visually accessible structures in the environment; so that the former cannot fulfill their function in the absence of the latter. However, what makes this a dual-component interpretation is the idea that the probing, exploring, and exploiting of environmental structures is not itself a genuinely representational component. It may *facilitate* the representational component in performing its representational function, and, indeed, it may be essential to its performing this function. But the external component is not itself representational. Rather this external, action-based component functions only to allow the perceiving subject to causally impinge on the environment in additional ways. This interpretation of the enactive approach falls foul of the third form of the myth of the giving.

One important entailment of the enactive approach is the claim identified in the previous chapter: *the normatively constrained content of a representation exceeds that which can be provided by the internal, genuinely representational, component alone.* The content of my visual experience does not consist merely in the *gist* of a visually presented scene—a sketchy outline devoid of the richness and complexity we usually take our experience to possess. On the contrary, in the having of visual experience, I encounter the world as rich, detailed, and complex. I experience the wall of Marilyns precisely *as* a wall of Marilyns, not as two or three Marilyns surrounded by a collage of indistinct shapes and colors. However, the richness, complexity, and detail of the experience are not, according to the enactive approach, features that can be constituted by internal representations alone. On the contrary, these typically provide only the gist of the visually presented scene. Therefore, at least part of the content of my visual experience is not, and cannot be, provided by the internal representation. Therefore, the content of my visual representation of the world exceeds that which can be provided by the internal component alone. Part of the content of my experience is constituted by my ability to act on—probe, explore, and otherwise exploit—structures in the world around me.

If this is so, then we should reject a certain conception of this action-based component of representation. The conception is that embodied in the third form of the myth of the giving. The contribution that the action-based component makes to representation cannot simply be a causal one. The action-based component plays a role in constituting the content of the representation. This content is normative. Therefore, the action-based component, in addition to playing a causal role, must also play a normative one. The action-based component, in addition to allowing us to causally impinge on the world in extra ways, must also have a normative function. And to accept this is to reject the dual-component interpretation of the enactive approach.

11   The Power of Myth Revisited

If we are to avoid the first form of the myth, then, in our attempt to understand representation, we cannot appeal to a concept of action that presupposes representation. If we do, then our explanation will be *circular.* The interpretation of the enactive approach as hostile to any form of representation ultimately falls victim to this myth. In effect, representation sneaks in through the back door via the appeal to knowing or acting. Thus, the concept of action we employ must, it seems, be a nonrepresentational one. However, if we are to avoid the second and third forms of the myth, then, in our attempt to understand representation, we cannot appeal to a concept of action that does *not* presuppose representation. If we do, then our explanation will be inadequate. We simply reiterate a conception of action as merely enhancing our ways of causally impinging on the world. And these, as the third form of the myth tells us, can never accommodate the normative character of representation.

There is, however, a way out of this dilemma, and it involves looking more closely at the first horn. The appeal to a normative or representational concept of action will be circular only if the action acquires its normative or representational status from something else—for example, from a prior intentional state. If it does, then we shall, of course, be assuming representation to explain representation. But suppose that the representational status of the action is not derived from anything else. Suppose the action is representational because of what it is in itself, and its relations to the world, and not because of its relation to a prior, or distinct, representational state. Then, the appeal to this type of action would avoid the problem of circularity.

Moreover, in employing this concept of action we would not be reiterating the sort of boundary between representation and action that is implicated in the second form of the myth of the giving. Both the representational and action-based components of representation would be, in fact, normative and representational. Thus, there can be no issue of whether the boundary between these components is of a sort bridgeable by causal impingements alone. And, in employing a normative and, indeed, representational conception of action we would avoid the third form of the myth—the mistake of supposing that the contribution action makes to perception is merely one of enhancing a subject's abilities to causally impinge on the world.

Does the requisite concept of action exist? Are there such things as actions that possess representational status but do not acquire this status from any other intentional state? In the remainder of this book, I shall argue that there are. These are not actions in the traditional sense. They are what I shall call *deeds*. Deeds provide the basis of a more radical interpretation of the enactive approach, and of vehicle externalism in general. This interpretation denies the sort of separation of representation and action that was, in effect, common to both eliminativist and dual-component interpretations. We cannot separate, not even logically, representation from action. There is no possibility of separating, as the dual-component interpretation would have it, the genuinely representational from the action-based components of visual perception. Therefore, *a fortiori*, there is no possibility of eliminating representation in favor of action. Actions and representations do not make even notionally separable contributions to the overall task of representing the world. Representation and action are, indeed, essentially connected—because acting can be a form of representing. Representation does not stop short of its objects: representation is representation *all the way out.*

The book so far has tried to provide reasons to look favorably upon this thesis of representation in action. The remainder of the book attempts to motivate and defend the thesis independent of these reasons. The argument developed in the remaining chapters is that certain forms of actions—deeds—satisfy all the criteria traditionally required of something for it to count as representational and, crucially, they satisfy these criteria independently of any connection they bear to other representational states. The first task is to clarify the notion of a deed, and this will be the subject of the next chapter.

6 Actions, Doings, and Deeds

1 Two Constraints on Action

I have argued that the attempt to involve the concept of action in one's account of representation needs to satisfy two desiderata:

1. The concept of action employed cannot presuppose any other prior intentional or representational states. A corollary of this is that if an action were deemed to share a feature or features—such as *normativity*—with intentional states, it must not have acquired or inherited this feature from those states. If either of these conditions are not met, then the attempt to use the concept of action to cast light on the concept of representation would be *circular*. As we have seen, many recent attempts to explain representational capacities in terms of action—either bodily or psychic—do seem to take action as an unproblematic given. In this, they fall victim to the first version of the *myth of the giving*.

2. The concept of action must possess certain key features of intentional or representational states. In particular, the type of action to which we appeal cannot be thought of as making a purely *causal* contribution to representation. Increasing our repertoire of causal impingements upon the world makes no contribution to understanding our representational capacities because it makes no contribution to understanding the normative dimension of those capacities. And this dimension is essential to anything that is to count as a representation. The idea that action makes a purely causal contribution to representation provides us with a dual-component interpretation of our representational grip on the world, a grip constituted by both normative and nonnormative vectors. And this vision of the role of action in representation falls victim to both the second and third forms of the myth of the giving.

Therefore, I have argued, we seem to be presented with a potential dilemma. If we want to appeal to action in helping us understand representation, the concept of action to which we appeal must both share certain essential features of representation yet cannot share those features. The escape from the dilemma is provided by the idea that the contribution that action makes to representation is one that is itself representational, hence normative. However, crucially, this is not because the action that falls under this concept acquires its representational status from prior intentional or representational states but, rather, because it is itself representational. Representation, in this nonderivative sense, extends all the way into action and, therefore, action is, or can be, a form of representation.

The claim that representation extends into action is the claim that action, in at least some of its forms, can be representational. But, as we have seen, in one sense this claim is utterly mundane. We use bodily movements and postures to represent situations all the time. In an expression of grief, someone might cover her face with her hands. This is, in the first instance, an expression, rather than a representation, of grief. However, suppose the same person makes the same bodily movements because she is an actor playing a role. In this case, we have a simulation of grief—the utilization of various bodily movements to represent someone grieving. Her actions are, pretty clearly, representational. However, equally clearly, their representational status is a *derived* status. What makes the re-presentation of grief-behavior in the absence of its typical eliciting stimulus a representation of grief is its connection to other intentional states, both on the part of the actor and his audience. In Gricean fashion, she intends that we take her behavior as a representation of grief, and we understand that she intends us to take her actions in this way, and so on.

Therefore, to further develop the case for the representational status of action—the second desideratum—we need to identify a class of behaviors that do not threaten this case with triviality. That is, we need to identify a class of behaviors such that, *if* they were to count as representational, *then* they could not, plausibly, be thought to derive their representational status from other, logically prior, representational states. And this is precisely what is specified in the first desideratum.

This chapter is going to deal with the first desideratum—developing a concept of behavior such that, if it were to share certain essential features of intentional states, it could not have inherited those features from such states. The remainder of the book is going to deal with the second desideratum. I shall argue that actions of this sort—*deeds* as I shall call them—are representational items.

Deeds, I shall argue, are quite different from actions in the traditional philosophical sense. In particular, they stand in a quite different relation to intentional states. However, although I shall argue that deeds are representational states, this should not be taken to imply that actions are not. On the contrary, I think that actions, in the strict sense, might be representational for precisely the same sorts of reasons as deeds. My focus on deeds serves a strictly dialectical function. As we have seen, actions are intimately bound up with other intentional states: both the status of an item as an action, and its identity as the particular action it is, depends on its standing in some or other appropriate relation to a prior intentional state or states, where what counts as an appropriate relation is defined by way of one's preferred theory of action. Given this intimate relation between actions and intentional states, if actions were found to be representational, or to share certain essential features of representations, then the overwhelming temptation would be to suppose that this status, or the possession of these features, had been inherited from those intentional states with which the action is so closely bound. And this makes actions, in the strict sense, dialectically useless for the purposes of this book. Therefore the first task is to identify a type of action that stands in a much looser relation to intentional states and where, consequently, the threat of inheritance is considerably reduced.

2   The Strict Concept of Action

There is a certain, *strict*, conception of action, according to which the concept of action is logically connected to that of the intentional, hence to the representational. Roughly speaking, actions are constituted as actions by their entering into appropriate relations with intentional, hence representational, states. The precise nature of this relation will vary, depending on one's view of action, but there are, broadly speaking, four possibilities. According to one view—a basic causal theory of action—actions are to be identified with bodily movements that are caused in an appropriate way— by a prior intention, belief-desire couple, or *trying* on the part of the agent. Another view claims that actions are to be identified with the inner antecedents of bodily movements—inner tryings of some sort being the usual candidate. A third view has it that actions are made up of a combination of tryings and movements. The trying does not cause the action (as on the first view). And the action is not (as on the second view) constituted by the inner trying alone. Rather, the action incorporates both inner trying and resulting bodily movement. The fourth view claims that actions are identical with *successful* tryings. A trying becomes an action when, and only when, it is successful and brings about the appropriate bodily movement. So, actions are identical with tryings individuated in terms of the movements they cause. The difference between the third and fourth theories, thus, consists in the difference between composition and individuation.

Adjudicating between these rival accounts is not essential to our present purposes. What is important is that all of these, in one way or another, reiterate the basic connection between the concept of action and the concept of the intentional. As we shall see shortly, unlike intentions, beliefs, and desires, we need not assume that tryings are intentional states—we can make sense of a nonintentional construal of this concept. However, what I am referring to as the *strict* view of action asserts a logical connection— of one of the forms described above—between the concept of action and the concept of the intentional. To the extent that tryings figure in such a view, therefore, it will be tryings construed intentionally.

As we have seen, the basic idea behind the strict view of action is that both the *status* and *identity* of action-tokens is constituted by their connection to intentional states. Suppose you are rubbing your stomach while, at the same time, patting your head. First, what makes what is going on here an action—or part of an action—as opposed to a (mere) bodily movement? What I have called the *strict* view tells us that it is elevated to the status of an action either by its being produced by a prior intention, or trying, or by the movement and these sorts of intentional states forming appropriately related proper parts of a larger entity, the action properly understood, or by the intentional state being individuated in terms of the movement, and so on. In each case, the intention, or trying is understood as an intentional state. Thus, in each case, the status of an event as an action is underwritten either by its connection to intentional states or, in fact, by its being an intentional state.

Second, how many actions are there here? The strict account of action tells us that the various movements will constitute—or form a proper part of—one action rather than two if the intention, trying, and so forth from which they derive (or with which they couple) is one rather than two. Thus, if you intend or are trying to pat your head while rubbing your stomach—in other words, you are the subject of a single intentional state— then the corresponding action is one action rather than two. If, on the other hand, you were the subject of two intentions, tryings, and so forth— trying to pat your head and trying to rub your stomach—which just happened to be contemporaneous, then you would be performing two actions.

The same sort of points about status and individuation, rehearsed in the previous chapter, can be recast in belief-desire terms, rather than in terms of intentions or tryings. If you succeed in performing an action out of a desire and belief, which together function as your reason, the content of the belief and desire transfer into the description under which the act emerges as intentional. This is because your belief is a belief about your action. For example, if you believe that pulling the trigger will kill your enemy, this content transfers into the description under which the act appears as intentional, that is, "pulling the trigger," "killing."

The strict concept of action, therefore, asserts a constitutive connection between actions and intentional states. As long as we realize that what we are dealing with here is, partly, a matter of stipulation, there is nothing wrong with the strict concept of action. Indeed, I propose to defer to the strict concept and, henceforth, allow that nothing counts as an action in the absence of the sort of connection to intentional states envisaged by the strict concept. What this does mean, however, is that most of what we do does not count as action. Most of what we do, I shall now argue, falls under one of two categories. These categories are significantly different, and require two names. I am going to refer to these as *doings* and *deeds*. Consider, first, the notion of a *doing*.

3   The Subintentional Act

Doings, as I shall use the expression, correspond to what Brian O'Shaughnessy calls *subintentional acts*—the concept of which was largely introduced into recent philosophical consciousness by his work. According to O'Shaughnessy, an act counts as subintentional if:

We perform it; we know of or are aware of it neither in the conscious nor unconscious sector of the mind; we do it out of a feeling-like; it is not performed for any reason that is our reason; and the faculty of reason plays neither a *positive* nor *negative* causal role in its genesis. (1980, 2: 62, emphasis his)

By way of unpacking, take O'Shaughnessy's primary example of a subintentional act. He writes:

If [the reader] will attend, at this very moment, to his tongue, he may well discover that it is in motion; and if not, let him attend to it on another occasion; or else attend some time to his toes or fingers; etc. In the end he must eventually come across an example of movement that is possessed of a special property, viz. the property of *not being intended*. (Ibid.: 60, emphasis his)

The following claims, O'Shaughnessy argues, are true of events such as this tongue movement:

1   We perform it   Such an event is something we do or perform. When you become aware of the movement of your tongue, for example, it is not as if you become aware of your tongue moving of its own accord. That would be a very strange, and disturbing, occurrence indeed. When you become aware of the movement of your tongue, you become aware of it as something that you are doing. Such an event may fall far short of action in the strict sense, but it is nonetheless something that you do. It is what we might call a *doing*.

2   We know of or are aware of it neither in the conscious nor the unconscious sector of the mind   Your noticing that your tongue is moving has the character of a discovery. So, prior to this noticing that, your tongue was moving without any conscious awareness of the movement on your part. Perhaps, then, your awareness was unconscious? Here O'Shaughnessy appeals to a version of the familiar distinction between *knowing that* and *knowing of*. If one wants to assert unconscious awareness of the movement of one's tongue, then one would be hard put to defend the idea that this unconscious awareness is awareness that. For, normally, we do not remember what we did with our tongue not just a minute ago, not just five seconds ago, but, in fact, not even a second ago. It would be pushing the idea of knowledge that or awareness that to questionable lengths to claim that we have a kind of knowledge that is extinguished the very instant it comes into being. As O'Shaughnessy puts it, "Short-term memory is one thing, instant forgetting another!" (1980, 2: 64). There is, in fact, a sense in which you might unconsciously know of the movement of the tongue prior to your noticing that it is moving. This is the sense in which we might have bodily awareness of the orientation of our body, the dispositions of our limbs, and so on. O'Shaughnessy need not dispute such knowledge because, as he sees it, it is *nonconceptual*. Thus, he can merely reformulate his claim: prior to noticing that one's tongue is moving, there does not exist a concept-using state of knowledge (or awareness) that this movement is occurring. Given his assumption that intentional action is conceptually individuated ("action that, for its owner, falls under preferred concept-headings" [1980, 2: 66]), the absence of a concept-using state of awareness is all he needs to establish his primary claim: that the movement of the tongue is a subintentional, rather than intentional, act.

3   We do it out of a feeling-like   The movement of one's tongue might typically be caused by something like restlessness—a state that manifests itself in momentary urges (for example, the urge to alter one's posture). Some of one's beliefs might play a *causal* role in the genesis of this movement. For example, the movement of one's tongue might be, in part, caused by the frustration attending the failure to adjudicate certain of one's beliefs (in, for example, the process of working out a difficult puzzle). However, these beliefs do not play a *rational* role in the genesis of the tongue's movement. Indeed, in this genesis the rational faculty is entirely bypassed.

4   It is not performed for any reason that is our reason; and the faculty of reason plays neither a positive nor negative causal role in its genesis   There are two ways in which reason might have played a role in the genesis of the tongue movement. First, there is a strict sense of rational according to which some action is rational because it contributes to satisfying certain of your (rational) aims, either directly, or indirectly via its contribution to the bringing about of means that are necessary for satisfying those aims. In this sense of rational, the faculty of reason plays what O'Shaughnessy dubs a *positive* role in the genesis of the action. There is another, somewhat less strict, sense of rational. Suppose you are drumming your fingers across the table. This act can be rational in the sense that you have decided it will do you no harm. (As opposed to a situation in which, for example, you have judged that it will do you harm in virtue of irritating your coworkers). This is what O'Shaughnessy means when he talks of the faculty of reason playing a *negative* role in the genesis of an action. In the case of the moving of one's tongue, reason plays neither a positive nor negative role in the genesis of the action. You are not doing it to further—either directly or indirectly—any of your rational aims. And you are not doing it because you have judged it to be harmless. The moving of your tongue is neither rational nor irrational. It is a primitive nonrational *doing* (O'Shaughnessy refers to it as a *deed*; but I want to reserve that usage for something else).

If we combine conditions (1) through (4), we arrive at the concept of the *subintentional act*. The concept of subintentionality gains its purchase from the strict concept of action. Recall how, given that concept, it is the content of the relevant intentional state that transfers into the description under which the action emerges as intentional. Thus, it is in its connection to intentional states that the status of a bodily movement as an action (or part of an action) is to be found. The relevant intentional state may be, depending on one's concept of action an intention, belief-desire coupling, or trying, but the underlying idea remains the same. However, in the case of one's tongue movement, there is no relevant intentional state. There is no intentional state that functions as *my* reason for moving my tongue. Therefore, no such descriptive transfer is possible. Thus, there is no description under which the moving of my tongue counts as intentional. Therefore it does not count as an action in the strict sense. Nevertheless, it is something I do or perform. O'Shaughnessy, therefore, refers to it as a *subintentional* act.

To claim that the subintentional act is not intentional is not to claim that it is not the result of a trying: as long, crucially, as we are willing to reinterpret the concept of trying in nonintentional terms. O'Shaughnessy is willing to do this, and a nonintentional concept of trying plays a crucial role in his overall account (1980, 2: 95ff.). Consider, again, his example of moving one's tongue. Suppose scientists have attached an inhibitory mechanism to the relevant part of the tongue mover's neural supply, a mechanism that prevents tongue movement. So, at a particular time, we might suppose that the usual neural buildup, an increase in activity in a certain region that will typically result in tongue movement, occurs. But at the last moment prior to this movement the inhibitory mechanism kicks in, and so the tongue does not move. O'Shaughnessy comments:

Then what happened? I suggest that this man *tried to move his tongue*. That is, *subintentionally* he strove to move it. For what else could one say? After all, we must say something less than "he moved it" and something more than "the motor mechanism was activated most of the way." Only "he strove" seems to meet these requirements. (1980, 2: 96)

So, trying or striving does play a role in the causal genesis of the act, and, according to O'Shaughnessy, this is precisely what makes it something we *do*. But trying or striving in this sense is not an intentional act. Intentional states possess either truth conditions or conditions of a related sort, and this is precisely what makes them intentional. In the case of tryings or strivings, the relevant conditions would seem to be satisfaction conditions. If tryings or strivings were to be intentional states, they would have to be essentially directed toward as yet unrealized futures. But the strivings involved in the subintentional act do not, O'Shaughnessy claims, seem to be thus directed. He claims:

After all, such acts elude awareness, and, since there exists no such thing as completing or failing to complete them, the sub-intentional act cannot be directed towards any temporally removed goal; and the same must hold true of any putative sub-intentional trying. (1980, 2: 95)

These remarks are less than clear. First of all, the fact that such acts elude awareness will merely invite the retort that the tryings are fully intentional but merely unconscious. So, the fact that they are unconscious cannot be what is crucial to their nonintentional status. O'Shaughnessy's appeal to the idea of nonconceptual awareness (in defending claim 2 above) might lead us to suspect that he might try to infer their nonintentional status from the subject's nonconceptual (and, incidentally, unconscious awareness) of the subintentional act. Unfortunately, I am somewhat more suspicious of the idea of the nonconceptual than O'Shaughnessy, and so cannot go down that route. So, here is another possible defense of the nonintentional status of the subintentional act.

The crucial point, I think, is not simply that the subject has no awareness of what would or would not count as completion of the act, nor that if the subject were to know this, that her knowledge would be nonconceptual. What is crucial involves the idea of a "temporally removed goal"; for without this, there is no nontrivial answer to the question of what would or would not count as completion of the act. To see this, consider, first, a standard intentional case of action, where there is a temporally removed goal, albeit minimal. One switches on the light by flicking the switch on the wall. If one did want to understand this in terms of the concept of trying—in this case an intentional version of that concept—then, in the first instance, what one is trying to do is achieve a temporally removed goal, namely switching on the light. The movements of one's hand and arm are the means by which one does what one is trying to do. Because there is a temporally removed goal of this sort, we have a clear sense of what would count as success or failure. And, this goal is perfectly compatible with variations, within a certain limit, in the way one moves one's hand and arm. What individuates the act is the overall goal.

However, in the case of the subintentional act of one's tongue moving, there is no similarly defined goal. So, there is no similar conception of what would count as success or failure in the subintentional act. There is a trivial sense in which the moving of one's tongue constitutes completion or success of the trying. However this trying or striving is not sufficient to individuate the movement. Moving one's tongue in manner X might constitute completion of the trying, but so too might moving one's tongue in manner Y or Z. Moving one's tongue for duration A might constitute completion of the act, but so too might moving it for duration B or C. There is an indefinite number of movement types whose tokening might constitute success of the striving. In the absence of a temporally removed goal, there is, as we might put it, an *indeterminacy* of satisfaction conditions for the striving.

However, even worse, this indeterminacy of satisfaction conditions infects the individuation of the striving itself. Suppose, as O'Shaughnessy reasonably speculates, that the movement of one's tongue is caused by something like restlessness—a state that manifests itself in various fleeting urges to modify one's posture. Then, what fact of the matter determines the trying as a trying to move one's tongue, rather than a trying to modify one's posture in a way that relieves the restlessness? But, if there is no fact of the matter with regard to the identity of the striving, then there can be no fact of the matter as to whether some other modification of one's posture might satisfy the striving also.

Thus, with regard to the satisfaction conditions of strivings, we need to do better than the claim that the satisfaction conditions of trying to move one's tongue are the moving of one's tongue. In the absence of a temporally removed, nontrivial, goal, we seem to be left with a general indeterminacy of satisfaction conditions for strivings, and a general indeterminacy of strivings themselves. It is this absence of a temporally removed, nontrivial, goal that marks the difference between subintentional strivings and genuinely intentional states. And this is why, I think, strivings fall short of intentional status.

Henceforth, I shall refer to subintentional acts in O'Shaughnessy's sense as *doings*. The change in terminology is, in part, intended to highlight a danger: that we shall fall into the trap of thinking of intentional and subintentional as poles of a dichotomy when it is, I think, far more helpful to think of them as positions on a spectrum. In the next section, I shall identify a class of events that fall in between intentional actions in the strict sense and subintentional acts in O'Shaughnessy's sense. We might refer to these as *preintentional acts*, or, as I shall use the expression, *deeds*.

4   The Preintentional Act

Here are two examples of something that I am going to label *deeds*, or, *preintentional acts*. The idea is that they occupy a logical position somewhere between actions in the strict sense and O'Shaughnessy's subintentional acts.

1. Suppose you are catching a cricket ball. In fact, suppose you are fielding in a position where the cricket ball comes to you very quickly. You are fielding at first slip, and the bowler is very quick—Brett Lee, for example, or Shoaib Akhtar. Typically, you will have less than half a second before the ball, which may be traveling in excess of 100 mph, reaches you. So, the ball flies toward you: if you are lucky you will see this. However, the ball is also flying toward you at the height all slip fielders hate: lower-chest height. To make the catch you will have an awkward decision to make: whether to point your fingers upward or downward.

2. You are playing Chopin's *Fantasie Impromptu in C# Minor,* and your fingers have to traverse the keys in the sort of bewildering display necessary to successfully negotiate this notoriously difficult piece.

The first point to note about pointing your fingers up or down, or throwing your keys around the keyboard in the way mandated by Chopin, is that both of these are things we do, rather than things that are done to us. They are, as we might say, *deeds.* We can establish this in a similar manner to that in which O'Shaughnessy established the active character of the subintentional act. Unlike the case of one's tongue moving, it is difficult, in the two cases described above, to turn one's attention to what one is doing in the commission of those acts—doing so will almost certainly result in a failure of such commission. However, suppose you turn your attention to what you did afterward. To the extent that you remember what you did, it will be, precisely, a case of remembering what you *did.* You, manifestly, do not remember it as a case of your body doing certain things. It is not as if you remember your fingers doing things of their own accord—that would be a very strange, and presumably disturbing, sort of memory indeed, and not one that is typically prevalent in one's recollection of one's sporting or musical endeavors. So, I think we should conclude that in such cases we are dealing with *acts* of some sort. The relevant events fall into the category of activity rather than passivity. They are things we do rather than things that befall us.

However, now look more closely at the relevant events. The acts of playing Chopin's *Fantasie Impromptu* can, fairly obviously, be broken down into various subacts—primarily involving one's fingers hitting the right key at the right time. Each of these is, for the reasons outlined above, something that we do or perform, rather than something that happens to us. Almost as obviously, the act of catching the ball can be broken down into a succession of subacts—pointing one's fingers up or down, leaping or crouching further, and so on. Each of these subacts consists in a succession of online, feedback-modulated adjustments, where incoming sensory information is correlated with the required motor response. And these subacts, although clearly being things we do or perform, do not fit into the strict conception of action outlined earlier.

In these sorts of cases, what we have is (i) a general *antecedent* intention (to catch the ball, to play the piece, or some variant thereof), and (ii) an array of on-line, feedback-modulated adjustments that take place below the level of intention but, collectively, promote the satisfaction of the antecedent intention. Let us call the events identified in (ii) as *deeds.* The claim that deeds do not fit the strict conception of action is, therefore, entailed by the conjunction of two claims: (A) the direct antecedents of these deeds are not themselves intentional or representational states, and (B) the general antecedent intention is not sufficient for the relevant doings to be individuated in the way that actions are individuated.

The defense of (A)   The evidence for (A) is both phenomenological and neurophysiological. At the level of phenomenology, less than half a second is simply not sufficient time to form the intention to move one's fingers in the way demanded by the exigencies of the ball's trajectory. Still less is there sufficient time to form intentions to move one's fingers in a way required by the genius of Chopin. In such situations, we simply find ourselves acting. It is not, as Wittgenstein put it, that our reasons have given out and we find ourselves acting without reasons. It is rather that we did not have the time to consciously entertain the reasons in the first place.

Of course, someone may want to object that all these considerations indicate is that we do not *consciously* form or entertain intentions to point our fingers up or down, or to hit a certain piano key at a certain appropriate time. But we may, nonetheless, unconsciously intend these things. I think this sort of appeal to unconscious intentions in these sorts of cases is the last refuge of a scoundrel caught in the grip of a strict conception of action, but nonetheless the objection does, in effect, make a valid logical point about the limits of phenomenological argument. Phenomenological considerations can, obviously pertain only to what one experiences. Therefore, apart from some considerations pertaining to the burden of proof, they are powerless against the sort of person who, come what may, wants to postulate *unexperienced* intentions. So, with a view to strengthening the argument, let us turn now to the neurophysiological evidence.

The neurophysiological evidence for (A) consists in the widely accepted Milner–Goodale hypothesis (Milner and Goodale 1995), itself a development of the even more widely accepted distinction between the *what* and *where* components of the functional architecture underlying vision. Milner and Goodale have argued that visually guided action is supported by neural and functional systems quite different from, and at least partially independent of, those that support conscious visual experience, imagistic reasoning, and visual categorization. More precisely, they argue that human cognitive architecture is made up of two distinct *visual brains*. One, the more ancient, specializes in the visually based control of motor action that must be accomplished rapidly. The other, more recent, is dedicated to the explicit selection of deliberate and planned actions on the basis of knowledge and memory. Milner and Goodale argue that the former system is located in the dorsal visual processing stream leading to the posterior parietal lobule, while the latter is located in the ventral stream projecting to the inferotemporal cortex.

Several considerations support this thesis. At the level of functional organization, a division of labor of this sort is plausible: the acute control of action requires rapidly processed, egocentrically specified, and continually modified information about form, orientation, distance, and so on. Conceptual thought, on the other hand, requires the identification of objects and states of affairs according to significance and category, and irrespective of excessive or irrelevant details such as retinal image, size, and so on. It seems that computationally coding either one of these—in any sort of efficient way—rules out the implementation of the same code for the other. In each case, as Milner and Goodale note, we need to eliminate different aspects of the signal, and to perform very different kinds of computational transformations.

In addition to considerations of functional organization, three types of neurological evidence support the Milner–Goodale hypothesis. First, recordings of single-cell activity indicate that cells in the two streams respond very differently to stimulation. For example, posterior parietal neurons appear to react maximally to visual cues combined with motor actions. Inferotemporal neurons, on the other hand, respond better to complex object-centered features irrespective of their location in egocentric space.

Second, the hypothesis is supported by various pathologies. D. F. is a ventrally compromised patient who claims to have no conscious visual experience of the shape and orientation of objects but who can nonetheless perform quite fluent motor actions. For example, although claiming to have no conscious experience of a visually presented slot in front of her, she is quite capable of correctly orienting a letter so as to post it through the slot. Significantly, D. F.'s performance declines if a time delay is introduced between presentation of the slot and selection (with the slot now out of sight) of an orientation. Such a delay, Milner and Goodale speculate, relocates the processing burden from the undamaged dorsal stream to the damaged ventral processing stream dedicated to memory, planning, and deliberate action. On the other hand, optic ataxics show a converse behavioral syndrome. Such ataxics are dorsally impaired and, despite the fact that they are unable to engage objects by fluent actions, they claim to see these objects perfectly well.

Third, certain visual illusions seem to affect even normal subjects. For example, the Tichener circles illusion seems to work by affecting our conscious perceptions without impairing our visuomotor capacities. Milner and Goodale suggest that the illusion arises through processing idiosyncrasies in the ventral stream, and therefore, the nonconscious dorsal stream, which controls the fine-tuned motor actions, is unaffected.

Milner and Goodale probably overemphasize the extent to which the dorsal and ventral streams work in near isolation. Nevertheless, a weakened version of the Milner–Goodale hypothesis has widespread acceptance. Such a version will recognize that there exist complex feedback-modulated interactions between the two systems, but preserve the essential insight: significant amounts of acute action-guiding visual processing are independent of the processing that underlies conscious visual awareness. The two visual brains interact at the level of intentional agency. The ventral stream is (in part) responsible for the selection of the types of action to be performed. But the nonconscious dorsal stream is left with the task of working out how to implement these plans and ideas. In short, the ventral stream is responsible for *actions*, in the strict sense; and the intentions, belief-desire couplings, and (intentionally individuated) volitions that might be responsible for these are denizens of the ventral stream. The dorsal stream, on the other hand is responsible for *deeds*—pointing one's fingers up or down, hitting the right key at the right time, and so on. The neural mechanics of actions and deeds are, thus, quite distinct, and the former involve intentional states that are, in fact, quite absent in the latter.

In short, when we look at our *deeds* both from the *inside* and the *outside*—in terms of what it seems like to perform them, and in terms of the neural mechanics underlying them, we (a) find no evidence for any role played by intentions, and (b) find convincing evidence that intentions play no role, other than providing a general antecedent intention that the dorsal stream has the job of implementing in ways that are intention free. This concludes the defense of (A).

The defense of (B) Let us now move on to the defense of (B): the claim that the general antecedent intention is not sufficient for the relevant deeds to be individuated in the way that actions are individuated. According to the strict conception of action, the individuation of actions is essentially bound up with the individuation of intentional states. It is antecedent intentional states that determine whether a sequence of bodily movements counts as one action rather than two, or three, or *n* (or whether such a movement counts as *part* of one action, rather than, two, three, or *n*). Actions are individuated by way of the content of their associated intentions, volitions, or belief-desire complexes. Thus, both the *status* of an event as an action (as opposed to mere bodily movement) and its *identity* as the particular action it is, derive from its connection to an intentional state that has a certain identifiable content. Rubbing one's head while patting one's stomach is an action, or part of an action, if there is an associated intentional state—an intention or volition—that is responsible for it. And it is *one* action, or part of one action, if the intention or volition responsible for it is one intention or volition.

It is difficult to see how the general antecedent intention underlying the catching of the ball or the playing of the piece could play this sort of role in the individuation of the relevant deeds. The general problem is that any number of on-line, feedback-modulated adjustments—deeds—can be involved in satisfying an antecedent intention. Several different adjustments can go into catching the ball, and many thousands can be involved in successfully negotiating a work of Chopin. Thus, the appeal to antecedent intention is not capable of individuating—separating—one deed from another. If it is the antecedent intention that is supposed to individuate deeds (as it does in the case of actions), then we are left with no criteria of identity for deeds, other than the hopelessly coarse-grained criterion according to which all deeds performed in the satisfaction of a general antecedent intention are the same deed.

One might think we can circumvent this problem by way of a respecification of the relevant general antecedent intention. For example, perhaps the relevant general antecedent intention is not the intention to catch the ball, but, rather, the intention *to do whatever it takes to catch the ball*? The problem with this suggestion, however, is that the problem of individuation remains. There are an indefinite number of deeds the performance of which would, in the appropriate circumstances, be what it takes to catch the ball. So, if this antecedent intention were supposed to individuate the deeds—as it does in the case of strict actions—we would still be left with a hopelessly coarse-grained criterion of identity for deeds.

Suppose, however, we modify the general antecedent intention in the following way. We see the general antecedent intention as a Boolean conjunction of simpler intentions. Since Boolean operations are closed under conjunction, a conjunction of simpler intentions is itself an intention. The antecedent intention now has the following form: I have the intention to do X in circumstance Y and do X^1 in circumstance Y^1 and so on, where X specifies a certain movement and Y a certain trajectory of ball, and so on. In this way, in catching the ball, could I not have an intention to do whatever it is I in fact do?

The problem with this suggestion, however, is that it leads to another, slightly different, problem of individuation; but it is still, in essence, a problem of *grain*. One way of understanding the Milner–Goodale hypothesis is this: *there are discriminations that can be made in action that cannot be made in thought*. Suppose, for example, that we have two ball trajectories that differ only in that, relative to the fielder, the second is one millimeter to the left of the first. The dorsal stream, doing what the dorsal stream does best, will be able to discriminate between these trajectories, and the adjustments the fielder makes will be the result of the feedback-modulated response from this stream. But intentions are not, as we have seen, denizens of the dorsal stream. So, in formulating one's intentions, the ventral stream doing what it does best, how can one formulate intentions to do things that are, as we might put it, *invisible* to the ventral stream and its processing?

In other words, there are all sorts of discriminations made by the dorsal stream to which the ventral stream is insensitive. Intentions are denizens of the ventral stream, and the fielder can have no intentions with respect to those discriminations invisible to it. So, in the case described, the deeds are different, but the intentions cannot be different. Therefore, once again, we cannot use intentions to individuate deeds.

This is, in general true, for the relation between intentions and deeds. Take the everyday action of picking up a glass. The general antecedent intention may be to pick up the glass, or whatever, and in virtue of this I reach out to grasp it. But then the dorsal stream springs into action, and the movement is rendered successful by an array of feedback-modulated adjustments emanating from that stream. It is not simply that I *am*, in fact, unconscious of exactly what my fingers, and so forth, are doing. I cannot, in the normal course of events, *be* conscious of them—they are invisible to ventral stream processing. And it is only under very unusual circumstances—for example, someone showing me a magnified, slow-motion film clip of my action—that they might become accessible to ventral processing. But, in the absence of such unusual conditions, the fine-grained, feedback-modulated *deeds* I perform are invisible to the ventral stream, hence invisible to my intentions. Therefore, such deeds cannot be individuated in terms of my intentions.

Therefore, the conjunction of (A) and (B) is satisfied. The direct antecedents of such deeds are not themselves intentional or representational states, and the general antecedent intention—whatever form it takes—is not sufficient to individuate deeds in the manner of actions. Therefore, we should, I think, accept that deeds are not a form of action in the strict sense.

One objection to this argument might be based on the idea that the role played by intentional states in individuating the status of actions might be played, in the case of deeds, by *motor representations*. That is, we might explain the status of a deed as a deed in terms of its connection to a general antecedent intention, but then individuate the deed in terms of the motor representation that causally produces it. However, if this line is to be convincing, two questions need to be addressed. First, do motor representations possess content of a sort sufficient to individuate deeds? Second, if so, what is the source or basis of this content? In answering the second question, we will be required to tell a certain story about how motor representations come to satisfy the essential conditions of, or constraints on, representation: how they carry information about the environment, how they have the function of tracking environmental items, or enabling the organism to achieve some task in virtue of tracking such features, how they are capable of misrepresentation, and so on. In short, we will have to tell precisely the same story about motor representations as I am, in the remainder of this book, going to tell about deeds. So, the case for thinking that motor representations possess content that they pass onto the deeds they produce is, in fact, no stronger than the case for thinking that deeds possess content in themselves. Therefore, we cannot use the former claim as an objection to the latter.

Since deeds are things that we do or perform, but since they do not fit into the strict conception of action, the temptation is to assimilate them to subintentional acts. However, this assimilation does not seem correct either. To see this, recall O'Shaughnessy's characterization of such acts: we perform them; we know of or are aware of them neither in the conscious nor unconscious sector of the mind; we perform them out of a feeling-like; they are not performed for any reason that is our reason; and the faculty of reason plays neither a positive nor negative causal role in their genesis.

The most obvious divergence between subintentional acts—doings—and deeds concerns the role played by reason in their genesis. According to O'Shaughnessy, in the case of subintentional acts such as moving one's tongue, reason plays neither a positive role—in that the act does not directly or indirectly further one's rational aims—nor a negative role—in that one has judged the act to be harmless. The subintentional act that is the moving of one's tongue is, therefore, neither rational nor irrational.

However, in the case of the sort of deeds identified in this section, reason does seem to play both a positive and (arguably) negative role. When one is making the various on-line, feedback-modulated, adjustments required to catch the ball or play the piece, one is, in a clear sense, doing these because of one's goal of catching the ball or playing the piece. The various adjustments that constitute deeds do play a definite and identifiable role in furthering one's rational aims. So, reason plays a positive role in the genesis of such actions. Also, although it would be difficult to form an occurrent belief about the effects of such deeds while in the process of commissioning them, it is almost certainly true that, while in the process of commission, one does believe, in a dispositional sense, that the adjustments one is making are, at the very least, not harmful in the accomplishing of the goals one wants to accomplish. So, arguably, reason can also play a negative role in the genesis of such actions.

Therefore, deeds do not seem to be insulated from reason in the way that subintentional acts—doings—are insulated from rational considerations and assessments. This point is, ultimately, scarcely contestable. For intuitively, it seems obvious that the sort of on-line, feedback-modulated, adjustments one makes in catching a ball or playing Chopin's *Fantasie Impromptu* are goal directed in a way that O'Shaughnessy's flagship example of tongue moving is not. Underlying deeds is a general antecedent intention of one form or another. Underlying doings is no such thing: instead there is, as O'Shaughnessy puts it, a vague "feeling-like," a visceral restlessness that manifests itself in an intention-free alteration of posture.

A preintentional act is not intentional in the way that actions are: it does not acquire its intentional status from its connection to prior intentional or representational states. Nevertheless, a preintentional act—a *deed*—is intentional in another sense, in a sense that mere doings are not. Deeds are done with intention, but not in the way that actions are done with intention. To say that an action is done with intention is to say that *both* the status of an action as an action *and* its identity as the particular action it is derive from its connection to prior intentional states. In the case of deeds, however, although the status of a deed as a deed might derive from prior intentional states—a general antecedent intention, for example— the identity of the deed as the particular deed it is does not similarly derive from this state. Deeds, therefore, occupy a middle ground between action in the strict sense, and doing in the subintentional sense.

Nonetheless, there is an important difference between the two examples of deeds—and the examples were, in fact, chosen partly with a view to making this point. Playing Chopin's *Fantasie Impromptu* is a highly intellectual activity in a way that catching a ball is not. Playing the piece requires months, even years, of intentionally directed activity—of correlating notes on a page with keys on a piano, and so forth. At each step, one will hit a particular key because one has looked at the page, *recognized* the note as an instance of a particular type, *believed* this note to correlate with a particular key, and therefore, formed the *intention* of hitting this key at this time. Catching a ball, on the other hand, is typically a matter of on-line adjustments made through a process of trial and error that acts independently of intention formation. So the deeds involved in playing Chopin are, one might argue, far more closely bound up with intentions than those involved in catching a ball.

Therefore, if we do not want to engender further worries about the inheritance of representational features by deeds from intentional states, we would be advised to deal with deeds located at, as we might put it, the lower end of the intellectual spectrum. Happily, playing a difficult composition on a piano is an entirely atypical example of a deed. The vast majority of deeds are, in fact, located at what, from our point of view, is the right end of the spectrum. As we shall see, it is deeds formed independently of intentional states that provide far and away the best examples of our representational activities and, certainly, the case for the representational status of deeds will be based on deeds of this sort.

In the remaining chapters, I am going to be dealing in deeds, rather than actions or doings. These are the most likely candidates for behavioral items that can have a representational function, and, crucially, can have this function independently of any relation they bear to other representational states. Deeds are such that any representational status they bear cannot have been inherited from antecedent intentional states. If they were to acquire representational status in this way—in the way that strict actions do—then they would have to acquire both their status as act (i.e., as active rather than passive), and, more important, their identities as the particular acts that they are by way of their connection to prior representational states. And the identity of deeds is not dependent upon such a connection. Accordingly, any representational status a deed possesses is not a status that has been acquired or derived from another representational state. If deeds possess representational status, this must come from somewhere else. In the remaining chapters, I shall argue that they do possess such status, and try to show where it comes from.

7 The Informational Constraint

1 Criteria of Representation

The notion of *body language* is usually taken to be a metaphor. I am going to argue that it should, in some cases, be understood quite literally. Certain types of behavior can, *in at least one clear sense*, constitute a language. That is, at least some sorts of behavior can form a genuinely representational part of the overall process of representing the world. And it can form such a part quite independently of its connection to prior intentional—hence, representational—states. The type of behavior on which I shall focus is, for reasons explained in the previous chapter, the category of *deeds*. However, to reiterate: there is no argument presented in this book that entails that actions—in the strict sense—cannot also be representational. On the contrary, I think that the type of arguments to be developed in the remaining chapters can also be applied to actions. However, given the connection between actions and prior intentional states—intentions, volitions, tryings, and so on—there will always be a temptation to suppose that actions acquire whatever representational status they have from those states. This temptation is undercut in the case of deeds—for the relevant connection to distinct representational states does not exist.

To claim that deeds are representational is to claim that they satisfy the criteria commonly regarded as necessary and sufficient for an item to qualify as representational. There are, it is generally accepted, *five* such criteria:

Informational condition   An item *r* qualifies as a representational item only if it carries information about some state of affairs *s* that is extrinsic to it.

Teleological condition   An item *r* qualifies as representational only if it has the *proper function* either of tracking the feature or state of affairs *s* that *produces* it, or of enabling an organism or other representational *consumer* to achieve some (beneficial) task in virtue of tracking *s*.

Decouplability condition   Item *r* qualifies as representing state of affairs *s* only if *r* is, in an appropriate sense, decouplable from *s*.

Misrepresentation condition   Item *r* qualifies as representing state of affairs *s* only if it is capable of misrepresenting *s*.

Combinatorial condition   For an item *r* to qualify as representational, it must occur not in isolation but only as part of a more general representational framework.

The precise content and logical status of each of these claims is not unambiguous, and part of the task of the following chapters is to provide some much needed clarification. Moreover, none of these constraints even approximates univocal acceptance; and some constraints are clearly more controversial than others. Worse, *on some readings*, some of the constraints are incompatible with others. However, I think there is general consensus that *if* any item were to satisfy all five (suitably rendered) conditions, *then* it would count as representational if anything does. For something that satisfied all five conditions, then it is simply not clear what *else* we could legitimately demand it satisfy for it to count as representational. If an inner configuration of a subject were to satisfy all five conditions, for example, there would be little hesitation in regarding it as a representational state. The argument to be developed in the remainder of the book is, then, this: *deeds can satisfy all of these criteria*. Deeds have as much right to representational status as any inner state or configuration.

At risk of repetition, it should be noted that these constraints pertain to the nature of the relation between a representational device and its represented object. Accordingly, they are intended as conditions a representing device must meet in order to be the sort of thing that can *have* a represented object. These conditions are not, necessarily, identical with those that must be met for a device to qualify as a representation. In the latter case, we would need to specify also the way the device functions in the overall psychological economy of the subject. My claim is that deeds are the sorts of things that can have representational status. I take no stand on the issue of whether deeds are representations. To do so would likely be unhelpful in at least one clear respect. The concept of representation is permeated, perhaps irredeemably, by its assimilation to the category of the *word*. One manifestation of this assimilation is to think that the capacity to *guide* behavior is an essential part of being a representation. This idea is the basis of causal or explanatory constraints on representation.

As we shall see, my position on this constraint has two facets. First of all, it is no part of the thesis of representation in action to claim that deeds guide behaviour in the same way that internal configurations guide behavior. My claim is that deeds are *representational* in that they satisfy the conditions necessary, and perhaps sufficient, for an item to be the sort of thing that can have a representational object. That is, they satisfy the sorts of constraints required for something to be *about* something else. My claim is not that deeds are *representations* in exactly the same way that internal configurations are, or have commonly been supposed to be, representations. Thus, I shall not argue that deeds guide behavior *in the same sort of way that internal configurations guide behavior*. Nevertheless, I shall argue that deeds *can* and typically *do* play a role in guiding behavior. This role is significant and unambiguous, and we discuss it properly in chapter 9, where we examine the decouplability constraint.

This chapter discusses the first of these constraints: the *informational condition*. I shall argue that deeds can satisfy this condition no less, and no more, than internal representations traditionally construed.

2   Information and Probability

Many people, though by no means all, claim that the idea of representation can be captured, at least in part, in terms of the concept of *information*. Information is understood as carried in, or as consisting in, relations of conditional probability. However, precisely *which* relations of conditional probability is a matter of dispute.

The most uncompromising account of information associates it with a conditional probability of 1 (Dretske 1981). So, for r to carry the information that s, the probability of s given r must be 1. And this relation of conditional probability will be underwritten by *strict* laws of the form: it is a law that s only if r. So, on this understanding of information, it is natural to see informational relations as identical with, or supervenient on, nomic relations of this sort. Thus, suppose that r consists in structure or mechanism M adopting configuration F; and suppose s consists in the world W being G. Then, roughly, very roughly: r (the fact that M is F) carries information about s (the fact that W is G) if and only if r depends nomically on s.

In other words, the informational constraint is satisfied in this case if, and only if, there is a strict law to the effect that M would not be F unless W is G. Thus, according to this stringent form of the informational constraint, what binds a representation r to a represented item s (where both are understood as states of affairs) is a relation of strict nomic dependence, and a resulting s/r conditional probability of 1.

There is, however, a weaker version of the informational constraint predicated on a less demanding conception of information (Lloyd 1989). This conception associates information with an increase in conditional probability, but not necessarily an increase to the value of 1. On this weaker view, r will carry information about s if the probability of s given r is greater than the probability of s given not r.

The differences between the two concepts of information are not insignificant. Indeed, as we shall see, they have important ramifications for the prospects of regarding information as a component of representation. However, there is a notable similarity between the two conceptions that allows us, at least to some extent, to further develop them in tandem. On either account of information, the concept of information can be further explicated in terms of the concept of *law*. However, the type of law in question will vary depending on the conception of information employed. If we adopt the stringent conception of information as associated with a conditional probability of 1, then the laws in question must be strict and exceptionless. If, on the other hand, we adopt the weaker conception of information as associated merely with an increase in conditional probability, then the laws in question need to be probabilistic rather than strict. But, in both cases, the idea of information can be further explained in terms of the concept of law.

3   Informational Approaches to Representation

Mental representation is typically understood as a relation that links an internal representing item (a mental representation) and an extrinsic (typically, external) represented item. With informational accounts, it is orthodox to think of the items in question as *states* or *facts*.[1] Thus, mental representations are typically thought of as states or configurations that internal mechanisms might assume given certain circumstances or exigencies. Thus, suppose:

(1)   Mental representation r is identical with state F of internal mechanism M.

That is, r is identical with M's being F (equivalently, it is identical with the fact that M is F). Suppose also we have the external represented item:

(2)   Represented item s is identical with state G of worldly array W.

That is, s is identical with W's being G (the fact that W is G). Then, the problem of representation, traditionally understood, is the problem of explaining in virtue of what r can be about s.

Informational approaches, of course, attempt to explain what makes *r* about *s* in terms of the concept of information. One way of understanding information might be as a converse causal relation. The idea is that if, say, fire causally produces smoke, then smoke carries information about fire. However, information cannot be understood simply in terms of *actual* causal relations. An actual causal relation between *s* and *r* may be necessary for the latter to carry information about the former—although this claim is itself controversial.[2] However, the existence of a causal relation between *s* and *r* is not *sufficient* for *r* to carry the information that *s*. The reason is that *r* may be *equivocal*.

The concept of equivocation is a child of communication theory. Let us, in line with this theory, refer to *s* (*W*'s being *G*) as the *source* and *r* (*M*'s being *F*) as the *signal*. Consider first the source: that *W* is *G* rather than some other way (*H*, *J*, . . .) means that *W*'s being *G* already eliminates certain alternative possibilities. Thus, the obtaining of this state of affairs at the source—the fact that *W* is *G*—itself carries information. Some of this information may not be transmitted from source *s* to signal *r*. If the fact that *W* is *G*, rather than *H* or *J*, generates a certain quantity, *Q*, of information, we may ask how much of *Q* is still present in *M*'s being *F*. The information generated by *W*'s being *G* at the source that is not carried over to *M*'s being *F* is the *equivocation* of *r*. The primary reason why the existence of an actual causal relation running from source to signal is not sufficient for information is that *r* may be equivocal.

The equivocation of a signal stems from the fact that the actual causal processes running from source to signal by themselves need reveal nothing of alternative possible causes of the signal. The way to capture the contribution made by possible causal processes to the information carried by signal *r* is by appeal to the concept of nomic dependence:

(3)   *r* (the fact that *M* is *F*) carries information about *s* (the fact that *W* is *G*) iff it is a law that *r* only if *s*.

In other words, the fact that *M* is *F* carries the information that *W* is *G* if and only if it is a law that *M* is *F* only if *W* is *G*. Then, depending on whether one thinks of information merely in terms of an increase in conditional probability or in terms of a conditional probability of 1, one is free to think of this law as probabilistic or strict respectively.

Informational approaches to representation are committed to regarding information as a perfectly objective commodity. The strategy is to explain the representational in terms of the informational. This strategy would be obviously circular if the informational were dependent on the representational; on, for example, intentional states of a subject. The objectivity of information is also evident in the informational approach to what's known as the problem of the *relativity of information*. The information that *r* carries about *s* may, it seems, vary depending on what information, *Q*, is already available to the subject of *r*. Dretske (1981: 78–81) provides what has by now become a well-known illustration. Consider four shells, beneath one of which is a peanut. Suppose person A has already turned shells 1 and 2 and found them empty; person B has not. If so, then finding shell 3 empty does not supply A and B with the same information. Finding 3 empty informs A that the peanut is under shell 4, but only informs B that it is under shell 1, 2, or 4.

This relativity of information seems, *prima facie*, to provide a problem for the attempt to reduce the representational to the informational. The difference in information acquired by A and B derives from the fact that prior to the turning over of shell 3, A *knew* things that B did not, or was aware of things of which B was not. But knowing, or being aware of, are intentional, hence representational, states. And so the relativity of information seems to indicate that the attempt to reduce the representational to the informational is circular.

It seems to me that Dretske's attempt to deal with this problem is exactly right. According to Dretske, we must clearly distinguish the idea that the information contained in a signal is relative from the idea that it is relative to the representational states of a subject. In the case of the shells, the information is, in the first instance, relative simply to further information. There is information contained in the various configurations of the shells and in their history (being turned over or not, etc.), and the information contained in the turning over of shell 3 and finding it empty is relative to this information. However, this does not mean that the information is relative to representational states of a subject. Subject A may have acquired more of the relevant information than subject B—and so more of the relevant information is *available* to A. But the idea of information being *available* does not threaten the objectivity of information in a way that could undermine the attempt to reduce the representational to the informational. The concept of availability, while relative, is not an intentional concept. It is relative in much the same way that the concept of velocity is relative: relative to a frame of reference. But it is not relative to the intentional states of a subject. Therefore, Dretske argues, the information contained in the signal is, in the first instance, relative to further information contained in the configurations of the shells and their history, and not to representational states of these subjects.

Another important implication of the concept of information as nomic dependence is that information, in addition to being objective, is *ubiquitous*. It exists wherever there are nomic dependencies of the required sort. Such dependencies may exist between an internal configuration, as a mental representation is commonly taken to be, and an external state of affairs. But, equally, it can exist in the relation between two external, and non-mental, states of affairs. The fact that the trunk of a tree contains n rings carries the information that the age of the tree is n years. The presence of smoke carries information about the presence of fire, irrespective of whether there is any subject around to access this information. Both the objectivity and ubiquity of information are, thus, fairly uncontroversial entailments of the concept of information as nomic dependence.

4 The Problem of Misrepresentation

Any adequate account of representation must be able to explain the phenomenon of *misrepresentation*. This follows from the normative character of representation. Anything that qualifies as a representation of the world, it is generally accepted, must possess a content that makes a claim about the way the world *should* be if the representation were true. It is easy to see why the more stringent version of the informational approach—the approach based on associating information with a conditional probability of 1—would have difficulty satisfying this desideratum. Consider, again, representation r, consisting in M's being F. If the informational content of this representation derives from the relation of nomic dependence between property F and property G (as in W's being G), and if we understand nomic dependence in strict, exceptionless terms, then, it would seem, r cannot misinform about its source. The root of the problem is that representation is normative in a way that nomic dependence is not.

Consider a mental representation of a horse (Fodor 1990). Adopting common practice, I shall refer to this by way of the capitalized HORSE to show that we are talking about the representation and not the horse itself. The representation HORSE, it seems, means "horse." And, at the very least, this means that that the tokening of the representation makes a normative claim about the way the world should be. When the representation is tokened, the world should contain, in an appropriate way, a horse. This is most obvious in the case of a visual representation. In this case, the world should contain, at the beginning of the relevant causal chain, a horse rather than anything else (a donkey, or a cow, for example). If it does not, then we have a case of misrepresentation. The same is true of other types of representation, though in a less obvious sense. If the representation is one of memory, for example, then it should be produced by a horse, rather than anything else. And if it is not so produced then, again, we have a case of misrepresentation. That it makes a normative claim about the way the world should be is what makes *r* the representation it is, and not the representation of something else.

However, it also seems possible, indeed likely, that the representation HORSE can be caused by things that are not horses. Donkeys in the distance and cows on a dark night might, in certain circumstances, be equally efficacious in causing a tokening of the HORSE representation. Now, according to an informational account, representation is to be explained in terms of nomic dependence. However, if the representation HORSE can be tokened in the absence of horses, then HORSE does not seem nomically dependent on horses. Rather, what HORSE does seem nomically dependent upon is not the property of being a horse but the disjunctive property of being a horse or a donkey-in-the-distance or a cow-on-a-dark-night. Thus, if information is a matter of nomic dependence, and if representation is a matter of information, then we seem forced to say that what HORSE represents is not the property of being a horse but the above disjunctive property.

Anything that qualifies as a representation makes a normative claim about the way the world should be. If HORSE is tokened then the world *should* contain, in the relevant way, a horse. But nomic dependence is not normative in this way. The representation HORSE is nomically connected to whatever *does*, in fact, produce it, and not what *should* produce it. Hence, there is a problem of misrepresentation. Representations can misrepresent because their content specifies that the world should be a certain way—must be a certain way if the representation is to be true—and sometimes they occur when the world is not that way. But nomic dependencies cannot specify the way the world should be at all. A given item, such as *r*, is nomically connected to whatever it is nomically connected to. We can make no sense of the idea of what it *should* be nomically connected to.

It might be thought that we could avoid this problem simply by abandoning the stringent version of the concept of information—the version that associates information with a conditional probability of 1. Then, the fact that HORSE is not correlated in a strict, exceptionless way with horses would not count against the former carrying information about the latter. However, this response fails to understand the real problem. This is a problem concerning the normativity of representation, and, as such, is indifferent to the character of the laws thought to underwrite the concept of information: for both strict and probabilistic laws fail to accommodate this normative dimension. To return to our above example, it is true that the tokening of HORSE in a subject might increase the probability of there being a horse in the environment. However, the tokening of HORSE, we are supposing, can also be caused by donkeys-in-the-distance and cows-on-a-dark-night but not, presumably, by other things—a chocolate cupcake, for example. Therefore, the tokening of HORSE also increases the probability of there being a cow or a donkey in the environment. Nonetheless, HORSE means "horse" because this is what is *supposed* to cause its tokening. Thus, the less stringent, probabilistic, construal of the informational approach also fails to accommodate the normativity of representation.

Even if we retreat to the more sophisticated idea of *relative* increases in conditional probability—the idea that HORSE means "horse" because the probability of the latter given the former is greater than the probability of the presence of cows or donkeys given the latter—the problem of normativity remains. In such cases, the problem can be made graphic by considering various *Twin-* or *inverted*-Earth-type scenarios where malign or unfortunate environmental circumstances have conspired to remove horses from the environment while making subjects incapable of registering this fact. The baseline fact remains the same: HORSE is *supposed* to occur only when horses are present. Neither strict correspondences nor increases in conditional probability are ever sufficient to delineate the content of this word "supposed." Correlations between items—whether strict or probabilistic—only ever pertain to the way things are. They cannot tell us anything about the way things are supposed to be.

The problem of representation is, then, essentially a problem of normativity. For us to arrive at an adequate account of representation we need to inject an element of normativity that is lacking on the purely informational approach. This has led many to suppose that informational accounts need *either* supplementation with *or* replacement by a *teleological* account. We shall look at teleological approaches in the next chapter. The remainder of this chapter is, however, not concerned with evaluating the informational approach. Rather, I shall presuppose the truth of this approach; I shall assume that the informational approach can give us at least part of the correct story concerning representation. What I am now going to argue is that deeds can satisfy the informational constraint—at least they can do so to no lesser (and no greater) extent than internal representations traditionally construed.

5 The Perfect Slip Fielder

Do deeds carry information about environmental states of affairs? The inevitable answer—given the differing conceptions of information we have identified—is: yes and no. However, crucially, they can carry information about such states of affairs to no *lesser*, and also no *greater*, extent than mental representations, traditionally construed. The reasons for this will depend on which conception of information we adopt; specifically, whether we associate information with a conditional probability of 1 or with merely an increase in conditional probability. So let us first work with the stringent view that information is carried in the relation between two items r and s only when the s/r conditional probability is 1.

I shall return to one of the flagship examples of deeds; catching a cricket ball. Imagine, now, the case of the *perfect slip fielder*. The perfect slip fielder successfully completes every catch that comes to him. He does this because he succeeds in getting his hands and fingers in exactly the right position given the velocity and trajectory of the incoming ball. We need not worry overly about how the perfect slip fielder came into being. Perhaps he was divinely created—God, of course, being a big cricket fan. Because of God's omnipotence, his creation is such a perfect fielder that he always gets it right, and, indeed, his catching performances support subjunctives and counterfactuals in the way characteristic of laws. In fact, the correlations between the position of his hands and the ball's trajectory have a modal status inherited from God's infallibility: necessarily, the fielder never gets it wrong because, necessarily, God never gets it wrong. In virtue of this, the orientation of his hands and fingers is nomically correlated with the trajectory of the ball.

In these circumstances, there would be little credibility to the denial of the claim that the orientation of the hands and fingers carries information about the trajectory of the ball. If r consists in a particular orientation of the hands/fingers, and s consists in a certain ball trajectory, then r carries information about s in a standard and familiar way: in virtue of the fact that it is a law that r only if s. The conditional probability s/r is 1. I am assuming, for simplicity's sake, that each distinct ball trajectory requires a unique orientation of the hands/fingers for a successful catch to be made. If this assumption is false, as it almost certainly is, matters do, admittedly, become more complicated, but only in a technical sense—no point of principle need be surrendered. We merely understand s as referring to a certain range of trajectory. So, in the case of the perfect slip fielder, hand/finger orientation does carry information about the trajectory of the ball. The perfect slip fielder and the ball form a complex interactive system, part of a wider system that involves the batsman, surrounding fielders, and the like. As the ball flies toward the perfect slip fielder, the system unfolds in a way susceptible to the sort of mathematical modeling appropriate to complex dynamic systems. In the unfolding relationship between the movement of the ball, the position of the fingers, and subsequent unfolding of the system, information is contained, and this information can be expressed in the form of differential equations that describe these relationships. The orientation of the hands and fingers, therefore, carries information about the trajectory of the ball in virtue of the information contained in this unfolding system.

The claim that finger orientation does, in these circumstances, carry information about ball trajectory is, I think, scarcely contestable. Indeed, it is simply an expression of a familiar idea, one that, as we have seen, is entailed by informational approaches to representation: the *ubiquity* of information. If information is realized by relations of nomic dependence between items, then information is instantiated wherever the requisite relations are instantiated. Information does not necessarily reside only in relations between inner representing items and outer represented ones. Information can be anywhere the appropriate nomic dependencies are to be found. And in the case of a divinely created perfect slip fielder, the appropriate nomic dependencies are to be found in the relations between finger orientations and ball trajectories.

6   The Less-Than-Perfect Slip Fielder

There are, of course, no perfect slip fielders. Even the best of them fall short of this sort of perfection. In the real world, there is no nomic correlation between hand/finger orientation and ball trajectory—that's one reason why so many balls are dropped in the slips. So, in the absence of the sort of nomic correlation that is thought to underwrite the more stringent concept of information, how can finger position carry information about ball trajectory? The answer is (a) that it can't, and, more important, (b) that this renders it no worse off than mental representations traditionally construed.

We have, in fact, already seen that if information is to play a role in explaining the concept of representation, it must be possible to make sense of the idea of information obtaining in the *absence* of the sort of nomic correlation that yields conditional probabilities of 1. Consider, again, the celebrated example of Fodor's that we discussed earlier. I have, let us suppose, the HORSE representation. How is this representation individuated? That is, what makes it a representation of horses (as opposed to donkeys, cows, etc.)? If we do want the concept of information to play a role in explaining what makes HORSE a representation of horses, then we are going to have to accommodate the obvious fact that HORSE can be tokened in the absence of horses—for example, in the presence of a donkey-in-the-distance or a cow-on-a-dark-night. So, we are going to have to divorce our informational constraint on representation from the idea that representations are *strictly* nomically correlated with what they represent. That is, we are going to have to abandon the idea that a representation, r, is nomically correlated with what it represents, s, in such a way that the s/r conditional probability is 1. So, at the very least, strict laws would have to be replaced by probabilistic ones. And, as we have seen, this is tantamount to replacing the stringent concept of information with the more relaxed concept that associates information with a simple increase in conditional probability.

So the problematic for internal representations precisely parallels that for deeds. We might imagine, of course, a perfect HORSE-tokener—divinely created—who, as a matter of nomic necessity, tokens HORSE in the presence, and only in the presence, of horses. But most of us are no closer to being this than we are to being the perfect slip fielder. So, in this respect deeds—for example, the orientation of one's hands/fingers—are in no worse a position than straightforward internal representations. That is, when the imperfect HORSE-tokener gets things wrong—when he tokens in the presence of a donkey-in-the-distance or a cow-on-a-dark-night—then, *from the perspective of the informational constraint*, this parallels the situation where the fielder tokens a particular hand/finger configuration in the presence of an inappropriate ball trajectory.

When we switch from the stringent to the relaxed concept of information, the parallels between internal representations and deeds are reiterated. The tokening of HORSE in an accomplished, or even modestly accomplished, horse-spotter increases the probability of there being a horse in the environment. But, similarly, the tokening of a particular hand/finger configuration in an accomplished, or even modestly accomplished, ball catcher increases the probability of there being a given ball trajectory in the environment.

However, as we have also seen, the tokening of HORSE in even an accomplished horse-spotter also increases the probability of there being a cow or a donkey in the environment. Indeed, it increases the probability of there being any item in the environment that might, under suitable unusual circumstances, be mistaken for a horse. Similarly, the tokening of a particular hand/finger configuration in even an accomplished ball catcher increases the probability of there being in the environment any ball trajectory with which—because the differences between the two are difficult to discern—the anticipated trajectory might be confused.

Of course, if things are going well for the horse-spotter, his or her tokening of HORSE increases the probability of there being a horse in the environment more than it increases the probability of there being a cow, donkey, or other item in the environment. But even with this sophisticated version of the informational account, the parallel for the case of deeds is maintained: if things are going well for the ball catcher, then his or her tokening of a particular hand/finger configuration increases the probability of one ball trajectory more than it increases that of any other trajectory.

The phrase "if things are going well" is, of course, telling; and it points to the inadequacies of the purely informational approach. HORSE is *supposed* to occur only when horses are present. Similarly, the particular hand/finger orientation tokened by the catcher is *supposed* to occur only when the ball has a certain trajectory. And, as we have seen, neither strict correspondences nor increases in conditional probability are ever sufficient to delineate the content of this word "supposed." Correlations between items—whether strict or probabilistic—only ever pertain to the way things are. They cannot tell us anything about the way things are supposed to be.

This feature of representations—the divergence of their content from that with which they are strictly or probabilistically correlated—is often taken to show that the informational approach can never furnish us with a complete account of representation. If this is true, then the informational constraint is, at best, in need of supplementation, and at worst in need of replacement. Of course, the arguments of this book do not require that the informational approach be incomplete or otherwise inadequate and, accordingly, I do not pretend to have made a compelling case for that here. I am concerned not with the adequacy or otherwise of the informational approach, but whether a case for the representational status of deeds can be made in terms of that approach; I have argued that it can. However, many have supposed that a purely informational approach is incomplete or inadequate, and, for them, the appeal to information, in any complete account of representation, needs to be supplemented, or even supplanted, by an appeal to the concept of *teleology*. This brings us to our next condition on representation: the *teleological* constraint.

8 The Teleological Constraint

1 Teleosemantics

Many people suppose that any adequate account of representation must satisfy a teleological constraint. Roughly:

Teleological condition An item r qualifies as representational only if it has the *proper function* either of tracking the feature or state of affairs s that *produces* it, or of enabling an organism or other representational *consumer* to achieve some (beneficial) task in virtue of tracking s.

This will, of course, take considerable unpacking; and this section attempts to do so.

Absolutely central to teleological approaches is the concept of *proper function*. The proper function of some mechanism, trait, state, or process is what it is *supposed* to do, what it has been *designed* to do, what it *ought* to do. More precisely, consider the following simplified version of Millikan's already simplified version of her definition of proper function given in *Language, Thought, and Other Biological Categories*.[1]

An item X has proper function F only if (i) X is a reproduction of some prior item that, because of the possession of certain reproduced properties, actually performed F in the past, and X exists because of this performance; or (ii) X is the product of a device that had the performance of F as a proper function and normally performs F by way of producing an item like X.

This definition, simplified though it is, requires considerable explication. First, the concept of a proper function is a normative concept. The proper function of an item is defined in terms of what an item *should* do, not what it normally does or is disposed to do. The concept of proper function, being normative, cannot be defined in causal or dispositional terms. What something does, or is disposed to do, is not always what it is supposed to do. This is for three reasons. First, any mechanism, trait, or process will do many things, not all of which are part of its proper function. A heart pumps blood; it also makes a thumping noise and produces wiggly lines on an electrocardiogram. But only the first of these is its proper function since only pumping blood is something performed by hearts in the past that explains the existence of hearts in the present. Second, a mechanism, trait, or process can have a proper function even if it never, or hardly ever, performs it. To use a flagship example of Millikan's, the proper function of the tail of a sperm cell is to propel the cell to the ovum. The vast majority of sperm-cell tails, however, do not accomplish this task. Third, a mechanism, trait, or process may have a proper function and yet not be able to perform it properly. A person's heart may be malformed and, thus, not be able to pump blood properly. Nevertheless, pumping blood is its proper function because ancestors of the person whose heart it is had hearts that pumped blood and this (in part) explains why they survived and proliferated and, thus, why the person in question possesses a heart (although not why that heart is malformed). The concept of proper function is, thus, a normative concept. The proper function of an item is its *Normal* function where, following Millikan, the capitalized "N" indicates that this is a normative sense of normal and not a causal or dispositional sense.

What underlies the normativity of the concept of proper function, and this is the second key feature of teleological approaches, is that the concept is essentially *historical* in character. The proper function of an item is determined not by the present characteristics or dispositions of that item but by its history. In particular, the possession of a proper function *F* by an item depends on that item existing because it possesses certain characteristics that have been selected for because of the role they play in performing *F*. This is the import of (i). Hearts have the proper function of pumping blood because hearts possessed by our ancestors succeeded in pumping blood, and we have hearts today because the hearts of our ancestors were successful in this regard. That (i) be satisfied is a necessary condition of an item possessing what Millikan calls a *direct* proper function. Such possession is essentially a matter of history. There are no first-generation direct proper functions.

There is, however, an important distinction to be observed between (1) *direct*, (2) *adapted*, and (3) *derived* proper functions. An example will help. Chameleons are able to camouflage themselves. They do this by way of a pigmentation mechanism that alters the distribution of pigment in the chameleon's skin:

1. The *direct* proper function of the pigmentation mechanism is to cause the chameleon's skin to match its immediate surroundings. The chameleon possesses this (token) mechanism because its ancestors possessed (token) mechanisms that performed this function. It is the performing of the function that explains why such mechanisms *proliferated*.

2. Suppose, now, that the chameleon is placed in a particular immediate environment. In fact, let's make the chameleon work hard and place it on a Jackson Pollock *Number 4*. The chameleon's skin, therefore, takes on a "Pollockian" arrangement.[2] In these circumstances, the pigmentation mechanism has the *adapted* proper function of producing a Pollockian skin pattern. This is not a direct proper function of the device: the device has not proliferated as a result of producing, specifically, Pollockian skin patterns. Producing such a pattern is a proper function only *adapted* to a given context. Such a pattern is what Millikan calls an *adapted device*.

3. Adapted devices possess *derived* proper functions. The derived proper function of the "Pollockian" arrangement of pigmentation in the chameleon's skin is to match the chameleon to the Jackson Pollock *Number 4* on which the poor chameleon has been placed. In general, the proper functions of adapted devices are derived from the proper functions of the mechanisms that produce them.[3]

Unlike direct proper functions, there can be first-generation adapted and derived proper functions. The pigmentation mechanism has the adapted proper function of producing a Pollockian skin pattern, and the pattern has the derived proper function of matching the chameleon to the Pollock *Number 4*, even if no chameleon has been placed on a Pollock *Number 4* before, hence even if the pattern has never been produced before.

Like direct proper functions, however, both adapted and derived proper functions are normative in character. Adapted devices can malfunction or be maladapted. A device is *maladapted* to a particular context—its *adaptor*—if it does not bear the relation that it is supposed to bear to that adaptor. If the chameleon's pigmentation mechanism is simply not up to the job of reproducing a Pollock *Number 4* it may produce a skin pattern that fails in its derived proper function. And if, because of some unusual optical contingencies, the chameleon takes itself to be on a Pollock *Number 4* when it is in fact not, then the pigmentation mechanism does not really have, as an adapted proper function, the production of the Pollockian skin pattern.

The proper function—whether direct, adapted, or derived—of many evolved items is often *relational* in character. A device has a *relational proper function* if it is its function to produce something that bears a specific relation to something else—for example, the relation "same color as." The direct proper function of the chameleon's camouflage mechanism is to make the chameleon the same color as its immediate environment. If the chameleon has been placed on the Pollock *Number 4*, then the mechanism has the adapted proper function of producing a skin pattern that is the same as the painting. And the derived proper function of this pattern is to match the chameleon to the painting. All of these proper functions are, therefore, relational. More generally, many evolved devices have proliferated precisely because they enable the organism to cope with its environment: to locate food, evade predators, protect itself against heat and cold, and so on. This is what underwrites their relational character.

The core idea of the teleological approaches to representation is that the mechanisms responsible for mental representation are evolutionary products, and that we can therefore understand both representation and representations (i.e., the relation and one of its relata) in terms of the apparatus of direct, adapted, derived, and relational proper functions. Consider a representational mechanism M:M is capable of going into a variety of states or configurations. Mental representation r, let us suppose, consists in M's being in state F. According to teleological approaches, r counts as a representation if the following conditions obtain. World W, let us suppose, is G. The *direct* proper function of mechanism M is to allow the organism to track various environmental contingencies. In the event of environmental contingency s, which consists in W's being G, M has the adapted proper function of entering state or configuration F. And M's being F has, therefore, the derived proper function of occurring only when W is G. This is what makes M's being F represent W's being G. If we represent W's being G as s, then this is what makes representation r *about s*.

The normativity of proper functions is crucial to this story. M is *supposed* to enable organism O to track various environmental contingencies. To this end it is *supposed* to go into state F when and only when W is G. It is this element of normativity that is supposed to allow teleological approaches to account for the possibility of misrepresentation—and so avoid the problem that was the downfall of purely informational approaches. The elegant solution to the problem of misrepresentation is a distinct strength of teleological approaches.

According to teleological approaches, HORSE represents the property of being a horse and not the disjunctive property (horse v donkey-in-the-distance v cow-on-a-dark-night) because the direct proper function of the mechanism M is to adopt certain configurations contingent upon the presence of certain environmental states of affairs. Therefore, M also has the adapted proper function of producing HORSE in the presence of horses. That is what (presumably among other things) the mechanism has been selected for. It does not have the adapted proper function of producing HORSE in the presence of donkeys or cows, whether in the distance or on a dark night. And, on a teleological account, the content of HORSE derives from the adapted proper function of M. Thus HORSE is about horses and not about donkeys, cows, or disjunctions of the three. Providing a solution to the disjunction problem requires, in effect, detaching the content of a representation from the property with which it is maximally correlated. And this is precisely what the teleological account allows us to do. Representation, on this view, derives from function. And proper function, being normative, cannot be defined in causal or dispositional terms. The fact that HORSE is tokened not only in the presence of horses but also in that of donkeys and cows, and that it is maximally correlated with a disjunction of the three, is, therefore, irrelevant. What determines the representational content of HORSE is not what environmental item in fact does causally produce it, but what *should* causally produce it. And this is determined by the adapted proper function of its producing mechanism.

2   Stimulus and Benefit in Teleosemantics

Teleological accounts of representation are often referred to as *teleosemantic* accounts, and the preceding section provided a general introduction to the main features of such accounts. However, this section also slid over a crucial ambiguity in the concept of a proper function—whether direct, adapted, or derived. Consider an example, made famous by Dretske (1986). Some marine bacteria have internal magnets, called magnetosomes, that function like compass needles: they align the bacteria parallel to the earth's magnetic field. The result is that bacteria in the northern hemisphere propel themselves in the direction of geomagnetic north. In the southern hemisphere, the magnetosomes are reversed, and southern bacteria propel themselves toward geomagnetic south. The survival value of these magnetosomes, it seems likely, consists in their allowing the bacteria to avoid the oxygen-rich surface water that would be lethal to them. In the northern hemisphere, movement toward geomagnetic north will take the bacteria away from oxygen-rich surface water toward the comparatively oxygen-free water lower down. Movement toward geomagnetic south has the same effect in the southern hemisphere.

What is the adapted proper function of the magnetosomes? Is it to indicate (in the northern hemisphere) the direction of geomagnetic north?

Or is it to indicate the direction of oxygen-free water? Geomagnetic north provides the *stimulus* that allows the magnetosomes to perform their proper function: the magnetosomes track geomagnetic north, and track oxygen-free water only insofar as this is correlated with geomagnetic north. But, it is oxygen-free water that provides the *benefit* to the organism of the magnetosomes tracking geomagnetic north. The question then is this: is representation determined by stimulus or benefit? Dretske endorses a stimulus-based account:

When an indicator, C, indicates both F and G, and its indication of G is via its indication of F . . . then despite the fact that it is the existence of G that is most directly relevant to explaining C's recruitment as a cause of M (F is relevant only in so far as it indicates that G exists), C acquires the function of indicating that F. It is F—the (as it were) maximally indicated state—that C comes to represent. (1990: 826)

The magnetosomes, thus, represent geomagnetic north. This is the stimulus for the magnetosome, and representation tracks stimulus not benefit. Millikan, on the other hand, endorses a benefit-based approach:

What the magnetosome represents is only what its *consumers* require that it correspond to in order to perform *their* tasks. Ignore, then, how the representation . . . is normally produced. Concentrate instead on how the systems that react to the representation work, on what these systems need in order to do their job. What they need is only that the pull be in the direction of oxygen-free water at the time. For example, they care not at all how it came that the pull is in that direction. . . . What the magnetosome represents, then, is univocal; it represents only the direction of oxygen-free water. (1989: 93)

The notion of a representational *consumer* is of absolutely central importance to Millikan's account. However, the problem is, I think, that it is crucially ambiguous. Appreciating this ambiguity can not only point us in the direction of a more satisfying account, but also allow us to see that there is no necessary incompatibility between stimulus- and benefit-based accounts of representation.

The notion of a representational consumer, and the associated idea of a representational consumer performing its task, is ambiguous between *personal* and *subpersonal* levels. Here is one of Millikan's examples. The beaver's tail splash indicates danger—typically, the presence of a predator. When a beaver splashes its tail, other beavers quickly return to the water. If we allow that the tail splash is a representation, what, in this case, is the consumer of the representation? The most obvious answer is: other beavers. The consumers of the representation are, thus, other organisms. The same is true of another example commonly employed by Millikan: the dance of the honeybee. Here, the consumers are other bees. In the present semitechnical terminology, both these examples are cases of *personal*-level consumers.[4] The crucial idea is that the representational consumers are organisms, and not internal, subpersonal, mechanisms possessed by organisms.

However, beavers don't just jump into the water upon hearing the tail splash. Their motor response is mediated by way of various mechanisms. The acoustical properties of the splash have to be registered and transmitted to the brain, and in the brain a link has to be set up with the motor cortex. At this level too we have representational consumers. These are the mechanisms whose operation will eventually allow the beaver to dive into the lake. So, in addition to *personal* consumers—other beavers—we also have *subpersonal* consumers.

This ambiguity passes over and infects the notion of a consumer *performing its allotted task*, and the related idea of what it *needs to do its job*. The allotted task of the beaver, in this case, is evading predators. What it needs to do its job is that the splash be, within certain limits, reliably correlated with the presence of predators. So, in the case of personal consumers, one could plausibly argue that representation tracks benefit. And as we have seen, this is precisely Millikan's claim. However, when we switch to subpersonal consumers, an entirely different story emerges. What do the acoustic mechanisms responsible for registering the tail splash require to do their job? Basically, it seems, they require that the splash have certain appropriate acoustical properties. What do the motor mechanisms that produce the beaver's rapid motion into the lake require to do their job? Basically, they require that a message of a certain type has been transmitted from the beaver's perceptual cortex. No part of their job requires sensitivity to the benefit associated with the splash. Personal-level consumers are sensitive to the benefit of a representational item; subpersonal consumers are not.

The possibility of there being both personal and subpersonal consumers of a representation is obscured in the example of the bacterial magnetosome. The magnetosome functions by literally pulling the bacterium into alignment with the earth's magnetic field. It's pretty much like winding up a toy and letting it go. They are no mechanisms internal to the bacterium that read off the information contained in the magnetosome and then send the message on to the appropriate locomotory centers. In other words, in the example of the bacterium, there is only one representational consumer, an exclusively personal one: the bacterium itself. In this regard, the example is entirely atypical. We might imagine, for example, a more complicated organism. Instead of simply being pulled into alignment by the magnetosome, this organism possesses various internal mechanisms that are sensitive to the information embodied in various states of the magnetosome. Having registered this information, they then transmit it to various locomotory structures that, in this example, we will suppose the organism to possess. In this case, it would make sense to speak not only of the organism, but also of the relevant internal mechanisms, being the consumer of the representation.

What are the allotted tasks of the internal mechanisms in our imagined creature? And what would they need to do their jobs? The allotted task of one mechanism, for example, might be to measure the distribution of magnetic field over the magnetosome. This task has nothing to do with the (personal-level) benefit of oxygen-free water. And to do its job, it would need to be appropriately sensitive to such fields. Again, this sensitivity has nothing whatsoever to do with the benefit of oxygen-free water.

It is notable that only in the second sort of case—where we have both personal and subpersonal consumers of a representation—that we would be willing to contemplate the possibility of a genuinely representational level of description of the organism. The presence of internal mechanisms performing various diverse functions on information they receive is necessary for the sort of multiple-deployability (deployability in a variety of contexts so as to accomplish a variety of tasks) that is characteristic of a fully fledged representational system.

3   Personal and Subpersonal Proper Functions

The notion of a representational consumer is, then, ambiguous. There can be both personal and subpersonal consumers of a representation. Personal consumers, arguably, track the benefit of a representation. But, subpersonal consumers track the representational stimulus. Therefore, *pace* Millikan, we cannot use the concept of a representational consumer to defend a benefit-based account of representation over a stimulus-based alternative. Nevertheless, the ambiguity in the notion of a representational consumer does point us in the right direction. The crucial distinction, I think, is not between producers and consumers of representations but between *personal* and *subpersonal* proper functions. In fact, not only does this distinction point us in the right direction, it will also allow us to reconcile stimulus- and benefit-based accounts of representation.

Suppose mechanism M of organism P goes into state r in the presence of environmental item s. Going into r in the presence of s is, let us suppose, an adapted proper function of M. Then, the orthodox teleosemantic story is that state r has the derived proper function of occurring in the presence of s, and thus *represents*, or is *about*, or *means* s. The distinction between personal and subpersonal proper functions applies to the derived proper functions of r thus:

Subpersonal r has the subpersonal derived proper function of tracking s.
Personal r has the personal derived proper function of enabling P to φ in virtue of tracking s.

Generally, a subpersonal derived proper function will be to track (i.e., occur in and only in the presence of) some or other feature of the environment. A personal derived proper function will be to enable an organism to accomplish some or other task in virtue of tracking that feature. Each distinct derived proper function will license the attribution of a distinct content. And, crucially, they will license the attribution of this distinct content to distinct individuals. Subpersonal derived proper functions license the attribution of content to subpersonal mechanisms. Personal derived proper functions license the attribution of (a distinct) content to the organism ("person") as a whole.

In a little more detail: suppose we have an organism P sensitive to (i.e., able to detect) some feature of the environment s. On the basis of this sensitivity, let us suppose, we can attribute a content C_p to the organism. However, P's sensitivity to this feature of the environment is underwritten by mechanism M whose direct proper function is to track a certain range of environmental features, and whose adapted proper function is to enter state r in the presence of s. Therefore, the derived proper function of r is to track s, and, on the basis of this, we can attribute the content C_M to r. It does not follow, however, and indeed is usually false, that $C_P = C_M$. This is true even though it is M's being r that allows P to be sensitive to its environment in a way that warrants the attribution of content C_p it. That is, even though it is the adapted proper function of M that allows the attribution of C_M to r, and even though it is the fulfilling of M of its adapted proper function that allows the content C_p to be attributed to P, it does not follow, and indeed is almost always false, that $C_P = C_M$. The content attributable to a state r of mechanism M and the content attributable to the organism that possesses the mechanism that has adopted this state do not generally coincide, even where it is the state of the mechanism that underwrites the attribution of content to P (Rowlands 1997).

To see how this works, consider another well-known example. Rattlesnakes have certain cells that fire only if two conditions are satisfied. First, the snake's infrared detectors, situated in its nose, must be stimulated. Second, the visual system must get positive input. The former condition is satisfied when there is a localized source of warmth in its environment, the latter when there is a localized source of movement. When these two systems are contemporaneously activated, the snake's hunting mechanisms are engaged. In the snake's ancestral home, there will indeed be food about, since the combined input is typically caused by a field mouse, the snake's usual prey. Of course, the rattlesnake can be fooled easily. An artificially warmed imitation mouse on the end of a stick would do the trick. So, what is the adapted proper function of the snake's prey-detection mechanism? What does it represent? Stimulus-based accounts would focus on what activates the mechanism—that is, localized warmth and movement—and claim that the relevant state of the mechanism represents those features. Benefit-based accounts would focus on the benefit associated with the mechanism performing its proper function—the snake gets to eat—and claim that the relevant state of the mechanism represents food.[5] However, the distinction between personal and subpersonal derived proper functions allows us to see that these answers are not incompatible.

First, there is the personal derived proper function of the state r of the rattlesnake's system (r is, in this case, understood to be a conjunction of states, one in the infrared-detection mechanism and one in the movement-detection mechanism). The personal derived proper function of r is to enable the rattlesnake (the "person") to do something—namely, to detect a certain affordance of the environment: r enables the rattlesnake to detect that the environment affords eating. Thus, the personal derived proper function of r is sensitive to the benefit of the prey-detection mechanism fulfilling its adapted proper function.

Second, there is the subpersonal derived proper function of r. The prey-detection mechanism's fulfilling of its personal derived proper function is what enables the rattlesnake to detect that the environment affords eating. However, it does this by way of a certain method or *algorithm*: the detection of warmth and movement. The subpersonal derived proper function of the state r of M is to track warmth and movement. This latter proper function is, therefore, sensitive to the stimulus, rather than the benefit, of the mechanism fulfilling its adapted proper function.

Each proper function licenses the attribution of a distinct content to a distinct individual. The personal derived proper function warrants the attribution of content such as, "eatability, there!" to the rattlesnake as a whole. The subpersonal derived proper function licenses the attribution of the content "warmth/movement, there!" to the state r of mechanism M. So not only do we have attributions of distinct contents, those attributions are also made to distinct things.

Seen in this light, stimulus- and benefit-based accounts are not competing accounts of representation. They correspond to two distinct types of derived proper function. And they are concerned with the attribution of distinct contents to distinct things. Stimulus-based accounts are appropriate to states of subpersonal mechanisms, and the attribution of content that they license to such mechanisms is underwritten by the subpersonal derived proper function of states of such mechanisms. Benefit-based accounts are appropriate to the personal level—to organisms ("persons") as a whole. The attribution of content that they license is underwritten by the personal derived proper function of appropriate states of subpersonal mechanisms possessed by such organisms. Both stimulus- and benefit-based accounts, therefore, have a legitimate role to play in a teleological account of representation.

4   A Few Added Wrinkles

The above reconciliation of stimulus- and benefit-based accounts is, I think, correct in the essentials. However, it does assume an overly simplistic conception of the relation between the personal and subpersonal levels. The distinction was presented in something of the manner of a dichotomy. However, there are, in fact, many distinctions to be made here. There are as many personal–subpersonal distinctions to be drawn as there are appropriate levels of specification for a biological proper function—and there are many such levels. To see this, consider David Papineau's (2003) critique of attempts to attribute content to simple mechanisms.

Papineau argues that attempts to attribute content to simple mechanisms suffer from a crippling problem of indeterminacy. The same is not true for beliefs and desires. Therefore, beliefs and desires, and associated items such as sentences, are, he argues, the only true representations. To see the problem, consider the standard problem of indeterminacy illustrated by way of a familiar example: the frog's sight-strike-feed mechanism. The firing of this mechanism, it is argued, could represent any number of things. There is a certain, useful, order in which we can represent these possibilities: (1) small, black, moving thing, (2) fly, (3) stomach filler, (4) nutrient source, and (5) reproduction enhancer. The problem, as Papineau sees it, is how do we choose between these simply on the basis of evolutionary benefit?

I am going to use the distinction between personal and subpersonal proper functions to defend the claim that (1) and (4) are the key items in the list (although, as we shall see, this claim will be subject to qualification later). The firing of the frog's strike mechanism has *two* proper functions, one that involves small, black, moving things and one that involves an affordance: *eatability* (to be distinguished from edibility). It is (4) on Papineau's list that corresponds most closely to this. Therefore, I am going to have to rule out (2), (3), and (5). Even if this were achieved, the fact that I am allowing the firing of the mechanism to have two proper functions might be thought to entail a problem of indeterminacy—precisely the problem that concerns Papineau. I shall argue, however, that this is not so.

The *personal* derived proper function of the firing of the frog's mechanism is to enable the frog to detect that the environment is eatable (indicative) and enable it to consume this eatable part of the environment (imperative). The former is what is often referred to as an *indicative* proper function; the latter is often called an *imperative* proper function. The distinction is well understood, and although important in some contexts, it plays no significant role in the arguments to follow. So, I shall largely gloss over it in the development of those arguments.

The *subpersonal* derived proper function of the firing of the frog's strike mechanism is to detect the presence of a small, black, moving thing. Detection of an item with these properties is, in effect, the *algorithm* with which the mechanism fulfils its *personal* derived proper function. The mechanism detects the presence of small, black, moving things, and the organism, thereby, detects that the environment is eatable. Both abilities are underwritten by the mechanism, but each ability corresponds to a distinct proper function of that mechanism.

Why does the admission of two distinct proper functions not engender a problem of indeterminacy? The first point to note is that indeterminacy is, I think, best construed as a worry about *content*, and not as a worry about *function*.[6] In particular, *multiplicity* of functions does not entail *indeterminacy* of functions. Two distinct but determinate functions never, by themselves, add up to one indeterminate function. The worry is not about function but about *content*. If the content attributable to a state of a mechanism derives from the proper function of that mechanism, and if the state of that mechanism has multiple proper functions, then there seems to be no way of deciding which of these functions is the determinant of content. We would seem to have as many contents as there are proper functions, and no fact of the matter determining which is the *real* content.

However, this worry rests on an assumption we should not endorse. To see this, consider: what is the difference between one indeterminate content and two distinct, but perfectly determinate, contents? A necessary condition for there being one indeterminate content is that both contents are attributed to the same thing. If this is not the case, then we simply have a case of two perfectly determinate contents being attributed to different things.

Suppose, as we did earlier, that we have an organism P sensitive to (i.e., able to detect) some feature, s, of the environment. On the basis of this sensitivity, let us suppose, we can attribute a content C_p to the organism. However, P's sensitivity to this feature of the environment is underwritten by mechanism M whose direct proper function is to track a certain range of environmental features, and whose adapted proper function is to enter state r in the presence of s. Therefore, the derived proper function of r is to track s, and, on the basis of this, we can attribute the content C_M to r. As we have seen, however, it does not follow, and indeed is usually false, that $C_p = C_M$. This is true even though it is M's being r that allows P to be sensitive to its environment in a way that warrants the attribution of content C_p to it. That is, even though it is the adapted proper function of M that allows the attribution of C_M to r, and even though it is the fulfilling of M of its adapted proper function that allows the content C_p to be attributed to P, it does not follow, and indeed is almost always false, that $C_p = C_M$. The content attributable to a state r of mechanism M and the content attributable to the organism that possesses the mechanism do not generally coincide, even where it is the state of the mechanism that underwrites the attribution of content to P.

The moral of the story is that, on the basis of *one* proper function of the frog's mechanism, we can attribute a content such as "eatability, there!" to the *frog*. And on the basis of the *other* proper function of the frog, we can attribute a content such as "small, moving, black thing, there!" to the mechanism. Crucially, we do not attribute these contents to the same thing. Therefore, we have a case of two perfectly determinate contents rather than one indeterminate one. The claim that the firing of the strike mechanism has two distinct proper functions does not entail the indeterminacy of content.

It remains to rule out interpretations (2), (3), and (5) as interpretations of the proper function of the mechanism. With regard to interpretation (5), I think the strategy developed by Karen Neander (1995) is correct. Neander accepts, in my view correctly, that any trait with one biological function will typically have a whole "concertina" of them. Nonetheless, she argues, one of these functions will have a special status.

The idea is that most of the functional effects of any given trait will depend not just on that trait alone, but also on the wider system within which it is embedded. For example, the lungs can have the function of getting oxygen to the blood but also, in virtue of the wider system in which it is embedded, of getting oxygen to the muscles. The frog's strike mechanism can have the function of catching prey, but also of getting prey to the stomach, or of getting prey within the influence of the frog's digestive juices. However, this does not alter the fact that the mechanism can possess a function that is peculiar to it. The function that is peculiar to it is that for which the mechanism is *directly* responsible. We can work out for which function a mechanism is directly responsible by shifting our attention from function to *malfunction*.

For example, if my lungs fail to send oxygen to my muscles, this might not be because my lungs are failing but because my heart is. But oxygenating the blood is the function peculiar to the lungs since this is the effect whose absence implies that the lungs are malfunctioning. If the frog's strike mechanism fails to get food into its stomach, this may not be because of a failure of the mechanism but because of, say, some blockage in its throat. But enabling the frog to detect eatability is the personal proper function of the mechanism, and detecting small, moving, black things is the subpersonal proper function of the mechanism because these are the effects whose absence implies that the mechanism is malfunctioning.

In general, the function for which a mechanism is directly responsible is that function whose absence entails that this mechanism, rather than any other, is malfunctioning. Therefore, reproduction enhancement (5) cannot be regarded as a proper function of the frog's strike mechanism. This effect might not occur, due to some other problem with, say, the stomach, or the reproductive system.

This leaves us with interpretations (2) and (3). Interpretation (3), that the proper function of the mechanism is to fill the frog's stomach, can be ruled out for the same reason. The failure of the frog's stomach to be filled might be due not to a failure of the strike mechanism itself, but, instead, to a blockage in the frog's gullet. In this case, however, there are *additional* reasons to reject this interpretation. It can, in fact, be ruled out on straightforward teleological grounds independently of Neander's innovations. The filling of the frog's stomach does not explain why the mechanism is extant today. If it had filled the frog's stomach with BBs, for example, then frogs would not have survived and prospered and the mechanism would not be around today. What is crucial to the mechanism is that it fills the frog's stomach with the *right stuff*—that is, with *eatable* stuff; a nutrient source of some sort.

This leaves us interpretation (2)—*flies*. This, I think, we can rule out. The mechanism's function is not just to catch flies; any eatable thing will do.

It may just happen to be that in the environment of the frog, flies are the only eatable thing. But, it is nonetheless true that if other similar eatable things had been present—gnats, midges, and so on—these would have done just as well in promoting the frog's survival. And, crucially, it is not the ingestion of flies per se that explains the frog's survival, but the fact that these ingested flies are eatable. Detecting flies should not be regarded as a proper function of the trait, but rather as a *consequence* of the trait performing its proper function: enabling the organism to detect that the environment is eatable.

Papineau thinks there is a problem with applying this general scheme to simple systems—we cannot avoid the problem of indeterminacy. The objection is directed specifically at Neander's account, and given the use I have made of Neander, I might be thought vulnerable to it also. On my account, the strike mechanism has the subpersonal proper function of detecting small, moving, black things, and the personal proper function of enabling the organism to detect that the environment is eatable, because these are the functions that are peculiar to it. And these are the functions that are peculiar to the mechanism because a failure in any downstream effect is not, necessarily, the fault of the mechanism. Perhaps the stomach is not working properly, perhaps the reproductive system is not working properly, and so forth.

Papineau's objection is that this makes representational content crucially dependent on the system in which we choose to locate the mechanism:

[T]his depends crucially on viewing the relevant signal as *part of the prey-catching system*. And this by no means seems mandatory. After all, why not regard the frog's sensory signal as part of the prey-stomaching system, or as part of the prey-digesting system. . . . This then promises to render the content of the sensory signal indeterminate once more. (2003: 121)

We want to say that the trait is part of the prey-catching (eatability-acquiring) system. But what makes it part of this rather than the prey-stomaching system? Or the prey-digesting system? The effects occasioned by the firing of the strike mechanism do not typically stop with the eatable object being caught, but also "stomached" and, eventually, digested. The indeterminacy now arises in, and derives from, the system to which we attach the mechanism in question, for the content of the firing of the strike mechanism is relative to this.

There is something right about Papineau's objection, but also, I think, there is something wrong. The objection is, of course, predicated on certain thorny issues about the reality or otherwise of biological categories. To what extent, if any, is the prey-catching system a more real biological cat-egory than the prey-stomaching system, or prey-digesting system? And what is the source of this greater reality? This is not the place to decide these issues, even if I could. So, I am going to accept the assumption that there need be no fact of the matter determining in which system we should locate the strike mechanism. The systemic location of the mechanism, I shall assume for the sake of argument, is indeterminate.

Where Papineau is wrong, however, is to think that this indeterminacy of systemic location yields indeterminacy of representational content. Multiplicity of proper functions does not, of course, entail indeterminacy of proper functions. And multiplicity of proper functions yields indeterminacy of associated contents only if these contents are attributed to the same thing. But this latter condition does not hold.

To see this, recognize, first, that the prey-catching system is numerically distinct from the prey-stomaching system, which, in turn is distinct from the prey-digesting system, and so on. Now, recall the distinction between personal and subpersonal proper functions. One valuable feature of Papineau's objection is that it makes us acutely aware of the fact that the personal–subpersonal distinction is a relative one. There is no such thing as *the* personal–subpersonal distinction, just various levels of description whereby a subpersonal mechanism is embedded in a larger "personal" system, which in turn counts as a subpersonal mechanism relative to a larger embedding system, and so on. Nonetheless, the general distinction between personal and subpersonal, relative though it is, is still a useful one.

Suppose the strike mechanism fires in the context of the prey-catching mechanism. Then, the subpersonal proper function of the mechanism is to detect the presence of small, black, moving things. In fulfilling this proper function, it enables the prey-catching mechanism to achieve its "personal" proper function of catching prey. However, the same subpersonal proper function—the firing of the mechanism—can enable the prey-stomaching system to achieve its *personal* proper function (i.e., relative to the subpersonal proper function of the prey-catching system) of stomaching prey. And it can enable the prey-digesting mechanism to fulfill its *personal* proper function (i.e., relative to the subpersonal proper function of the prey-stomaching mechanism) of digesting prey, and so on.

In each case, we have the content, "small, black, moving thing, there!" attributable to the firing of the mechanism. This is content licensed by the subpersonal proper function. But in each case we also have a distinct content that is licensed by the relativized personal proper function. The content, "catchable, there!" might be attributed to the prey-catching system. The content, "stomachable, there!" might be attributed to the prey-stomaching mechanism. And the content, "digestible, there!" might be attributed to the prey-digesting system.

What is crucial, however, is that this multiplicity of personal proper functions does not entail the indeterminacy of content because they underwrite the attribution of content to *distinct* things—prey-catching, prey-stomaching, and prey-digesting systems respectively. Far from being a case of indeterminacy, this is an example of three perfectly determinate contents being attributable to distinct things.

5 Learning and the Historical "Because"

Now that we have identified the principal features of the teleosemantic approach, and have addressed the usual concerns over this approach, it remains to argue that this general framework can be applied to deeds. That is, the remainder of the chapter will argue that deeds can satisfy the teleological constraint.

As a beginning, let us return to Millikan's definition of proper function, introduced earlier:

An item X has proper function F only if (i) X is a reproduction of some prior item that, because of the possession of certain reproduced properties, actually performed F in the past, and X exists because of this performance; or (ii) X is the product of a device that had the performance of F as a proper function and normally performs F by way of producing an item like X.

Each clause presents a sufficient condition for something to possess a proper function. It is clause (i) that is most relevant to the case of deeds, and so I am going to focus on that. Clause (i) contains two occurrences of "because"; it is the second one that is of concern here. I shall refer to this as the *historical because*. How is it, precisely, that a deed can exist today because of the performance of a proper function by a token-distinct deed of which the former is a replica? When we are talking about biological mechanisms—hearts, prey-detection mechanisms, and the like—the basis of the historical because is a reasonably familiar one: genetic transmission. Deeds, of course, are not thus transmitted. And so the first task that we face is delineating the concept of the historical *because* as it applies to deeds.

Generally speaking, deeds can be transmitted by some or other combination of mechanisms of individual and social learning—to be discussed in more detail in chapter 10. Four mechanisms are, I think, of particular importance:

Instruction The most obvious reason that a deed might be exhibited by a person today is because it was exhibited by someone else yesterday, and was passed on to the person today by way of explicit instruction on the part of the latter. In the context of an athletic activity, for example, one might be given explicit instructions on how to perform some relevant task. Typically, however, explicit instruction of this sort is more appropriate for explaining the transmission of *actions*, and barely scratches the surface of the explanation of the transmission of *deeds*.

In a sporting activity such as cricket, for example, one might be given general instructions on how to catch the ball, and these instructions might be geared to the specific area of the field in which one is fielding, since the precise method will vary with the type of ball trajectory one can expect to face, and this will vary with the area of the field in which one is positioned. These instructions might cover how to stand, how to position one's hands and fingers, and so on.

Instruction of this sort will, of course, only take you so far—and this is for several reasons. Most obviously, every ball trajectory is different, even if slightly, and you are going to have to make adjustments to bring your movements into line with the exigencies of the current trajectory. But even if this were not so, even if every ball trajectory were exactly the same, and each fielder were standing in exactly the same spot relative to that trajectory, were of the same height, adopted the same stance, and so on, each catch would rely on fine-grained adjustments of the fingers, hands, eyes, and so forth, that we have no idea we are making. This, in effect, is one of the morals of Milner and Goodale's work. These sorts of adjustments cannot, in general, be passed on by instruction because the instructor, in effect, has no idea of their existence.

In this sort of case, we have two different categories of act. There is, on the one hand, the *action* of catching the ball. This is an action because it is individuated by the general antecedent intention to catch the ball. On the other hand, there are the various fine-grained adjustments that go into satisfying this general antecedent intention—subtle or gross movements of the hand, fingers, eyes, legs, and so on. These cannot be individuated by way of the general antecedent intention, or, for that matter, by way of any intention. Nonetheless, they are intentional in one clear sense of that term: they are done for a reason that the agent *would* endorse, and help satisfy an intention that the agent *does*, in fact, have. They are what I have called preintentional acts, or *deeds*.

Generally speaking, explicit instruction does not take one far below the level of actions. Deeds, we might say, are largely instruction insensitive. And this is not an unexpected conclusion. Deeds are located below the level of intention. Since instructions are going to be built up from reflecting upon an agent's awareness of what he or she did in performing a particular action, deeds are not, generally, the sort of thing to be captured in explicit instructions about how to perform that action.

Nevertheless, instructions do perform an important role relative to deeds, and thus do play a role in explaining the transmission of deeds: they put the agent in the sort of position where the requisite deed or deeds can be performed. A fielder is not in a position to perform the deed of pointing his fingers up or down to catch a ball hurtling toward him at lower chest height unless he has absorbed the instructions about stance, foot position, and so forth. Instruction puts you in the right position for performing deeds. Or, switching to a more continental mode, instruction is the *horizon* against which the possibility of certain sorts of deeds emerges.

Imitation   Often the acquisition of a skill is facilitated by imitation rather than explicit instruction. The role of imitation is most obvious in contexts of innovation. To continue with the sporting theme, consider, for example, Muhammad Ali's method of avoiding punches that involved swaying backward out of their reach, as opposed to the received wisdom of using lateral movement to "slip" punches, or simply blocking them with one's gloves. Or consider Vivian Richards, the great West Indian batsman, who, in effect invented a new cricket stroke—one that involved him stepping across his stumps and flicking a straight ball away through midwicket. Ali's and Richards's innovations caught on—with mixed results for those with less natural ability. And this seems largely to be a result of imitation. Their propagation can scarcely be regarded as the result of explicit instruction— since they were at the time of their inception regarded as flaws in technique. Any explicit instruction involved was aimed at their eradication rather than propagation.

However, in these cases, of course, the type of imitation involved is that of actions rather then deeds. And the primary role of imitation is, undoubtedly, to explain the transmission of actions not deeds. Nonetheless, as with explicit instruction, imitation does play a role in providing a framework or *horizon* within which the possibility of certain sorts of deeds emerges.

And to this extent, imitation plays a role in explaining the transmission of deeds; it is a component of the historical because.

Consider, for example, the way in which, in cricket, a batsman learns a new shot, or a new way of playing a previously acquired shot. The shot is, arguably, an action. For example, one might have the general antecedent intention to play a shot known as an *off-drive* to a ball that lands in a given area of the pitch. One's subsequent off-drive, at least arguably, can be individuated in terms of this antecedent intention. That is what makes it a single action, hence a single shot. However, this action, if that is what it is, is one that is made up, in part, of deeds—fine-grained, feedback-modulated, adjustments of hand, eye, shoulders, arms, feet, and so on. These adjustments are things you do, and that help satisfy the general antecedent intention to play the off-drive. However, they are not, themselves, individuated by any prior intentional state.

Imitation, in addition to instruction, can play a role in explaining the acquisition, hence transmission of the action of playing the off-drive. Often a shot like this is best learned by watching someone else perform it. But, in thus facilitating the transmission of the action, imitation also plays a role in explaining the transmission of deeds. In imitating the gross form of the shot—the off-drive—certain contingencies or exigencies present themselves to the batsman. Sometimes these are options, sometimes they are requirements. Perhaps the batsman finds his feet naturally moving into a certain position as he leans his shoulder into the ball, for example. Perhaps he finds his head moving in a certain way. It is not clear whether these are good things, or tendencies that should be eliminated. However, these options only present themselves to the batsman in the context of playing the shot, and not when observing the shot played by another. But what these options allow the batsman to do is return to the observation, and potential imitation, of another with, in effect, a new *vision*. In presenting the batsman with new facets of the action—new contingencies that can now be made the subject of observation—playing the shot allows the batsman to appropriate new avenues for imitation that were not initially available.

The relation between imitation and deeds is, therefore, a complex one, and not at all captured by the simple linear scheme whereby deeds are acquired through imitation. They can be acquired in this way, but, more often, they are acquired by way of the sort of feedback loop described above, where imitation and deed are mutually reinforcing moments of a wider process. Imitation provides a framework for the performance of deeds, and these deeds can then go on and provide a framework against which new possibilities for imitation can emerge, which leads to the acquisition of further deeds, and so on.

Stimulus enhancement   Stimulus enhancement is the tendency to pay attention to, or aim responses toward, a particular place or object in the environment after observing a conspecific's actions at that place or toward that object (Byrne and Russon 1998). As a result of this narrowing of behavioral focus, the individual's subsequent behavior becomes concentrated on these key variables. And this will increase the chances of the individual gaining the same reward as its conspecific, often by performing the same actions.

Stimulus enhancement plays a less obvious, but nonetheless important, role in the transmission of deeds. For obvious reasons, its role is probably most easily exhibited in (what can be) solitary sports—such as surfing. Suppose, for example, that a region of surf, because of certain salient features that it possesses, affords the opportunity for a certain type of maneuver, say a *cutback*. As a result, a group of experienced surfers have congregated in that particular area. You don't know how to do a cutback, you might not even know what one is, and, standing on the beach, you are too far away from the other surfers to see exactly what they are doing. Still you know that a congregation of this sort indicates some useful feature of the breaks, even if you don't yet know what. So, you head out to the same general area. But being drawn to that area of surf gives you the opportunity to learn how to perform the maneuver. You may acquire this skill from imitating the other surfers when you get out there. Or, equally likely, since while lying on your board on the back of the breaks, your spectatorial opportunities are strictly limited, you might simply fall into this, acquiring the skill, as it were, by accident—a form of fortuitous trial and error.

Fortuitous or not, this acquisition still satisfies Millikan's historical *because*. The previous generation of surfers performed the cutback because it possessed a certain (useful) proper function—taking you back toward the pocket of the wave, where the power center is, from out on the face where power is diminished. These surfers are in this region of surf because it affords them the opportunity of this maneuver. You are in this region of surf because they are. And there you acquire the skill. So, the cutback is performed by you today because of the possession of a proper function by token-distinct versions of it performed in the past (i.e., by other surfers). The historical because is somewhat extended in this instance, but it is nonetheless there.

Trial and error   Instruction, imitation, and stimulus enhancement can, of course, only take you so far. The most obvious role they play is in explaining the transmission of actions, and they explain the transmission of deeds to the extent that they provide a horizon that is necessary for the performance of certain sorts of deeds—that is, a framework without which those deeds could not be performed. The remaining gaps—the content of this framework, if you like—are filled in by *trial and error*.

As Millikan has pointed out, trial and error is one way in which an action—or deed—might have a history. It is one way in which the historical because might be realized. And, for deeds, it is, I think, the preeminent way. A deed that has been acquired through trial and error is a deed that is performed today because it was performed in the past—by the same individual—and achieved a certain end when it was thus performed in the past. Often, trial and error is a conscious, intentional, process—for example, when one arrives at a given strategy through the elimination of alternative strategies. However, it need not be like this at all. The fine-grained, feedback-modulated, adjustments that go into catching a ball, hitting a ball with a bat, transferring one's weight on a board in the way required to perform a cutback, are all examples of deed acquired through trial and error. These deeds are not performed consciously, nor are they individuated by way of a general antecedent intention. Nonetheless, they possess a history, and in virtue of this history they possess a function.

Again, I should emphasize that it would be overly simplistic to regard trial and error as an entirely separate process from each of the other three. Trial and error is bound up with instruction, imitation, and stimulus enhancement in the sort of mutually reinforcing feedback loop that we have already seen emerge. This is not to say that *all* of these must be present in any given case of the historical because. But, if we want to understand the historical *because* for the case of deeds, then, typically, it is to these complex webs of instruction, imitation, stimulus enhancement, and trial and error that we shall have to look.

It is important to realize of course, that the location of deeds in this complex web of relations does not in any way undermine their status as deeds. No one is, of course, denying that deeds are located in a complex web of relations—some of which are intentionally constituted. That much is obvious, and, indeed, is entailed by the basic idea that deeds are performed because of an intention that the agent does or would endorse. Rather the claim that is preserved through this insight is that these deeds are not individuated in terms of the intentional component of this web. The tokening of a given deed might, in part, be caused by intentional states. However, such intentional states are incapable of individuating the deed.

6 The Function of Fingers

Deeds, as we have seen, are *preintentional* acts, and as such they stand somewhere in between actions, in the strict sense, and subintentional doings. Deeds are acts that are intentional in the sense that they are done for a reason (or with an intention) that their agent would endorse, but where this general antecedent intention is not sufficient to provide for their individuation, and therefore, not sufficient to imbue them with any representational status that they might possess.

Let's return to one example of a deed introduced earlier. You are a slip fielder attempting to catch a ball hurtling toward you at high speed. Its trajectory is going to bring the ball to you somewhere in the region of lower chest height, and you have an awkward decision to make—whether to point your fingers up or down. Pointing your fingers up or down, then, would be two examples of deeds. What makes them deeds is the fact that the "decision" you have to make is not really a decision in the traditional sense. If you decide in that sense, the ball will be upon you far too quickly for you to do anything about it. Rather, if you are at all competent, you will find yourself just acting. Your general antecedent intention to catch the ball (or some variant thereof) is not sufficient to individuate this deed—for there is any number of such deeds that might serve or satisfy this intention. But your deed is certainly not a random doing of O'Shaughnessy's tongue-moving variety. Its connection with your overall intentions, plans, goals, and so forth, is much closer than that exhibited by subintentional acts.

To what extent does it make sense to attribute a proper function to a deed of this sort? To see the sense in which it might, consider the following question: what is the difference between a situation in which a trained slip fielder points his fingers upward as a (dorsally initiated) response to a certain ball trajectory, and one in which a novice cricketer with no training exhibits the same bodily movements in the same circumstances? Imagine a bystander, who has accidentally strolled into the middle of the game and is languishing somewhere in the vicinity of the slip cordon. The ball flies toward the bystander, he or she vaguely sees something out of the corner of his or her eye, throws up his or her hands for protection, and as a matter of the sort of cosmic coincidence for which philosophers will be eternally grateful, the hands form precisely the orientation required to catch the ball. The ball sticks, and the catch is made. In both cases we have examples of deeds. But is there any difference between them? More precisely, is there any sense in which the deed performed by the trained fielder has a function that the deed performed by our imagined accidental tourist lacks?

The above scenario is, in effect, a *swampman* case for our imagined cricketing deed. Swampman is a creature dreamed up by Donald Davidson as an objection to teleosemantic accounts of content. Swampman is created, by another of the aforementioned fortuitous coincidences of cosmic proportions, when a bolt of lightning strikes a swamp. The molecules coalesce into exactly the same configuration as those present in some living human—say you. The objection to the teleological theory is that it is committed to claiming that swampman has no representational states—even though it is a molecule-for-molecule replica of you. The reason swampman has no representational states is that his various internal mechanisms have no history, and because they have no history they have no (direct) proper function. And without proper function, there is, on the teleosemantic account, no representation.

The purpose of this book is not to evaluate the teleosemantic account of representation. Rather, it is to show that the claim that deeds are representational is compatible with this account. Accordingly, I do not propose to take a stand on the swampman issue in general. However it is useful for throwing into sharp relief the relevant difference between the deed performed by the slip fielder and that performed by the cosmically lucky trespasser.

There are two obvious differences between the case of the slip fielder and the lucky trespasser. The first difference is *intention*. The fielder intends to catch the ball if he or she can; the latter has no such intention. This difference in general antecedent intention can certainly explain the difference in the *actions* performed by the two. However, if the arguments of chapter 6 are correct, it can play no role in explaining the deeds they perform—whether these are the same or different in each case. There are many deeds—online, feedback-modulated, adjustments that might serve the same general antecedent intention. Accordingly, the intention is insufficient to individuate each of these deeds. And as these deeds are performed beneath the level of intention, neither can intentions be used to explain why the particular deeds are performed.

For our purposes, the important difference between the slip fielder and the trespasser is *history*. The fielder has been trained to catch the ball, and this training adds a history to the movement, a history in virtue of which the movement can have a *function*. Roughly, in broad caricature, the story will be something like this. In the past, slip fielders who pointed their fingers up when balls had a certain trajectory t_1 and pointed them down when balls had a certain trajectory t_2 tended to catch the ball more often than those who did not. Thus, the former slip fielders survived and prospered at the expense of the latter (who were banished to the drudgery of the *long-leg* and *third-man* boundaries). The expertise of the successful slip fielders was then passed onto the next generation in the form of a regimented training regime designed to make cricketers good catchers of balls.

Of course, the bystander's movements will also have a function—presumably protection of some sort. But, this is a different function, and it is a different function precisely because it has a different history—one presumably involving the differential survival rate of humans who protected themselves with their arms when foreign objects were flying toward them and those who didn't. So, although the bystander's deed may well have a proper function; it is not the *same* proper function as the corresponding deed performed by the trained fielder. In both cases, the same movement may be involved. But the deed performed is different in each case.

Our story of the evolutionary history of the slip fielder may be caricatural—and there are no doubt *ceteris paribus* clauses aplenty that need to be thrown around to make it remotely plausible. But, in broad outline, the story is correct. The whole point of training regimes in high-velocity sports is to make you do the right things in the right circumstances so that your differential rate of success is improved—even, indeed especially, when you don't have time to think about it. And if you don't shape up, then, in one way or another, you ship out.

The upshot of the right sort of regime, then, is that slip fielders of the present generation point their fingers up when the ball has trajectory t_1 and point their fingers down when the ball has trajectory t_2 because in the past slip fielders who directed their fingers in these ways in these circumstances survived and prospered at the expense of those who did not. In other words:

Finger-position P (i.e., up/down) is a reproduction of some prior item (the finger position adopted by a cricketing ancestor) that because of the possession of certain reproduced properties (the creation of contours suitable for the reception of a cricket ball with a certain trajectory), actually performed function F (enabling/facilitating the fielder to catch the ball) in the past, and P is adopted now because of this past performance.

What this means, however, is that the finger position satisfies a sufficient condition for having a proper function in the etiological sense. In fact, it satisfies what was earlier identified as clause (i) of Millikan's definition: an item X has proper function F only if (i) X is a reproduction of some prior item that, because of the possession of certain reproduced properties, actually performed F in the past, and X exists because of this performance.

Therefore, the deed of pointing one's fingers up when the ball has a given trajectory, when it is backed by a suitable training regime, satisfies a sufficient condition for having a proper function in an etiological sense. There is, in general, no reason to deny proper functions to at least some deeds. If a deed has a history, in the sense that it is passed on from generation to generation (or from individual to individual within a generation) because it has certain beneficial effects, then it can have a function in virtue of this history.

7   Personal and Subpersonal Proper Finger Functions

Earlier in the chapter, we saw that there was an important distinction between *stimulus-* and *benefit-*based accounts of proper function, and consequently between stimulus- and benefit-based accounts of representation. Recall the magnetosomes that have provided much of the focus for this dispute. What is the adapted proper function of the magnetosomes? Is it to indicate (in the northern hemisphere) the direction of geomagnetic north? Or is it to indicate the direction of oxygen-free water? Geomagnetic north provides the *stimulus* that allows the magnetosomes to perform their proper function: the magnetosomes track geomagnetic north, and track oxygen-free water only insofar as this is correlated with geomagnetic north. But, it is oxygen-free water that provides the *benefit* to the organism of the magnetosomes tracking geomagnetic north. Geomagnetic north is what *produces* the relevant alignment in the magnetosomes. And according to stimulus-based accounts of representation, the function of a given state, S, of a representational mechanism, M, is to track whatever produces it, that is, whatever causes M to go into S. However, oxygen-free water is what the *consumers* of the representation, in this case the marine bacteria, need to do their job, namely survive. And according to benefit-based accounts of representation, the function of a state S of representational mechanism M is to track whatever benefit accrues to the consumer of S, whatever that may be.

I have described a way of reconciling stimulus- and benefit-based accounts of representation. This was based on a distinction between *personal* and *subpersonal* proper functions. Suppose mechanism M of organism P goes into state r in the presence of environmental condition s. Going into r in the presence of s is, let us suppose, an adapted proper function of M. Then, the orthodox teleosemantic story is that state r has the derived proper function of occurring in the presence of s, and thus *represents*, or is *about*, or *means* s. I argued that, subpersonally, r has the derived proper function of tracking s, and, at the personal level, r has the proper function of enabling P to Φ in virtue of tracking s. Each distinct derived proper function will license the attribution of a distinct content. And, crucially, they will license the attribution of this distinct content to distinct individuals. Subpersonal derived proper functions license the attribution of content to subpersonal mechanisms. Personal derived proper functions license the attribution of (a distinct) content to the organism ("person") as a whole.

The account I shall now describe of the proper functions of the hand/finger position will proceed against the background of this reconciliation of stimulus- and benefit-based accounts of representation. If, however, you don't buy into this reconciliation, it does not really matter. What is crucial is that we find a way of accommodating both stimulus- and benefit-based accounts, so that the representation-in-action thesis is not left hostage to one or the other. And I think the following will certainly accommodate both accounts.

We can regard the fielder's hands and fingers as a *mechanism*, M. Given a suitable training regime, this mechanism will enter a given orientation or configuration, C (e.g., fingers up or down), in the presence of certain environmental exigencies such as ball trajectory. As was argued in the previous section, given the appropriate regime, the hands/fingers can have the direct proper function of adopting configuration C in the presence of a certain ball trajectory, and C, accordingly, has the derived proper function of tracking this trajectory. However, in line with our need to accommodate both stimulus- and benefit-based accounts of representation, we need to identify two distinct derived proper functions possessed by C: one subpersonal, the other personal.

At the subpersonal level, the function of the hand/finger orientation C is to *indicate*: it is to track—covary with—the trajectory of the ball, where this constitutes the *stimulus* for the hand-finger orientation. In an accomplished fielder, the hand/finger orientation tracks the trajectory of the ball in a reliable, or at least semireliable, way (i.e., some or other degree greater than chance; some or other degree better than the other fielders vying for your position, and so on, ceteris paribus). And at the subpersonal level it tracks this stimulus because it has the *function* of tracking the ball's trajectory: this is precisely what the subpersonal proper function of the hand/finger orientation is: to track its environmental *producer*.

At the personal level, we find a distinct proper function: a proper function that tracks *benefit* rather than stimulus. The personal proper function of the hand/finger configuration, C, is to enable the slip fielder to make a successful catch. The benefit provided by C is a successful catch. The *consumer* of C is, at the personal level, the fielder. This personal proper function of the hand/finger configuration, C, is thus to track the benefit it provides the consumer. This benefit is that, in virtue of C, the relevant part of the environment becomes, as we might say, *catchable*. The hand/finger orientation, C, performs this personal proper function in virtue of performing its subpersonal proper function of tracking, in a reliable or semi-reliable way, the trajectory of the ball.

Compare this with the case of the rattlesnake discussed earlier.

First, there is the *personal* derived proper function of the state r of the rattlesnake's system. This is to enable the rattlesnake (the "person") to do something—namely, to detect a certain affordance of the environment. r enables the rattlesnake to detect that the environment affords eating. Thus, the personal derived proper function of r is sensitive to the benefit of the prey-detection mechanism fulfilling its adapted proper function. Second, there is the subpersonal derived proper function of r. This is to track warmth and movement. This latter proper function is, therefore, sensitive to the stimulus, rather than the benefit, of the mechanism fulfilling its adapted proper function.

Each proper function licenses the attribution of a distinct content to a distinct individual. The personal derived proper function warrants the attribution of the content, "eatability, there!" to the rattlesnake as a whole. The subpersonal derived proper function licenses the attribution of the content "warmth/movement, there!" to the state r of mechanism M. So not only do we have attributions of distinct contents, those attributions are also made to distinct things.

We have, in effect, taken a precisely analogous stance to the hand/finger position C. And if the analysis of proper functions possessed by the rattlesnake's prey-detection mechanism does indeed license the attribution of representational content to both the mechanism and the rattlesnake itself, then it is difficult to see how we could claim that it does not license a similar attribution in the case of the cricketer's hand/finger position. Thus, the analysis in terms of proper functions should license attributions of a form of content such as "trajectory t_1, there!" to the hand/finger position. And it should license the attribution of a form of content such as "catchable, there!" to the fielder.

Or, rather, it should do so, other things being equal. And not enough has yet been done to show that other things are, in fact, equal. In particular, it would be reasonable to maintain that the possession of a proper function of the sort described above is at most a necessary condition for the attribution of representational content to a mechanism or to its consumer, but that it falls well short of sufficient. And, of course, this is a claim with which I concur, and is what lies behind the list of the five constraints on representation identified earlier. For now, we should note however, that if other things do, in fact, turn out to be equal—that is, if the remaining constraints are satisfied—then the possession of personal and subpersonal proper functions by the hand/finger position, C, licenses the attribution of content to C, and (a distinct content) to the cricketer who consumes it: just as much as the possession of personal and subpersonal proper functions to the rattlesnake's prey-detection mechanism licenses the attribution of content to the relevant state of the mechanism and a distinct content to the rattlesnake that consumes this state.

If, of course, you don't buy into the reconciliation of stimulus- and benefit-based accounts presupposed here, matters are little changed. You can, then, simply adhere to your preferred account and run the analogy between the hand/finger position of the cricketer and the prey-detection mechanism of the rattlesnake to show that the possession of the relevant proper function by the former licenses your preferred version of content to it just as much as the possession of the relevant proper function by the latter licenses your preferred version of content to it. An account of what warrants attribution of *both* stimulus-based content and benefit-based content to an individual is an account of what licenses content of *either* sort.

8   Representing and Intervening

One point should be noted. The hand/finger configuration C not only has the function of tracking the trajectory of the ball, thus enabling the fielder to make a successful catch, it also *does* something to the world: it makes the relevant portion of the world, the portion that consists in the ball, *catchable*, in a way that it would not be if the hands/fingers had not gone into configuration C. At first glance, this might be thought to make the allegedly representational item C not sufficiently independent of the world for it to count as a genuine case of representation.

This thought, however, would be mistaken. The requisite hand/finger orientation does, of course, make that portion of the world that consists in the ball *catchable*—something that it wouldn't have been in the absence of that orientation. However, this does not impugn the independence of representing and the represented item. It is not as if the ball's trajectory changes in any way because of the hand-finger orientation—its trajectory is, of course, unaltered by its becoming catchable. To say that some portion of the world now becomes catchable is not to say something about that world as such; rather, it is to talk of the relation between the fielder and the ball. When the hand/finger orientation is correct, what changes is not the world, but the relation between the fielder and the world. And, it is difficult to see who would want to deny this anyway. It is difficult to see, that is, who would want to deny the general claim that the subject of a correct or true representation stands in a different relation to the world than the subject of an incorrect or false one.

In this modest sense of dependence—where the dependence is one of representation and relation to the world—the mutual dependence of representation and action is, in fact, a strength of the present account. It is precisely what we should expect for those cases of representation that consist in deeds. This is where our primitive epistemic grasp on the world lies, and here there is no distinction between representing the world and acting on it. *Here the world is represented in terms of what we can do to it precisely because it is represented in terms of what we do in it.*

In any event, deeds, hopefully, are beginning to look more and more like representations. Deeds can carry information about the world—at least to the extent that traditional representations do. They thus satisfy the informational constraint. And certain deeds, deeds that have a history, can possess a proper function—either of tracking some or other environmental feature, or of enabling their subject to do something in virtue of tracking such a feature. Thus, they satisfy the teleological constraint. There are three remaining constraints that need to be addressed. Chapter 10 examines whether deeds can satisfy the combinatorial constraint. The next chapter, however, looks at the *decouplability* and the *misrepresentation* constraints. We have already touched on these in a variety of ways. It is now time to look at them in detail.

9   Decouplability and Misrepresentation

1   A Controversial Constraint

It is often thought that for an item to be regarded as genuinely representational it must be *decouplable* from its wider environment and, in particular, from the state of affairs that it purports to represent. The guiding insight is that whatever else a representation might be, it must be the sort of thing that can be used, by an organism, to guide its behavior in the *absence* of the feature of which it is a representation. So, as John Haugeland puts it, to count as a genuinely representation-using system, that system must (i) be able to coordinate its behavior with environmental features that are not always reliably present to it, and (ii) do this by having something else stand in or go proxy for a signal directly received from the environment, and use this to guide behavior in its stead (1991).

The demand for decouplability is most obvious and pressing in *off-line* reasoning situations. As we have already seen (chap. 3), one important subvariety of such situations consists in the coordination of activity and choice with states of affairs that are *distal* or *counterfactual*. Examples of the former include planning a trip to Australia in six months time, or counting the windows in one's house while sitting several miles away in one's office. In the former case, the state of affairs is temporally distal; in the latter, it is spatially distal. Examples of where the state of affairs is counterfactual rather than distal include activities such as working out what would have happened if only you had done X instead of Y, or working out the likely consequences of a course of action on which one has no intention of following up. All of these cases are characterized by some form of physical disconnection or decoupling from the states of affairs that are the objects of one's cognitive states. Being distal or counterfactual, then, are two ways in which a represented state of affairs might be *absent* in the sense required by Haugeland's characterization.

There is, as we have also seen, another variety of offline reasoning situation: one characterized by the fact that the represented state of affairs is not distal or counterfactual, but *complex* or *unruly*—that is, nonnomic. The property of matching or clashing with a shirt, for example, is a nonnomic property that might be possessed by a tie. Our ability to selectively respond to nonnomic features seems to indicate that we are responding to more than straightforward physical features of the environment. Thus, to track a property such as *being a matching tie* we seem to use an indirect route—we track this property by first tracking more basic features of the world—color, shape, and so on—and their instantiation in shirt and tie. Once we have detected the presence of features such as these, we then *infer* the presence of a matching tie. But this seems to involve the use of a representation in the form of a hypothesis about what makes something a matching tie (e.g., relative to shirt X, something, Y, is a matching tie iff . . .).

Nonnomic properties provide another sense in which a represented state of affairs might be absent. Nonnomic properties, it might be argued, are less real than their nomic counterparts in at least one sense: nonnomic properties are supervenient upon, or constructed out of, nomic properties. Or, more precisely, although it is the case that *some* nomic properties are supervenient on other nomic properties, *all* nonnomic properties supervene on nomic properties. Therefore, in this sense, ontologically, nonnomic properties are asymmetrically dependent on nomic properties. Nomic properties can exist without nonnomic properties, but not vice versa. In this sense, then, one might argue that nonnomic properties are less real—and therefore less fully present in the environment—than their nomic counterparts. This inference is, of course, controversial, but nothing much turns on it for our purposes. To discuss the decouplability constraint, to the extent that we need examples of states of affairs that are *absent*, I shall focus on ones that are either distal or counterfactual.

In such *off-line* contexts, the demand for some form of decouplability can seem almost overwhelming. However, it does not follow from this that the demand is overwhelming *tout court*, because it does not, of course, follow from this that all representational contexts are offline. For example, the basic premise of the enactive model of visual perception, discussed in chapter 5, is that visual perception does not involve the coordination of activity and choice with features that are absent. On the contrary, the probing and exploration of environmental structures by way of the visual modality, and the resulting interplay between neural processes and environmental states of affairs, is constitutive of visual perception. Barring an eliminativist interpretation, this model may allow *some* role for decouplable internal representations; but, at best, these would merely provide the subject with the rough gist of a visually presented situation, and would not add up to visual perception in any genuine or familiar sense.

This point, however, can be defended independently of the enactive model of visual perception. Andy Clark (1997: 144–145) provides the following example. There is a population of neurons in the posterior parietal cortex of rats whose function is to carry, by way of an appropriate coding system, information about the direction in which the rat's head is facing. However, this population functions only in tandem with a continuous stream of proprioceptive information from the rat's body. Thus, it does not seem to satisfy the decouplability requirement. Nevertheless, the neuronal population's function is pretty clearly representational. Glossing states of the population as codings for specific head positions allows us to understand the flow of information within the system (for example, when we find other neuronal groups that consume the information encoded in the target population). Thus, as Clark points out, treating the neuronal encodings as representations buys us genuine explanatory leverage, and it is, therefore, unclear why we should deny these encodings the status of representations.

Therefore, we seem to be pulled in two directions. On the one hand, there are good reasons for assenting to the decouplability constraint for at least some cases of representation—those employed in off-line reasoning situations. On the other hand, it is far from clear that the constraint can be legitimately applied to all cases of representation. In this chapter I am of course, not concerned with attacking or defending the decouplability constraint itself, but, rather, with its applicability to deeds. This means that a defense of the representational status of deeds might take two forms. The first would be to defend the status of deeds by arguing against the decouplability constraint itself, and, by implication, arguing that the failure of deeds to meet this constraint is unimportant. The second form that a defense of the representational status of deeds might take is to accept the decouplability constraint and argue that deeds can, in fact, satisfy it.

I am going to adopt the second approach. Not only would a general attack on the decouplability constraint in the service of the representational status of deeds be suspiciously convenient; it would, from my perspective, also be dishonest. I do, in fact, think that there is a genuine role for decouplability in understanding the concept of representation. Once we properly specify the content of the decouplability constraint, however, I shall argue that it is the sort of condition that can be satisfied by deeds.

2 Behavioral Proxies

Recall Haugeland's formulation of the idea of decouplability: to count as genuinely representational, a system must (i) be able to coordinate its behaviors with environmental features that are not always reliably present to it, and (ii) do this by having something else stand in or go proxy for a signal directly received from the environment, and use this to guide behavior in its stead (1991). Some preliminary remarks are required concerning clause (ii). On one reading, this clause would immediately preclude deeds possessing representational status. This would be so if we read Haugeland's second requirement as claiming that what is used to guide behavior in the absence of a signal received directly from the environment, cannot itself be a form of behavior.

Of course, to advance this claim without defense would, with respect to the claims defended in this book, be question begging. If one wants to claim that *only* an internal configuration is the sort of thing can be used to guide behavior in the absence of a signal received directly from the environment, then one cannot afford to leave this as an undefended intuition. For then it would amount to nothing more than an internalist prejudice. Conversely, there are excellent reasons for thinking that certain sorts of behavior can be used to guide behavior in the absence of signals received directly from the environment.

The idea of behavior being used to guide further behavior vis-à-vis a certain state of affairs in the absence of a signal received directly from the environment concerning that state of affairs is, of course, in one sense an utterly familiar one. The sense involved is that in which, vis-à-vis state of affairs S, the behavior of *one* individual guides the behavior of another, *distinct*, individual in the absence of a signal directly received from S by that second individual. This, of course, is what language, in its many and variegated forms, achieves.

However, this clearly does not capture the relevant sense of "standing in for a signal directly received from the environment, and using this to guide behavior in its stead." For here it is the behavior of the same individual that is in question. Behavior can clearly be used to guide the behavior of others vis-à-vis S in the absence of a signal directly received from S. But what we require is a case where the behavior of an individual vis-à-vis S is used to guide the further behavior of the *same* individual vis-à-vis S. Such cases are far less familiar, but nonetheless do exist.

Perhaps the most obvious example is provided by the phenomenon of serial recall. In an excellent and wide-ranging study of strategies for remembering in oral or nonliterate cultures, David Rubin has drawn atten-tion to the role played, in such strategies, by *sound*.[1] Remembering in oral traditions depends on various constraints that cue memories and restrict choices. One of the most important features of Rubin's account is his emphasis on the role played by sound in this process. Two types of sound pattern are of particular significance: *rhyme* and *rhythm*.

Rhyme, as Rubin employs the term, coves three distinct types of sound pattern. *Rhyme* as it is ordinarily used, occurs when the last stressed vowel of a word repeats in sounds that follow it. When the initial consonant of a word repeats, the device is called *alliteration*. When a stressed vowel of a word repeats, the device is called *assonance*. All of these Rubin collectively refers to as rhyme. The existence of rhyming words in a song or speech will aid recall but, crucially, only after the first member of the rhyming set has been uttered and is available to cue recall of the later members. If a song, for example, has many rhyming words in its closing lines, this will not aid recall of the words until the closing lines have been reached (Rubin 1995: 76). Thus, rhyme, to fulfill its function of restricting memory choice, must be *externalized*: it must be turned into a sound pattern in the air around the speaker or hearer. A rhyme internalized in the speaker's mind plays no significant role in recall. This observation is central to the theory of serial recall developed by Rubin.

Rhythm functions in much the same way. The major function of rhythm is, again, that of a constraint, cuing memories and restricting choices. With rhythm, both word choice and the choice of larger units is restricted to those with the correct rhythmic pattern—that is, with the correct number of syllables and stress patterns. For example, in a Homeric epic, where the rhythmic constraints are relatively pronounced, words of three or more syllables in length can appear only in one or two places in a line (Foley 1990; Rubin 1995: 85). Memory for units larger than words also benefits from rhythmic constraints, especially units approximately the length of intonation units.

Rubin's theory of remembering for oral traditions is based on the idea that, in such traditions, recall is *serial*. That is, it starts at the first word and proceeds sequentially. At the beginning of a song, poem, or rhyme, fairly general cues are provided by the constraints of the genre. Then, as it is uttered, each word provides additional cues that are specific to the piece in question. To take a very—in many respects overly—simple example, con-sider the rhyme *Eenie Meenie*. On Rubin's view, as the recall begins, the entire sound pattern of the word *Eenie* will cue the word *meenie*, in which it is embedded. *Meenie* will cue *miney* through rhyme, and *miney* cues *mo* through alliteration. Once *mo* is recited, the first line is complete; the meter of the piece has been set and also, significantly, the *mo, toe, go, mo* end-rhyme pattern has been fixed. For a short piece like this, the serial nature of the unfolding of the cuing may not be necessary, but, as Rubin points out, for longer pieces it almost certainly is.

Whether or not Rubin's general theory of serial recall proves correct, what is important for our purposes is the role played by rhyme and rhythm in cuing memories and restricting choices. And their significance in this regard has been conclusively demonstrated by Rubin. This role is indifferent to whether the speaker of the rhyme is identical with or distinct from the hearer. The role they play in cuing memories and restricting choices in the speaker and hearer is the same, whether or not the speaker is the same person as the hearer.

In such cases of serial recall, the end of the song, poem, or rhyme is, at the beginning of the piece, *absent*, where, in this case, this means temporally distal. Let us refer to the ending of the piece as state of affairs *S*. The speaker, prior to reciting the piece, does not have the resources required to recall *S*. The recitation of the piece, and its consequent serial unfolding as patterns of sound in the air, provides the speaker with those resources. That is, as the speaker recites the piece, she is engaging in behavior that affords her the opportunity to engage in further behavior vis-à-vis *S*, the end of the piece—namely to recall and, hence, recite it. The speaker, therefore, uses her own behavior to coordinate her further behavior vis-à-vis state *S* and does so in the absence of a signal received directly from *S*.

In short, it is possible for the behavior of an individual vis-à-vis an absent state of affairs *S* to guide the further behavior of the same individual vis-à-vis *S*. Therefore, we should not interpret Haugeland's clause (ii) to preclude the claim that what guides behavior in the absence of a signal received directly from the environment may, in certain circumstances, be *other* behavior. To do so would be an undefended, and if the above argument is correct, *indefensible* internalist prejudice.

The other core aspect of the decouplability constraint is provided by Haugeland's clause (i): the ability of an organism to coordinate its behavior with environmental features that are not always reliably present to it. It is to a discussion of this that we now turn.

3   A Dynamicist Interlude

Despite our misgivings over whether decouplability can be regarded as a general feature of representation—that is, a feature necessarily possessed by all representations—when suitably formulated, the idea of decouplability can, nonetheless, play a legitimate, indeed important, role in our understanding of representation. One means of identifying this formulation is by working out precisely the sorts of situations that we should want the decouplability constraint to preclude.

As a start, consider again Van Gelder's attack on the notion of representation inspired by his discussion of the Watt governor.[2] One might be tempted to suppose that the angle at which the arms of the governor are swinging represents the speed of the engine. What makes this supposition a natural one is the fact that there is an intimate and interesting relation between the speed of the engine and the angle of the arms. However, van Gelder argues, correctly, that this relation is not a representational one. Crucially, the angle at which the arms are swinging is not only determined by the speed of the engine, it also determines the speed of the engine. Since the arms are directly linked to the throttle valve, the angle of the arms determines the amount of steam entering the piston, and hence the speed at which the engine is running. Thus, arm angle and engine speed are, at all times, mutually determining. Therefore, there does not exist the degree of independence that would allow us to talk of the arm angle "standing in for" engine speed, as would be required if the former was a genuine representation of the latter. There is nothing mysterious about this relation of codependence: it is perfectly amenable to mathematical analysis. The point urged by van Gelder, however, is that the concept of representation—of something standing in for some other thing—is too simple to account for the interaction between governor and engine (1995: 353).

This objection is, of course, predicated on the decouplability constraint. A representation, according to van Gelder, is a state of some system that, "by virtue of some general representational scheme, stands in for some further state of affairs, thereby enabling the system to behave appropriately with respect to that state of affairs" (1995: 351). The relation between arm angle and engine speed fails to satisfy this condition, and so fails to qualify as representational.

I think van Gelder is entirely correct on this point (though entirely incorrect to think that this underwrites a general case against representation). Thus, one form of decouplability that we should endorse is one that is required to rule out the essential mutual causal dependence of representing vehicle upon represented item. That is, the decouplability constraint must be satisfied to this extent: (a) the representing vehicle cannot be essentially causally dependent upon what it represents in the sense that the vehicle cannot, as a matter of physical necessity, occur in the absence of what it represents, *or* (b) what is represented cannot be essentially causally dependent upon the vehicle that represents it in the sense that it cannot, as a matter of physical necessity, occur in the absence of that vehicle. Note that (a) and (b) are disjoined, not conjoined. The failure of a relation to satisfy either of these is sufficient to disqualify that relation as a representational one. In the case of the Watt governor, the relation between arm angle and engine fails to satisfy either (a) or (b), and so clearly does not qualify as representational.

If this is what the decouplability constraint amounts to, however, then deeds are perfectly capable of satisfying it. The position of the fielder's hands/fingers does not causally constrain the trajectory of the ball. And the trajectory of the ball does not causally constrain the position of the hands/fingers. This is quite different from the arm angle/engine speed case. The angle of the arms of the governor essentially causally constrains the speed of the engine, and vice versa, because the two are physically connected in a way that is entirely absent in the case of the slip fielder—even when that fielder is perfect. The arm angle could not, as a matter of physical necessity, be of a certain value unless the engine speed was also of an appropriate value, and vice versa. And the corresponding claim for the relation between hand/finger orientation and ball trajectory would, quite obviously, be false.

4 Decouplability, History, and Normativity

The requirement of essential causal independence of representing vehicle from represented state of affairs—claim (a) above—is, in fact, a familiar constraint on representation; and we do not require dynamicist proclivities to understand its force. To see this, consider a naive *causal* theory of representation: a representation is about whatever causes it. Such a view is obviously misguided, which is why, presumably, no one holds it. As we have seen, the view entails that misrepresentation is impossible—a representation is about, "truly" about, whatever causes it. And thus, the view fails to accommodate the normativity of representation. In other words, the view fails to capture the distinction between what *in fact* causes the tokening of a representation and what is *supposed* to cause the tokening of that representation. What it also means, however, is that the type-identity of the representation-token is dependent, in this case, *logically* dependent on the item that causes this tokening. If the tokening is caused by environmental item s, then the representation-token will belong to one type. If it is caused by environmental item s^1 then it will belong to a distinct type. It is this latter form of dependence that we need to rule out to accommodate the normativity constraint.

To satisfy the normativity constraint, it must be possible for a representation of a given type to be tokened incorrectly. It must be possible for a
representation of type Φ to occur even if the immediate environment is
not, in fact, Φ. And for this to be possible, it must be the case that the type
to which a representation-token belongs does not, in general, essentially
depend on the character of its immediate environment.

Care must be taken in explicating this claim. The claim does not concern
the possibility of instantiating a representational type in general; but, rather,
of instantiating such a type in a given instance. And this distinction allows
us to avoid violating any general externalist scruples on content ascription;
and we need to avoid this because representations are typically typed by way
of their content. In fact, the claim can be explained in terms of a distinction
between two types of externalism distinguished by Colin McGinn (1989);
that between what he calls *weak* and *strong* externalism. Although employing the same labels, the distinction is, in fact, quite different from that
introduced in chapter 2. McGinn's version of the distinction is essentially
that between *existence dependence* and *environment dependence*—where
"dependence" refers to individuation dependence of the form explained in
chapter 2. Weak externalism is the claim that mental states are individuation
dependent on items that occur in the same *possible world* as the subject of
those states. Strong externalism is the claim that mental states are individuation dependent upon items that occur in the *environment* of their subject.
McGinn argues that strong externalism is an implausibly strong doctrine, at
best true of only a small proportion of mental states. Weak externalism, on
the other hand, is arguably true of all content-bearing states.

The claim that the type to which a representation-token belongs does
not, in general, essentially depend on the character of its immediate environment is, in effect, a denial of strong externalism concerning how representations are typed. It can allow that some representations are, or might
be, typed in this way. But the expression, "in general" is intended to preclude all of them being typed in this way. However, this claim is perfectly
compatible with a weak externalist account of how representations come
to be typed. One may not be able to instantiate the representational type
HORSE in a world where there are no horses.[3] But one can certainly instantiate a representation of this type in a world where there are horses but
where a horse is not currently causally producing the representation-
token. It is this latter form of independence of representational type from
environment that concerns us here. To satisfy the normativity requirement, we must accommodate this form of independence of representational vehicle from what it represents.

Therefore, on this interpretation of decouplability, the raison d'être for the decouplability constraint is that it is necessary to satisfy the normativity constraint. The former constraint is parasitic upon the latter. In any case of representation, there must be sufficient decouplability to satisfy the normativity constraint, but nothing more. And, if the arguments of the previous chapter are correct, we have reasons for thinking that deeds can satisfy the normativity constraint. If so, then we have precisely the same reasons for supposing they will satisfy the decouplability constraint.

Consider how deeds were shown, in the previous chapter, to satisfy the normativity constraint. Deeds satisfy this constraint because they have a *history* that provides them with a *function*. It is this function that provides for their being typed independently of the specific nature of their *immediate* environment, though not, of course, of their *historical* environment, or their environment *in general*. So, to the extent that deeds have a function, and satisfy the normativity requirement, we should expect them to satisfy the relevant form of the decouplability requirement and to satisfy this for precisely the same reasons.

The decouplability of deeds stems from the fact that they have a history. Consider the way in which a deed might be learned. This could be through practice that occurs, sometimes but not always, in absence of the typical eliciting environmental stimulus. Consider, for example, the way a batsman learns to play a particular cricket shot; say, the *off-drive*. In the heat of the game, the typical eliciting stimulus for this shot will be a half volley pitched on or just outside off-stump. But the shot will often be practiced in the absence of this stimulus. In such practice, the technique will be patiently refined, and the flaws ironed out. The position of the feet will be analyzed and adjusted if needed. The direction and angle of the shoulder will similarly be addressed and adjusted if necessary. This type of practice is essential to how the stroke is learned, perfected, and passed down from one generation to the next. In virtue of this process of learning and perfecting, when, in the heat of a match, an accommodating half volley presents itself just outside off-stump, what the batsman provides us with, in essence, is a *re-presentation* of an off-drive. It is a *re-presentation* of a product that has been acquired and perfected in a different arena, and decoupled from the environmental exigency with which it has been designed to deal.

The shot itself may be an action. However, it is composed of deeds. Consider just one of them—aligning the shoulder so that when the shot is played the bat, the arm, and the shoulder will form a straight line. This will, of course, only work if the shoulder stands in an appropriate relation to the ball. Specifically, the shoulders must be aligned at a specific angle to the ball. Let θ be the angle formed between the point of the bowler's delivery and the location where it crosses the plane of the batsman's stumps. And let ψ be the angle of the batsman's shoulders relative to the plane of the stumps. Then, if ψ/θ is too small, the batsman's attempt to play an off-drive will fail—the batsman will hit "inside" the ball. If, on the other hand, ψ/θ is too large, the attempt will also fail with the batsman hitting across the ball.

The connection between the decouplability and normativity of the off-drive is a close one. Specifically, the normative character of the shot provides the means of typing it independently of the presence of the typical eliciting stimulus. The off-drive has the function of enabling the batsman to successfully deal with a delivery that possesses a certain length and a certain line. It is the fact that it has performed this function in the past that explains why it is extant today. This function enables an instance of the shot to be typed as an off-drive—even when it fails to perform its proper function. Crucially, this way of typing the shot is *historical*. The shot is typed according to its history, and, therefore, independently of the presence or absence, in any particular case, of a typical eliciting stimulus. Thus, if the batsman plays the off-drive in inappropriate circumstances— the ball did not land in the requisite spot—and thus misses the ball, the shot is still an off-drive—just, in this case, a failed one. The shot is typed in terms of its history and thus in terms of what it is supposed to do, not in terms of what it does. This is all the decouplability we can reasonably require for the deed.

The same pattern is reiterated for any deed that possesses a proper function that is grounded in history. Consider, for example, the martial arts—particularly the highly regimented ones like karate. Consider a standard movement in karate: the front middle block. Different styles of karate will have slightly different means of implementing this block, so let's focus on one style—say, *Isshin-Ryu*. The arm is swung upward from the elbow, the elbow being used effectively as a pivot. The tough muscle of the outer forearm is pointed outward to protect the bone. The whole movement is fast and snappy.

This is a move that will be inculcated in a karate student through repeated repetitions (the student is being "trained up"). Faults in technique are identified by the instructor, who will point them out to the student and get him or her to keep repeating the movement until these faults have been ironed out. When the movement has been learned in an unopposed situation, limited contact will be allowed—the student will learn to use the move to block a punch thrown, with varying degrees of enthusiasm and severity, by a designated opponent. Following the successful completion of this stage, and the successful learning of this and a variety of other moves, the student will be allowed to move on to free sparring where—ideally— he or she will have an opportunity to practice these moves.

This is a slightly idealized version of the training process, but you probably get the point. First of all, the movement that constitutes the front middle block has a clear function, in both subpersonal and personal senses. Subpersonally, the function is to track an attack to the middle of the body. That is, the function of the movement, subpersonally, is to coordinate with an attack to the middle of the body so that the arm and the attack come to occupy the same place at the same time. The personal function of the movement is to enable the person to protect the middle part of their body—roughly from the waist to the shoulder—from attack by an opponent or assailant. Moreover, various subcomponents of the move can be identified, and these also possess clear functions. That the tough muscles of the outer forearm be pointed outward is to protect the bone—a blow to which can be extremely painful, and so on.

What grounds these functions is, of course, history. In the past, a person who blocks in the manner prescribed by the training will, theoretically at least, and all things of course being equal, have had more success in fending off an attack to the middle part of the body, and in avoiding damage to the arm while doing so. Thus, the reason the karate practitioner of today performs the various moves constitutive of his style today is because, in the past, the practitioner of yesterday who performed the moves in that way was differentially more successful than the one who did not. And training is what provides the link between the differential success of yesterday with the correct performance of the move today.

Function and history are connected in this tight manner in the practice of karate. As a result, we can legitimately talk of the way a move is *supposed* to be performed, and we can legitimately talk of the proper function of the move. This means, however, that the movement is typed in terms of its function, and hence in terms of its history. Whether or not a movement counts as a front middle block depends on its etiology, and not on the presence or absence of its typical eliciting stimulus. Thus, if the block is performed in inappropriate circumstances—perhaps because the attack was too high—it is still a front middle block—but a failed one. The movement is typed in terms of its history and thus in terms of what it is supposed to do, not in terms of what it does. And, again, this is all the decouplability we can reasonably require for the deed.

Therefore, to the extent that the decouplability requirement is a legitimate constraint on representation, it is no obstacle to regarding deeds as possessing representational status. The sorts of deeds that qualify as representational are ones that are individuated in terms of their proper function. This function is historically constituted. And so deeds are individuated in terms of what they should do, not in terms of what they in fact do. Equivalently, deeds are identified by way of their etiology, not in terms of the presence or absence of their typical eliciting stimulus. In this sense, deeds are decouplable from their environment. And this, I think, is the only sense of decouplability we can legitimately require.

5 Representation and Representing

Any adequate account of representation must account for the possibility of *misrepresentation*. It might be thought that this creates a problem for the claim that deeds are representational. After all, what would count as misrepresentation in the coupled system of the slip fielder and ball? The position of the fingers can represent the trajectory of the ball only if they can also *mis*represent the trajectory of the ball, and how, we might wonder, can they do that?

As we might expect, the key to understanding how deeds can misrepresent lies in their teleological character; the possibility of misrepresentation emerges as a consequence of a deed failing to perform its proper function. And, in this, the possibility of misrepresentation in the case of deeds parallels the teleological account of misrepresentation in general. Deeds are individuated in terms of their proper function—at least, they will be thus individuated if they are to qualify as representational—and this function is historically constituted. The possibility of deeds misrepresenting, therefore, lies in the possibility of divergence between what a deed is supposed to do, and what it in fact does; in the possibility of divergence between the eliciting stimulus to which the deed should be a response, and the eliciting stimulus to which it is in fact a response.

However, in the case of deeds, there are additional complications that may mask the ability of deeds to misrepresent. Most significantly, there are two distinct ways of thinking about representation, one that is amenable to the representational status of deeds, one that is far less so. Understanding how deeds can misrepresent requires us to clearly distinguish these ways.

The key to the distinction lies in the different stances each takes toward the concept of *genuine duration*. The two ways of thinking about representation are, in effect, recorded by the ambiguity of the word itself. On the one hand there is *representation*, and on the other there is *a* representation.

The first way of thinking about representation takes representations as primary, and sees representation as something to be built up out of representations, plus the relation of representation. So, if we are to understand representation, we must understand the relation that a representation bears to what it represents in virtue of which it so represents it. So, on this view:

Representation = representations + (the relation of) representation

Representations are typically regarded as neural configurations. And the instantiation or activation of a representation that stands in an appropriate relation to what it represents is something that has genuine duration. Accordingly representation of some or other fact takes place at a determinate, if perhaps difficult to determine, time. In effect, representation, thus conceived, has the character of a state, one whose instantiation begins at a determinate time, ends at a determinate time, and which has no intermittent lacunas. This, by a considerable distance, has been the standard way of thinking about representation. Representation is reducible to *a* representation standing in an appropriate relation to what it represents. If the activation of this representation has genuine duration, then so too does representation itself. This, as I argued in the opening chapter, is one manifestation of the assimilation of representation to the category of the *word*.

The alternative is to think of representation as, fundamentally, an *activity* rather than a state. This activity might involve the construction of internal configurations that stand in appropriate relations to things outside of them. But representation—the activity of representing—is not, in general, reducible to this. Rather, the activity of representing the world also involves action—broadly construed—on the world: the probing, exploring, manipulating, and exploiting of environmental structures by way of the organism's representational modalities. This, as we have seen, is the view of representation that underlies the vehicle-externalist model in general, and specific versions of that model such as the enactive or sensorimotor account of visual perception.

On this latter view, representation is fundamentally *representing*—and this is an activity. And like any activity, it may have unclear, perhaps even indeterminate, boundaries. Exploring is an activity, for example, and the activity of exploring does not stop just because the explorer sits down and takes a rest. Nor is it entirely clear where an exploration begins and where it ends. These are not just epistemological concerns. Exploration is not the sort of thing that need have precise spatial and temporal boundaries. It is not simply that these boundaries are difficult to identify; the problem is not primarily an epistemological one. Rather, there is no fact of the matter that could lend to the boundaries the sort of precision required to claim that the process of exploration possesses genuine duration. The same is true of manipulation and exploitation. When an organism manipulates structures in its environment to facilitate its representation of that environment, this manipulation is not the sort of thing that need possess precise spatial boundaries; nor need it possess precise temporal boundaries of the sort required for it to have genuine duration.

It is the second view of representation that is implicated in the vehicle-externalist account of representation and its specific incarnations. And, accordingly, this book defends that view. To claim that deeds are representations, as I have indicated before, would not be so much inaccurate as misleading—the danger is that it yields too much to the first way of thinking about representation and, by way of this, to the assimilation of representation to the category of the word. Rather, the idea is that deeds form part of the activity of representing the world, and, crucially, a part that is just as genuinely representational as any other part of that activity. It is not as if deeds are some nonrepresentational accompaniment, or even facilitator, of some genuinely representational core—representations traditionally understood, for example. Rather, the role played by deeds in the activity of representing the world is a role that is *itself* representational.

It is within the context of this overall view of representing as an activity that the account of misrepresentation is to be located.

6   Misrepresenting

Let us return to the worry concerning misrepresentation. Any adequate account of representation must account for the possibility of *misrepresentation*. This is a consequence of the normative status of representation. The content of a representation specifies how the world *should*, or is *supposed*, to be, but this must also accommodate the possibility that the world is, in fact, not that way. But, it might be argued, what would count as misrepresentation in the coupled system of the slip fielder and ball? The hand/finger orientation can represent the trajectory of the ball only if it can also *mis*represent the trajectory of the ball, and how can it do that?

One source of this worry—almost certainly the primary source—is the traditional view of representation, according to which representations are primary. The instantiation or activation of a representation, an item that stands in an appropriate relation to what it represents, is, it might be thought, something that has *genuine duration*. Accordingly, representation of some or other fact takes place at a determinate, if perhaps difficult to determine, time, and has no intermittent lacunas.

However, to assume that representation has genuine duration is to assume the view of representation that, it has been the burden of this book to argue, the vehicle-externalist account should reject. Therefore, the assumption of genuine duration cannot, without begging the question, be used as an argument against the vehicle-externalist account of representation. The situation would change, of course, if there were any *independent* reasons for thinking that representation must be the sort of thing that has genuine duration. So, the question is: are there such reasons?

Some, particularly those who assign a significant role to the concept of information in understanding representation, might think that we can derive the assumption of genuine duration from the nature of information. In particular, we might suppose that the information carried in nomic relations or relations of conditional probability is *synchronic* and/or *categorical* in a way that underwrites the genuine duration of representation. Thus, one might think that if the hand-finger position of the fielder is to carry information about ball trajectory, this information must be contained *at* a particular time, or through an identifiable, and relatively short, period of time, a period that has no intermittent lacunas. The information contained in the hand/finger position is, in this sense, synchronically constituted. Related to this is a view of the information relevant to representation as categorical, or categorically present at that time, or through that genuine interval of time. Thus, the information about ball trajectory carried by the hand/finger orientation cannot depend on certain contingencies that may or may not prove to obtain.

If information were synchronic and categorical in these senses, and *if* information were a constituent of representation, then there might well be a problem with the denial that representation possesses genuine duration. However, not only is the role of information in representation unclear (see chap. 7), there are no reasons at all for thinking that the information *must* be synchronically or categorically constituted. Certainly, neither the synchronic nor the categorical status of information is mandated by the basic Shannon concept of information.

The notion of conditional information, for example, is well understood, and is, in fact, a central component of the Shannon concept. The idea is simple: an item X can carry information about item Y conditionally upon the occurrence or failure to occur of contingency C. As we saw in chapter 7, it is the idea that information can be conditional in this sense that underlies the idea of the *relativity of information* we examined earlier.

Conditional information is, precisely, information that is relative to the obtaining or failing to obtain of given contingencies. The notion of conditional information, thus understood, entails that the information carried by X about Y is not information that is necessarily present at a given time—since the obtaining or failure to obtain of contingency is something that may well occur *through* time. Furthermore, since the obtaining or failing to obtain of a given contingency need not occur through any definite period of time—whether or not C obtains is not dependent on its obtaining at a particular time or during a particular period of time—neither need the information carried by X about Y to be constituted at or during any definite period of time. The time through which this contingency may obtain or fail to obtain need not have a determinate beginning or end, and need not be devoid of intermittent lacunas. This is not to claim that information can *never* be synchronically or categorically constituted; but it is to say that it is not *necessarily* thus constituted.

But if we distance ourselves from the claim that information *must* be synchronically and/or categorically constituted, then any role played by information in constituting representation does not entail that representation must have genuine duration. Certain instances of representation might have genuine duration; but there is no requirement that all representation is thus constrained. If this is true, then the information about the trajectory of the ball carried by the hands/fingers can, in part, be information that is essentially conditionally and diachronically constituted. The information concerning ball trajectory carried by the position of the fingers can be information that is conditional upon certain contingencies that are extended through a period of time that need have no determinate boundaries—such as, for example, what happens *after* the ball reaches the fingers.

The approach to misrepresentation defended here is, in effect, an extension of this specific point. If the extended view of representation defended in this book is correct, then representing the world is a process extended in both space and time. Representation of the world is not the sort of thing that need occur *at* a time; sometimes it can occur only *through* time. Equivalently, at least in some cases, there is no such thing as the representational content possessed by a representation at a given time. In such cases, content can only exist through time; it is diachronically, rather than synchronically, constituted, and it is conditional upon the way circumstances in fact unfold, rather than categorically present independently of such circumstances. Representation is fundamentally *representing*; it has the character of a process rather than a state, and a temporally untidy process at that.

Since part of what is at issue in the dispute between traditional and extended models of representation is precisely whether representation has the character of a state or of a temporally untidy process—that is, an activity—we cannot predicate an objection to the extended view on the assumption that representation must have the character of a state. But to suppose that it *must* be possible to distinguish cases of representation from cases of misrepresentation by focusing exclusively on what is occurring at given time, and ignoring what goes on through an interval of time, is to make precisely this assumption.

If the activity of representing is primary, and representations derivative, then the fundamental problem of misrepresentation is, in fact, a problem of *misrepresenting*. That is, the relevant question is not how misrepresentation is possible, but how *misrepresenting* is possible. And when we frame the question in this way, we see that the claim that deeds are representational—a genuinely representational part of the process of representing—is easily rendered compatible with the possibility of misrepresenting.

In what sense, then, might a deed count as a misrepresenting of the world? For example, in what sense might hand/finger orientation count as a misrepresenting of the trajectory of the ball? The answer to this is deceptively simple. If representing the world is a diachronic phenomenon whereby an organism acts on—probes and explores—structures in its environment, if, that is, representation is something that occurs through time rather than at a time, then there is a clear sense in which the hand/finger orientation can be a misrepresenting of the ball: the fielder drops the ball. More important, the fielder drops the ball in a way that carries information about the relative mismatch of the orientation and trajectory.

For example, if the fielder points his fingers down when he should have pointed them up, he will receive a painful knock on the bony part of the medial wrist just below the *mons veneris*. This is a case of misrepresenting. What happens *after* the fingers are positioned, and when the ball arrives, is part of the process of representing the trajectory. And the fact that the ball is dropped because it is hits the front wrist just below the thumb is a classic indicator of misrepresenting. The fingers were pointed down when they should have been pointed up. Similarly, if the fingers were pointed up when they should have been pointed down, the fielder receives a painful blow on the lateral wrist, below the little finger. The relevant fact pertinent to misrepresenting the trajectory is not simply that the ball is dropped—although that is important. Rather, it is the *way* in which it is dropped—for it is this that carries information about the relative mismatch of hand/finger orientation and ball trajectory.

The moral of the story is that if representing the world takes time—if it is a diachronically determined phenomenon—then *misrepresenting* the world also takes time. Misrepresenting the world is not, *in general*, the sort of thing achieved at a time, but only through time. And if this is true, deeds can misrepresent the world to the same extent as mental representations traditionally construed.

7 The Case So Far

Chapter 7 argued that deeds can satisfy the informational constraint. Chapter 8 added to this the teleological constraint. This chapter has argued that deeds can be decouplable from the environment and also misrepresent that environment. These possibilities, in fact, emerged as consequences of the satisfaction of the teleological constraint, given a few additional clarifications and qualifications. Therefore, it seems we are well on the way to allowing that deeds have representational status. They satisfy four out of the five commonly identified constraints on representation. Indeed, they satisfy these constraints to no lesser extent than do internal configurations of a subject. Therefore, from the perspective of the first four constraints on representation, if we want to accord representational status to internal configurations, it is difficult to see how we could legitimately deny this status to at least some deeds.

The next chapter considers the fifth and final constraint on representation: the idea that if any item is to qualify as representational, it must occur not in isolation but only as part of a more general representational scheme or framework.

10   The Combinatorial Constraint

1   Representational Systems

It is often claimed that for any item to count as representational, it must form part of a general representational scheme or framework (Haugeland 1991: 62). That is, a representational stand-in must be part of a larger scheme of stands-ins. This allows the standing in to occur systematically, and for a variety of related representational states. In other words, representational items are subject to what we might call a *combinatorial requirement*. This gives us our final constraint on the concept of a representational system:

Combinatorial condition   For an item *r* to qualify as representational, it must occur not in isolation but only as part of a more general representational framework.

The reasons for this constraint are clear and familiar. First, the capacity to represent any given state of affairs, *s*, is partly constituted by the ability to represent systematically related states of affairs. Any organism that is capable of representing the fact that Jane loves Dick *must* also be capable of representing the state of affairs Dick loves Jane. If the organism were not capable of representing the latter, then there is no real sense in which it could be said to represent the former. Representation is, in this sense, *systematic*. Second, some argue that the capacity to represent any given state of affairs, *s*, is partly constituted by the ability to represent states of affairs generated from *s*. Thus, any organism capable of representing the fact that Dick loves Jane *must* be capable of representing the fact that Dick loves *someone*. And any organism capable of representing the fact that Jane loves Dick, and of representing the fact that Dick loves Jane, must also be capable of representing the fact that Jane loves Dick *and* Dick loves Jane. Representation is, in this sense, *generative*.

The generativity requirement is more controversial than the requirement of systematicity: some regard it as an empirical, rather than constitutive, feature of representation (Fodor and Pylyshyn 1988). But whether motivated by the systematicity or generativity requirement, the idea is the same: we can only explain how systematicity or generativity is possible if we accept that no item qualifies as representational unless it forms part of a larger scheme of representations—a more general representational framework.

Note that it is no requirement of this combinatorial constraint that anything that is to qualify as representational must possess constituent structure. The constraint is compatible with the existence of primitive, unstructured, representational items. However, the constraint does require that where these items are complex—built out of simpler representational items—the structure that they possess must be adequate to accommodate features of representation such as systematicity and (perhaps) generativity.

Although the combinatorial condition is, in itself, not controversial, its entailments very much are. At one time it was thought that these were sufficiently serious to undermine the pretensions of entire research programs in artificial intelligence. Thus, for example, Fodor and Pylyshyn (1988) used the generativity and, in particular, the systematicity of representation to argue that connectionist models of cognition could at best be regarded as accounts of the implementation of cognitive processes, but not as accounts of the cognitive processes themselves. Happily, we need not become embroiled in such disputes. For our purposes, whatever controversy attends the combinatorial constraint can be sufficiently mitigated by careful attention to two related distinctions: (i) the distinction between *semantic* and *iconic* forms of representation, and (ii) the distinction between *vehicles* and *contents*.

2   Semantic and Iconic Representations

The most familiar example of a representational system that satisfies the combinatorial condition is, of course, human language. Indeed, it is the analogy between thought and language embodied in the language-of-thought hypothesis that, arguably, provides the principal motivation for the combinatorial condition. In virtue of its structure, linguistic forms are susceptible to certain sorts of transformation; the systematicity and generativity of language are grounded in the possibility of these transformations. As we have seen, these features are applicable, indeed arguably constitutive, of thought as well as language. So, the obvious idea would be that we should explain the systematicity and generativity of thought by way of the systematicity and generativity of language. The structure of language in virtue of which it is susceptible to these sorts of transformations is *semantic* structure. This structure is semantic in the sense that which modes of combination are permitted and which are not are determined by their relation to semantic concepts such as truth and reference.

Sentences are evaluable as true or false: they possess truth-conditions. Any language will contain mechanisms that allow complex expressions to be generated from simpler ones. The paradigmatic combinatorial mechanisms are the logical connectives: "and," "or," "not," "if-then," "some," "all," and so on. The truth-value of logically complex sentences varies systematically with the truth-values of its components. Thus, when we talk about the truth of a sentence or proposition, we are talking about a property that bears this sort of relation to the logical connectives. Second, the concept of reference, as applied to constituents of propositions, is a function of the contribution these constituents make to the truth-conditions of the propositions that contain them. Thus, any relation between a word and an object that is to count as reference must potentially satisfy clauses of the form: if F refers to dogs and a refers to Nina, then Fa is true iff Nina is a dog. A relation that did not meet this requirement would not count as reference, at least not of the sort that can legitimately be applied to subsentential components. And the reason is, of course, that this relation would not be appropriately connected to the concept of truth.

These claims are all, in this post-Tarskian age, utterly familiar. They show that what I have called semantic forms of combination are bound up with the concepts of truth and reference. First, the fact that the sentences of a language are truth evaluable entails that the language admits of structuring by way of the logical connectives in such a way that the truth-value of complex sentences varies systematically with the truth-values or references of its subsentential components. A language consisting simply of names and predicates may, or may not, be a logical possibility, and nothing that has been said here is intended to rule out this possibility. What is true, however, is that if there were a language consisting entirely of names and predicates, this language could be expanded by way of the logical connectives even if, in its extant forms, it had not been thus expanded. To talk of the truth of a sentence or proposition, is to talk about something that stands in the requisite relation to the logical connectives.

Second, the concept of reference, as it is applied to sentences or propositions, is also bound up with systematic patterns of the form identified above. Any relation between a word and an object that is to count as reference must potentially satisfy clauses like, if F refers to P and a refers to b, then *Fa* is true iff *Pb*. A relation that did not meet this requirement would not count as reference, at least not of the sort characteristic of sentences or propositions. And the reason is, ultimately, that this relation would not be appropriately connected to the concept of truth.

If we wanted to model the systematicity of thought on the systematicity of language, then it is to the interrelated concepts of truth, reference, and sentential structure we should appeal. And our representational system would have to possess semantic structure in this sense. However, such an appeal would be premature: it would be a mistake to suppose that all representational systems possess semantic structure. Some systems that clearly are representational are not structured in this way at all. Cognitive maps provide a case in point.[1] A cognitive map (or mental model), like any map, mirrors (is geometrically isomorphic with) the region it maps, and it does so if it accurately replicates the region's geometric features. In doing so, a cognitive map is clearly a representational item. But the notions of truth and reference that underlie the representational features of propositions are not applicable to cognitive maps. Crucially, the concept of geometric isomorphism does not interact in the same way with the logical connectives. The negation of a sentence is another sentence. But the negation of a map is not a map. To the extent that we can make sense of a negated map, the idea would be that a negated map is a different map. So, in this sense of negation, any map distinct from m would be a negation of m. Yet, it is not true that any sentence distinct from p is a negation of p. Similarly, what is the geometric analogue to disjunction? The disjunction of two maps is not itself a map—but the disjunction of two sentences is a sentence. If cognitive maps can be said to be true, or to refer to the region of reality that they map, this is only because "true" and "refer" mean something quite different in this context than in the context of semantically structured items such as sentences.

These sorts of points are familiar ones (see McGinn 1989, chap. 3). They are rehearsals of the idea that the way a model represents the world is different from the way a sentence represents the world. Nevertheless, a map is certainly no less a representational device than a sentence. And a cognitive map is no less a representational device than a thought. Where does this leave the combinatorial condition? In fact, it leaves it perfectly intact. We might accept that any representational item must be part of a general representational framework. But what we must emphatically deny is that the mode of combination appropriate to such a framework must be semantic. Maps—cognitive or otherwise—are not semantic representations. They are what we might call *iconic* representations. Correctness conditions for representations are not coextensive with truth-conditions; and the domain of representation is broader than the domain of reference.

The claim that deeds have representational status, therefore, does not commit us to certain claims that we should almost certainly want to reject. It does not commit us to the claim that deeds can be true or false; nor does it commit us to the claim that they refer to the world. Deeds are not semantically evaluable; but there is nothing in the thesis of representation in action that requires them to be. Their representational status is iconic, not semantic.

3 Vehicles and Contents (Again)

The distinction between semantic and iconic forms of representation is reinforced by the second distinction: that between the vehicles and contents of thought. The former distinction is one operative at the level of vehicles. And to claim that the vehicles of representation have iconic structure is not to deny that the contents possessed by those vehicles are semantically evaluable. On the contrary, the combinatorial possibilities evident in language are, clearly, mirrored by those evident in thought. And the basis of the possibilities is, in each case, identical: semantic structure. The attribution to thoughts of semantic relations such as truth and reference determines, and is determined by, their being susceptible to the sorts of combinatorial patterns responsible for sentences. Thus, it is fairly clear that certain paradigmatic examples of mental representations have semantic structure. However, one should be very careful in the conclusions one draws from this.

Most important, it is not possible to deduce, from formalized expressions of certain transitions undergone by the contents of representations, any claims about the structure of the representational vehicles that bear those contents. To do so would be to fall victim to a fairly blatant vehicle–content confusion. Thus, we cannot, legitimately, use these sorts of transformations to argue for a language-of-thought hypothesis. The representational properties of representations may be intimately bound up with patterns of semantic combination, but this does not entail that the vehicles that carry these properties are similarly structured. All we can conclude, in fact, is this: in the case of some representations, the representational vehicles need to be such that the content they bear is susceptible to the sort of transformations licensed by the logical connectives. This does not entail that the vehicles themselves be structured in the same way as the content.

Again, this point is a familiar one.[2] The content of thought is, indeed, truth-evaluable. Cognitive maps are not similarly truth-evaluable.

However, it does not follow from this that cognitive maps cannot provide the basis of truth-evaluable contents. Such maps are the vehicles of content, and what is required of such a vehicle is not that that it has the same properties as the content it bears, but rather than it has suitable properties to bear this content. Take, for example, a standard functionalist account according to which mental states are to be individuated in terms of their causal role. Causal roles cannot literally be the bearers of truth-value either; they are not the sort of thing that can be semantically evaluable. But, there is nothing in functionalism that requires that they be thus evaluable. All functionalism requires is that they be capable of mapping onto the propositions that provide the content of the states they individuate. Similarly, all we should require of cognitive maps is that they be capable of being mapped onto contents; not that they share the same properties as contents.

The claim that deeds are representational is a claim about the vehicles, not the contents, of representation. The thesis of representation in action, therefore, does not commit us to the idea that deeds share some or all of the properties of contents. It does not commit us to the claim that deeds possess a structure that might be conceptual or nonconceptual. And it does not commit us to thinking of deeds as primitive concepts. Deeds are not, and do not have, any of these things.

4   Structure, Learning, History, Function

In this chapter, I am going to argue that deeds can satisfy the combinatorial condition. The preceding sections have been engaged in the preliminary work of identifying what this claim does not entail. Thus, it does not entail that deeds are semantically evaluable—usefully characterized in terms of the concepts of truth and reference. It does not entail that deeds have sentential structure. It does not entail that deeds possess any of the properties of contents—conceptual or nonconceptual structure, and so forth. Finally, it does not even entail that deeds are themselves internally structured. This is an, as yet, open question: it may be that deeds occupy the same sort of role as primitive, unstructured, representations. All that is required is that deeds occur not in isolation but as part of a more general representational framework. This requires that deeds be combinable in ways that would allow them to be the bearers of content—to map onto the crucial features of content, such as systematicity and (perhaps) generativity, which the combinatorial condition has been introduced to explain.

The general claim to be defended in this chapter, then, is that behavior can, and typically does, exhibit combinatorial structure. That is, behavior is decomposable into a hierarchically structured sequence of deeds. As we have seen, that deeds themselves possess constituent structure is not a requirement of the combinatorial condition; and, accordingly, I shall not defend this claim. Rather, the claim is that deeds contribute to the structure of behavior in a way akin to that in which lexical elements contribute to the structure of language. Deeds are the constituents of behavior, and can be combined in ways that allow behavior to satisfy the combinatorial constraint.

In prosecuting this case, I am going to examine one—particularly important—form of behavior: imitative behavior. I shall argue that imitation, of anything other than simple forms of behavior, requires that the imitated behavior possess recombinant structure. Although important in itself, this argument, in effect, will take us back to the heart of the book, and to the teleology that I have taken to lie at the core of representation. Recombinant structure is what binds together the other core elements of representation—elements that form the basis of the case for the representational status of deeds. In all but the simplest deeds, structure is required for learning. But learning is required for history. History is required for function. And function is required for representation. It is within this circle of concepts—structure, learning, history, function, representation—that the thesis of representation in action is ultimately grounded.

Thus, the claim I shall defend in the following pages is that deeds form the lexical elements of imitative, hence learned, behavior, and the exigencies of learning complex forms of behavior require that this behavior be structured in a way that allows it to satisfy the combinatorial constraint. The first step in the argument is to show that it is, in fact, deeds—not actions—that form the lexical elements of imitative behavior.

5 Cavalry Charges

Despite their popularity in philosophical circles, actions, in the strict sense, form only a tiny part of human agency. The vast majority of what human beings do, rather than what happens to them, consists in doings and deeds—subintentional and preintentional acts—rather than actions. The reasons for this are well-known, and have been for some time, but perhaps are nowhere more elegantly summed up than by Alfred North Whitehead:

It is a profoundly erroneous truism, repeated by all copy-books and by eminent people making speeches, that we should cultivate the habit of thinking of what we are doing.

The precise opposite is the case. Civilization advances by extending the number of operations we can perform without thinking about them. Operations of thought are like cavalry charges in a battle—they are strictly limited in number, they require fresh horses, and they must only be made at decisive moments. (1911: 61)

One cannot help but think that Whitehead had his friend and colleague Bertrand Russell in mind—the Russell whose intellectual capacities discernibly declined after he spent five years in a library day after day working through the extremely abstract issues that were to form *Principia Mathematica*. Or perhaps Whitehead could sense a similar diminution in himself. But, whatever its source, Whitehead's point is correct, and has been the subject of extensive empirical confirmation in recent years.

It is not simply that conscious and intentional mental processing and its efflux in action is much slower and more difficult to perform than unconscious, automatic, processing and its behavioral results—although many writers have emphasized the impossibility of functioning effectively if conscious, controlled, and intentional mental processing had to deal with every aspect of life (Bateson 1972; Miller, Galanter, and Pribram 1960; Nørretranders 1998). In addition to being inefficient, conscious intentional processing, as a precursor to action, is costly. The cost of such processing has been amply demonstrated by Baumeister, Tice, and colleagues in a series of experiments on what they call ego depletion (Baumeister et al. 1998). Their experiments typically took a certain form. Subjects were asked to exert an act of control in one area—for example, not eating the chocolate cookies in front of them—and to then engage in another unrelated task—for example, trying to solve a particular puzzle. Baumeister et al. unearthed the following sorts of results:

1. Eating radishes instead of available chocolates made it more difficult to persist in attempting to solve unsolvable puzzles.
2. Making a choice between two options made it more difficult to persist in attempting to solve unsolvable puzzles.
3. Suppressing emotional responses to a movie made it more difficult to solve (solvable) anagrams.
4. Proofreading made it more difficult to take action (to stop watching a boring movie).
5. Suppressing emotional responses to a movie made it more difficult to squeeze a handgrip exerciser for a short time.
6. Suppressing thoughts (about white bears) made it more difficult to persist in attempting to solve unsolvable puzzles.
7. Suppressing thoughts (about white bears) made it more difficult to suppress signs of amusement while watching a comedy tape.

The phenomenon of ego depletion is an altogether unsurprising one. In fact, it's merely a formalization of something that will be all too familiar to most of us: thinking is hard! Or, more generally, conscious, intentional processing is hard, and is not the sort of thing you want to be doing willy-nilly. If you have to employ such resources in one problem domain, then you have less left over for other domains. Cavalry charges, indeed.

Intentional mental processing, of the sort involved in action, is both inefficient and costly; and presumably should be employed only when there is no other option. More difficult, however, is working out when there is and when there is not another option. One type of behavior that might be thought to require intentional mental processing is behavior that one organism has learned from another. Social learning, one might be tempted to suppose, is the result of conscious, intentional, processing. That is, learning behavior from another, seems, prima facie, to require an understanding of what they are doing, perhaps even an understanding of the intentions behind what they are doing.

However, although this understanding of social learning may be true for some cases, for the vast majority of cases it is simply false. Social learning, in general, does not work this way at all.

6   The Mechanisms of Social Learning

There are several varieties of social learning pertinent to the concerns of this book. Unfortunately, these are not always properly distinguished. The following fourfold distinction is now common coin in the field of cognitive ethology, in particular primatology, and it will be useful to begin here.

Stimulus enhancement   Stimulus enhancement is the tendency to pay attention to, or aim responses toward, a particular place or object in the environment after observing a conspecific's actions at that place or toward that object (Byrne and Russon 1998). As a result of this narrowing of behavioral focus, the individual's subsequent behavior becomes concentrated on these key variables. And this will increase the chances of the animal gaining the same reward as its conspecific, often by performing the same actions.

For example, suppose a monkey observes another monkey eating under a coconut tree. In virtue of this—and in this case, in virtue of the perceived reward—the observing monkey might focus its own attention on the large nuts on the ground under the tree. It begins to experiment with the coconuts, and eventually discovers how to crack them open—for example, by smashing them against an adjacent rock. In cracking open the coconuts, the observing monkey may end up using the same technique as the observed monkey. But what is crucial in making this a case of stimulus enhancement is that the observing monkey did not learn this technique by observing the first monkey. Rather, the technique was learned by individual trial and error. The contribution of the observed monkey consisted solely in narrowing down the observing monkey's field of exploratory activity.

Emulation   In emulation, an individual learns the affordances of objects disclosed by another individual's actions upon them (Tomasello 1990). Thus, if the monkey sees a coconut smashed against a rock, breaking to disclose edible flesh, then by stimulus enhancement she may focus her subsequent behavior in the region below the coconut tree, and by emulation she may now know certain affordances of the coconut—that it is brittle, and so affords breaking in certain ways, and that, once broken, it affords eating. It is common to distinguish emulation from true imitation (ibid.). In imitation, it is the action itself (e.g., smashing the coconut against the rock) that is learned. In emulation, it is the affordances of the objects that are discovered. This discovery may, of course, lead the monkey to go on and perform the same actions as the first—since smashing against a rock is a good way of dealing with a combination of brittleness and edibility. But, what makes it a case of emulation is that the monkey ends up performing these actions not through observing the first monkey performing those actions, but through learning the affordances revealed by that monkey's actions.

Response facilitation   Suppose that our observant monkey does replicate the behavior of the first monkey—that is, she smashes the coconut against the rock. Suppose, in addition, she does this because she saw the first monkey do it. This still does not, necessarily, qualify as imitation. It will not be imitation if the observing monkey already possesses this particular type of behavior in her repertoire. In the same way that one stimulus may be enhanced over another, increasing the probability that the individual would interact with it, or direct its exploratory searches toward it, so too may one type of response be enhanced over another by seeing it done. This phenomenon is known as response facilitation. This response facilitation is distinguished from imitation because the latter is seen to involve the acquisition of new behavioral traits or abilities, and not simply the facilitation—or priming—of behavioral traits or abilities already possessed.

Imitation   The core idea of imitation is still, perhaps, best captured by Thorndike's (1898) definition: "learning to do an act from seeing it done." Learning through observation is central to the concept. For a true case of imitation, our monkey must acquire the behavioral trait through watching the other monkey. That is, the monkey smashes the coconut against the rock because it saw the other monkey do this, and (presumably) because it realizes what it stands to gain from doing this.

At one time, imitation was regarded as, in effect, a likely sign of a lack of intelligence. Imitation was a cheap trick that allowed nonhuman species to simulate intellectual capacities they did not really have. The fourfold differentiation of stimulus enhancement, emulation, response facilitation, and imitation has facilitated a sea change in attitudes. The key to this is that stimulus enhancement, emulation, and response facilitation can all be regarded as instances of priming—a phenomenon that is familiar, well understood, and has broad application in psychological theorizing quite independently of mechanisms of social learning—and imitation cannot be thus explained (Byrne and Russon 1998). Thus, from cheap parlor trick, imitation has now been elevated to a hallmark of true intelligence.

However, this issue is clouded by the fact that the fourfold differentiation of stimulus enhancement, emulation, response facilitation, and imitation is often not adhered to—indeed sometimes seems to find no echo at all—in other cognate fields. Thus, in cognitive psychology, as opposed to ethology, one can find in the literature a wealth of well-known, and deservedly influential, experiments investigating the mechanics of imitation—all of which presuppose that imitation is a form of priming. This is because such experiments run together, at the very least, imitation (in the new strict sense) and response facilitation. This makes the waters rather murky, and care must be taken in navigating one's way around them. I shall draw attention to this issue again at appropriate junctures.

In the new, strict, sense of imitation, it has been remarkably difficult to demonstrate imitation in nonhuman animals. Any putative instance of imitation typically finds itself ripe for reinterpretation as a case of stimulus enhancement, emulation, or response facilitation. And since these can all be interpreted as cases of priming, these sorts of reinterpretation find themselves ahead on points, at least on the Lloyd Morgan system of scoring. Until very recently, those who regarded the capacity for imitation (in this strict sense) as exclusively human had the upper hand. For example, in 1993, Tomasello, Kruger, and Ratner argued that there exists no evidence of imitative learning in nonhuman animals. On the basis of this they proposed that it is the understanding of behavior as intentional that distinguishes human social learning from social learning in other species.

Such skepticism, however, now seems wrong on two counts. First, consensus is now emerging, or at least beginning to emerge, that shows imitation, in this strict sense, to be possible in the great apes (Whiten, Horner, and Marshall-Pescini 2004), in dolphins (Herman 2002), and in birds such as parrots (Pepperburg 1999, 2002, 2004) and others (Hunt and Gray 2003; Akins and Zentall 1996, 1998; Akins, Klein, and Zentall 2002).

Second, and perhaps more important, the claim that imitation requires an understanding of behavior as intentional is almost certainly false. Imitation can proceed on the basis of an understanding of behavior as intentional—but it does not necessarily do so. Indeed, it does not even usually do so.

7   Imitation without Intention?

In discussing the relation between imitation and intention, two issues must be distinguished:

1. To what extent is the capacity for imitation independent of the intentional actions of the imitator? That is, does the capacity for imitation, in any particular instance, require intentional action on the part of the imitating animal?
2. To what extent is the capacity for imitation independent of an understanding of the intentions with which the imitated animal performs the behavior that is to be imitated?

With the second issue, we are concerned with the presence, in the imitating animal, of a second-order intentional state—a state about the first-order intentional states of another, namely, an understanding of another's intentions. In the first issue, we are concerned with the presence, in the imitating animal, of intentional states, of any sort, that could provide the basis of the animal's performance of intentional imitative actions. I shall begin with the first, more general, issue.

Generally speaking, with regard to the possession of intentional states (of any order) on the part of the imitated animal, consensus converges around an already familiar picture: islands of intention in a sea of preintentional and subintentional processing. There is a huge body of experimental work all pointing to the claim that the vast majority of imitation is the result of processing that is unconscious, unintentional, and, in at least one sense of this term, automatic.

The underlying rationale for much of this work is to be found in Berkowitz (1984, 1997), who postulated that a tight perception-behavior sequence underlies so-called media effects on behavior. Thus, on his account, when one perceives the aggressive behavior of an actor in a movie or television show, this perception activates, in an entirely unconscious and unintentional way, one's own behavioral representations of aggressiveness, thereby increasing the likelihood of one exhibiting aggressive behavior. Carver et al. (1983) experimentally tested this hypothesis. In their experiment, some of the subjects—but not others—were exposed to (primed with) hostility-related words. This took the form of a "language experiment." Then, in what they were told was an entirely unrelated experiment, the subjects were put in the role of the "teacher" in a Milgram-style shock experiment. Those who had been primed with hostility-related stimuli subsequently gave longer shocks to the learner than did the control subjects.

These experiments were followed up and extended by Bargh, Chen, and Burrows (1996). In one experiment, subjects were first primed with words related to either rudeness (e.g., rude, impolite, obnoxious), politeness (e.g., respect, considerate, polite), or neither (in the control group) in an initial "language experiment." Having been told there was a further experimental task to be conducted, they were then given the opportunity to interrupt an ongoing conversation between experimenters to ask for the promised task. Significantly more participants in the "rude" priming condition interrupted (67%) than did those in the control condition (38%), whereas only 16 percent of those primed with "polite" interrupted the conversation.

A second experiment extended these findings to stereotype activation. In a first task, participants were primed (in the course of an ostensible language test) either with words related to the stereotype of the elderly (e.g., Florida, sentimental, wrinkle) or with words unrelated to the stereotype. Participants primed with elderly related material subsequently behaved in line with the stereotype—specifically, they walked more slowly down the hallway after leaving the experiment. Dijksterhuis, Bargh, and Miedema (2000) showed that these effects also hold for another central feature of the elderly stereotype—forgetfulness. Those participants whose stereotype for the elderly had been activated in the "first experiment" could not remember as many features of the room in which that experiment was conducted as could control participants. Incredibly, such priming effects also seem to extend to capacities such as intelligence. Subjects primed with words associated with intelligence, such as "college professor," perform better than control participants on a subsequent, and ostensibly unrelated, general knowledge test, and subjects primed with words associated with lack of intelligence, such as "soccer hooligan" or "supermodel," perform worse than control participants (Dijksterhuis and van Knippenburg 1998; Dijksterhuis 2004).

Such priming results are very robust. That is, they hold (i) across a wide variety of primes, both verbal and visual, (ii) across dozens of different stereotypes and general traits, and (iii) using a range of different priming methods—when primes are presented subliminally as well as when participants are conscious of them. Whether subjects are conscious of the primes or not, they are always unaware of any influence or correlation between the primes and their behavior. These results show what Dijksterhuis calls high-road imitation: exposure to traits and stereotypes elicits general patterns of behavior and attitudes, and influences the ways in which behavior is performed in a variety of contexts. These influences are rapid, automatic, and unconscious, they apply to both ends and means, and they do not depend on the subject's intentions or volitions. Indeed, they do not even depend on the subject having an independent goal that would rationalize their primed behavior. Imitation, in this broad sense, Dijksterhuis argues, is our default social behavior. Just thinking about or perceiving a certain kind of action automatically increases, in ways of which we are unaware, the likelihood of engaging in that type of behavior.

Conscious and intentional imitation, of course, can and does occur. But it is the small tip of a very large iceberg. Why is most imitation like this? Unconscious, unintentional, and automatic? The answer seems to be that it is this way because it is so important—far too important to be left hostage to the vagaries of consciousness and intention. Chartrand and Bargh (1999) tested the idea that this sort of high-road imitation has a social function. The experiment comes in two stages. Subjects are required to work on a task along with two confederates. The subjects believe the confederates to be fellow participants, but, in fact, they are colluding with the experimenters. In each session, the subject and confederate sat at right angles to each other and worked on a task that ostensibly involves developing a new projective task based on photographs. This task was chosen to minimize the risk of the subject forming a goal with respect to the confederate—for example, to become friends or form some other sort of relationship with them. Thus, the nature of the task is such that it requires the subjects to look mostly down at the photographs being discussed, thus minimizing eye contact. In session 1, the confederate either rubbed his or her face or shook his or her foot, and in session 2 the confederate performed whichever mannerism the first confederate did not do. The results showed that participants rubbed their face more times in the presence of the face-rubbing confederate than with the foot-shaking confederate and shook their foot more times with the foot-shaking confederate than with the face-rubbing confederate. No one had any awareness of engaging in these behaviors when asked at the end of the experiment. This is an example of what Chartrand and Bargh (1999) refer to as the chameleon effect. In a chameleon-like way, the subjects' behavior automatically changes as a function of their partners' behavior.

So far we merely have another example of the unconscious, unintentional, and automatic etiology of much of our imitative behavior. To test the function of this type of etiology, Chartrand and Bargh (1999) varied the experiment. As before, each subject worked with a partner—again, unbeknownst to them, a confederate—on the photograph-projective test. But this time it was the confederate who deliberately attempted to mimic the mannerisms and body posture of the participants without, of course, being too obvious about it. Upon completion of the task, subjects were questioned over their attitudes to the confederate/partner—specifically, how much they liked the confederate and how smoothly they thought the interaction had gone. Relative to those in the control condition, subjects whose mannerisms and posture had been mimicked found the confederate to be more likeable and reported that their interaction had gone more smoothly.

The explanation of the automatic, unconscious, and unintentional nature of most imitation, then, lies in two claims: (1) that imitation has the important social function of making other people like you and facilitating social interactions more generally, and (2) it would be inappropriate to cede this function to the vagaries of conscious, intentional, control. Social facilitation might not be quite up there with a beating heart in terms of importance, but it is not too far off. Ceding the beating of one's heart to conscious, intentional control would be inefficient for a variety of reasons. Most obviously, it is costly—it would be difficult to do much else if one had to concentrate on making one's heart beat roughly every second. And then, of course, any lapse of concentration on your part could have rather unfortunate effects. Similarly, if one had to always concentrate on mimicking one's conspecifics, one would have very little time to consciously and intentionally do anything else. And repeated lapses of concentration or endeavor on your part might have the rather unfortunate consequence of your social exclusion.

Whether or not this sort of explanation of the unconscious and unintentional character of our imitative tendencies is correct, one thing is clear: imitative tendencies of the sort described above are predominantly unconscious and unintentional (as opposed to nonintentional). And so, with

regard to the first issue—to what extent is the capacity for imitation independent of the intentions of the imitator—the answer seems to be that, in
general, the capacity is independent of the imitator's intentions. Imitative
behavior, in the sense employed in these experiments, is preintentional in
the sense defined in chapter 6. The behaviors in question are not at all like
O'Shaughnessy's subintentional tongue-waggling. On the contrary, they
are done for a reason that the agent would endorse if aware of it—getting
other people to like you, for example, is generally a useful thing to accomplish—but this reason is not sufficient to individuate the deed in question.
Many such deeds can, and even in these restricted contexts typically do,
facilitate this general antecedent intention.

These experiments also allow us to make headway on the second issue:
the extent to which imitation relies on an understanding of the intentions
of the imitated. Consider Chartrand and Bargh's (1999) second experiment. The sorts of behavior that the confederate sets out to mimic—
postures, mannerisms, and so on—are not intentional actions at all. They
are, in O'Shaughnessy's sense, subintentional acts. They are not performed
with any intention, and, indeed, are intentional under no description. So,
it can hardly be that the capacity to imitate these acts, in more natural set-
tings (i.e., outside the laboratory), requires an understanding of the intentions of the imitated person, because there are no such intentions.

In short, in the cases of imitation investigated in these experiments, the
imitative behavior consists in deeds, rather than intentional actions or
subintentional doings. However, the idea that the capacity for imitation
requires both intentional action on the part of the imitator and an understanding of the intentions of the imitated person or animal is going to
seem more appealing for complex, goal-directed, behavior. Indeed—and
here we return to the admonition made earlier—much of what is characterized, in these experiments, as imitative behavior does not, in fact, qualify as imitation all. At least, it does not qualify as imitation in the strict
sense imported from cognitive ethology. In the Chartrand and Bargh
(1999) experiments, for example, imitating bodily postures or mannerisms
scarcely involves the acquisition of new behavioral traits or abilities—it
simply involves the deployment of traits and abilities already possessed. In
other words, it is an example of response facilitation, rather than imitation
in the strict sense. Indeed, the divergence of the sense of "imitation"
employed in these experiments from the strict sense is exhibited in the fact
that these experiments all, in one way or another, involve the phenomenon of priming—and imitation in the strict sense, it is argued, cannot be
explained in terms of priming (Byrne and Russon 1998).

This being so, it might be thought that the connection between imitation and intention is at its tightest when we are dealing with behavior that is more complex than the simple types of behavior deployed in these experiments. For as the complexity of the newly acquired behavior increases, so the likelihood of explaining this behavior as a form of priming decreases. Beyond a sufficient level of complexity, one might think, acquiring new behavior by way of imitation requires both intentional action and an understanding of the intentions of the imitated animal.

However, in fact, even here the claim that imitation requires intentional action is not, in general, true. The reason is that complex, goal-directed behavior has a structure. Specifically, it has combinatorial structure. And it is sensitivity to this structure, a sensitivity that can be explained independently of the possession of intentional states on the part of the imitator, and independently of an understanding of the intentions of the imitated—that underwrites the ability to imitate. It is to this crucial issue that we now turn.

8   The Structure of Behavior

It is widely accepted that a certain sort of combinatorial structure pervades animal behavior in general, and skilled action in particular. As long ago as 1951, Karl Lashley argued that the apparent seamlessness and linear serial order of behavior concealed an underlying hierarchical structure (he thought this structure rendered stimulus-response models inadequate). More recently, Dawkins (1976) has proposed that hierarchical structure is pivotal to an understanding of the evolution of behavior. His case is based on two arguments:

1. An argument from analogy—specifically, an analogy with many other cases in developmental and neural biology.
2. An argument from efficiency. Hierarchical organizations of control are easier to repair when they fail, allow the economy of multiple access to common subroutines, and combine efficient local action at low hierarchical levels while maintaining the guidance of an overall structure.

For human behavior in particular, it has long been argued that hierarchical structuring is essential for many acquired skills, such as language production, problem solving, and everyday planning (Chomsky 1957; Newell, Shaw, and Simon 1958; Miller, Galanter, and Pribram 1960; Newell and Simon 1972). Thus, in general, the idea that behavior possesses a form of combinatorial structure has been with us for some time.

Typically, the type of organization is both modular and hierarchical. An apparently seamless string of behavior employed to achieve a certain goal can, typically, be parsed into a sequence of discrete modules, each of which can be iterated until the successful completion of the relevant subgoals. The hierarchical organization of the modules, then, ensures that subgoals are organized in such a way that they will culminate in the overall goal.

To see how this works, consider Richard Byrne's study of imitation in mountain gorillas (Byrne 2002, 2003, 2005; Byrne and Russon 1998). Mountain gorillas, *Gorilla g. beringei*, circumvent the almost entire absence of fruit in their habitat by exploiting various forms of herbaceous vegetation. Typically, however, such vegetation is defended by certain adaptations that reduce palatability—nettles, spines, hooks, and so on. So, the gorillas must develop certain techniques to undermine these defenses. These techniques involve several discrete stages of processing—modules— and within each module manual actions are organized into mechanically efficient combinations. The overall organization is hierarchical, with subroutines used iteratively at some stages.

It is overwhelmingly likely that these techniques are acquired through imitation. The techniques are remarkably standardized within local populations even though they are massively underdetermined by the nature of the task at hand. This makes it unlikely that the techniques would have been discovered by individual trial-and-error learning (stimulus enhancement or emulation rather than imitation). Indeed, even in the case of severe maiming in infancy—a not uncommon consequence of young apes' tendency to explore snares set for other creatures—the affected individuals nevertheless acquire a normal technique, that of their mothers, rather than devise a novel method better suited to their altered condition (Stokes and Byrne 2001; Byrne and Stokes 2002). There is, on the other hand, no serious possibility that these techniques are genetically transmitted. Techniques were developed to deal with certain types of herbs, and these are typically restricted to a limited altitudinal zone on just a few mountains. The result is that the techniques are localized in a way that precludes genetic explanations. Thus, in the absence of a genetic explanation, the high consistency of technique, coupled with the underdetermination of technique by task, strongly suggests that these techniques are acquired through imitation.

According to Byrne, the required imitation is made possible by the hierarchical organization of the behavior. Apparently smooth streams of bodily movement in fact possess recombinant structure. The problem of finding recombinant units within such streams parallels the problem of finding lexical items in the apparently continuous acoustic stream of speech. In both cases, the key is the ability to *parse* the stimulus into units and then identify the higher-order structural relations between those units. And the key to identifying such structure is the ability to detect statistical regularities in the stimulus. Thus, in the case of human language, there is strong evidence that human babies as young as eight months are able to detect statistical regularities in spoken strings of nonsense words (Saffran, Aslin, and Newport 1996). It is this sort of sensitivity to statistical regularities embodied in repeated offerings that underlies the capacity for imitation in general. The process can be broken down into two components.

1 The detection of lexical elements The first requirement is the ability to segment apparently seamless streams of action into building blocks, the analogues of lexical items. What is crucial here is that each block should *already* be within the repertoire of the observer. In one circumstance, a particular movement of a single finger might be seen as basic; but in another, it might be an elaborate sequence of bimanual movements that is taken as basic. What determines the *lexical* status of a sequence of behavior is not size or complexity but antecedent familiarity on the part of the observer. Typically, however, such lexical items will comprise fairly simple, goal-directed, movements.

The neural basis of sensitivity to such movements is, probably, provided by the mirror-neuron system, since this responds precisely to this class of actions (Gallese et al., 1996; Rizzolatti, Fadiga, and Gallese 2002; Iacaboni 2004). The principal feature of mirror neurons is that they fire both when a certain type of action is performed but also when another agent is observed performing the same type of action. That is, mirror neurons are sensitive both to others' actions and to equivalent actions of one's own; they are, thus, insensitive to the difference between one's own action and similar actions by others. For example, certain cells fire when a monkey sees the experimenter bring food to her own mouth with her own hand, *or* when the monkey brings food to his own mouth. The correspondence is not just visual: hearing an expression of anger increases the activation of muscles used to express anger (Gallese 2004; Iacoboni 2004).

Mirror neurons afford the detection of simple, goal-directed, movements in the monkey's own repertoire, whether the movement is performed by the monkey itself or by another monkey that it is watching. It is speculated that the primary function of such neurons is to reveal the demeanor and likely future actions of conspecifics. Whether or not this is true does not matter for our purposes. What is important is that mirror neurons provide a plausible neural basis for our ability to detect lexical elements in a stream of behavior.

2   The detection of recombinant structure   The detection of lexical elements is, of course, only the beginning. The next stage is to identify the recombinant structure that links these lexical items together. This structure will not be evident from the observation of a single performance. However, the observation of repeated performances will reveal certain statistical regularities, ones that reveal the organizational structure that underlies them. To see how this works, consider Byrne's analysis of an infant gorilla learning about nettle processing.

Unweaned gorillas spend a great deal of their time within a few feet of their mothers. Young gorillas first begin to process nettle leaves at around two years, largely because the stinging hairs discourage earlier attempts. So, by this time, they will have watched many hundreds of plants being processed expertly by the mother. Suppose the infant is antecedently familiar with each lexical item in the mother's stream of behavior (that is, suppose a mirror neuron exists for each element). They can then use their familiarity with these elements to mediate their repeated observations of their mother's behavior.

First, although each execution of the process will differ slightly from every other, the starting point is always the same—a growing, intact, nettle stem—and the final stage is always the same—popping a neatly folded package of nettle leaves into the mouth. With repeated observations, other regularities begin to emerge. The mother always makes a sweeping movement of one hand, held around a nettle stem that is sometimes held in the other hand, even though the nettle is still in the ground. And the result of this latter operation is a leafless stem protruding from the ground. She always makes a twisting movement of her hands against each other, and, following this, always drops several leaf-petioles onto the ground. She always uses one hand to fold a bundle of leaf-blades being held in the other hand, and always holds down this folded bundle with her thumb (Byrne 2003: 533). Moreover, these operations always occur in the same order: the order in which they are outlined above. These statistical regularities, therefore, serve to distinguish the essential components of the behavioral sequence from the many other inessential actions that occur during the nettle eating but that are not crucial to success.

Other statistical regularities reveal the modular and hierarchical organization of the behavior. Whenever the operation of removing debris is performed—by opening the hand that holds the nettle-leaf-blades and picking out debris with the other hand—it occurs at the same place in the string. Also, on some, but not all, occasions, a behavior sequence is iterated several times until a successful subgoal has been achieved. For example, the process of stripping leaves from a nettle's stem in a bimanually coordinated movement, then detaching and dropping the leaf-petioles, may be repeated several times before the mother proceeds to remove debris and fold the leaf-blades (Byrne 2003: 533–534).

Thus, in general, the underlying hierarchical structure of behavior leaves an observable trace in the form of certain types of statistical regularities. These include:

Interruptibility   The elements within modules are tightly bound together, as a result of their practiced and frequent cooccurrence. At the junction between modules, however, the link is weaker. Thus, interruptions at junctions will permit smooth resumption. Interruptions within a module will force the animal to start again, either at the beginning of the module or even of the entire program.

Omission   Behavioral elements that are unnecessary can be omitted, on the basis of local contingencies. Opening the hand to enable the removal of inedible debris is only done if there is indeed such debris. So, in iterated strings, certain sections will occur in some strings but not others. This gives further evidence of underlying modular structure. For example, observing numerous instances of the behavioral sequence A, B, C, D, E, F and also numerous instances of the sequence A, B, E, F carries the information that A and B are located within one module, and that C and D and E and F are located in distinct modules, and that there exist modular junctions between B and C and between D and E.

Repetition   Modules, used as subroutines in a hierarchical organization, may be employed iteratively until some criterion is reached, and repeated loops around a subroutine yield information about a distinctive sequence of modular elements. For example, numerous observations of the behavioral sequence A, B, C, B, C, B, C, D, E signals that B and C are located within the same module.

Natural end points and starts   In many cases, planned behavior leads to an observable conclusion or stopping point—for example, eating the nettles. In some cases, the proper start to a sequence might also be visible in behavior—for example, the grasping of a nettle visibly protruding from the ground—especially if no other activity occurred immediately beforehand.

Invariant elements   In nonessential ways, every execution of a token behavioral sequence is slightly different. However, there are certain characteristics that will always occur, in regular positions, in every string of elements leading to the same outcome, and that this is so can be revealed through repeated observation. These behavioral items are thereby revealed as necessary to the overall behavioral sequence; and the remainder, by default, are revealed as inessential. In this way, repeated observations of token behavioral sequences that lead to a common outcome can afford identification of the necessary and contingent elements of that behavioral sequence type.

Generativity   A behavioral subroutine may be used in more than one behavioral sequence. And an overall behavioral sequence may be used as a subroutine in a larger sequence. Once some behavioral strings have been identified as forming discrete modules, then these patterns can be picked out in as yet unparsed strings of elements.

As this overview should make clear, the claim that behavior has combinatorial structure is not, ultimately a controversial one. It is this structure that allows us to explain the ability of organisms to engage in imitation of complex behavior, indeed of anything other than the simplest motor responses, without supposing that this ability is underwritten by rich intentional capacities. This imitation requires not simply serial copying of action but, as Byrne puts it, *program-level imitation*. Attempting detail-by-detail duplication of precisely observed acts would seldom be a good way of acquiring an efficient technique. The perspective transformations that would be needed for an exact copying of finger movements, for example, would mean that this would inevitably be a slow and difficult process. The alternative of letting individual trial and error take care of each part of the process, and coupling this with imitation at the levels of program—or hierarchical structure—is far more efficient. So, imitation of complex behavior requires that the behavior possess recombinant structure. Thus, as one might imagine, the claim that behavior has recombinant structure has assumed the mantle of orthodoxy in fields such as cognitive ethology, primatology, and cognate disciplines.

  This structure is also what binds together many of the other core components of representation. It is because complex behavior has a structure that it can be imitated. But imitation is one form of social learning, and, as such, it supplies a behavioral sequence with a history or etiology. Thus, a token hierarchically structured sequence of behavior involved in the processing of nettles for food is employed by a particular mountain gorilla today because it was employed by another (or, indeed, the same) mountain gorilla in the past, and, when employed in the past it performed a certain function—that is, enabled the gorilla to achieve certain ends—and it is its performing this function in the past that explains why it is being performed on the present occasion. But in virtue of having a history in this sense, a behavioral item can also possess a proper function. And, as we have seen, the concept of proper function lies at the heart of representation, not only because it is crucial in itself, but also because it allows us to explain other features such as misrepresentation and decouplability. The recombinant structure of behavior is, therefore, the cement in which many of the other representational features of deeds are embedded. Structure, learning, history, and function are all connected in a tight circle that forms the basis of the representational status of deeds.

11   Representation in Action

1   Putting It All Together

The arguments developed in chapters 7 through 10 have been concerned, in effect, with providing an *existence proof* for the thesis of representation in action. That is, they have tried to show that there are at least some deeds that can satisfy all the relevant conditions of, or constraints on, representation: they carry information about items extrinsic to them; they have the function of tracking such items, or enabling an organism to accomplish some task in virtue of tracking such items; they are, in the relevant sense, decouplable from the items they track, and can misrepresent those items; they have combinatorial structure, of an iconic if not semantic form.

The argument has, of necessity, been theoretical. The thesis of representation in action is a counterintuitive one, and it is on the high and slippery slopes of theory that the battle must be predominantly fought. However, it is now time to put the arguments into practice. Accordingly, this final chapter examines a concrete case of deeds that are centrally involved in the visual representation of the world: the scan paths that subjects employ in accomplishing visual tasks. I shall argue that the same general principles we have identified in chapters 7 through 10 apply in this case also. Therefore, scan paths qualify as representational items, and do so for the same reasons as the internal configurations involved in vision.

2   The Yarbus Experiments

In a famous series of experiments, Yarbus (1967) asked subjects, prior to their viewing of a painting, to perform certain tasks. The painting showed six women and the arrival of a male visitor. Subjects were asked to either:

1. View the picture at will.
2. Judge the age of the people in the painting.
3. Guess what the people had been doing prior to the arrival of the visitor.
4. Remember the clothing worn.
5. Remember the position of objects in the room.
6. Estimate how long it had been since the visitor was seen by the people in the painting.

Yarbus demonstrated that the required task impacted on the visual scan path that the subject took: different tasks resulted in quite different visual scan paths. Subjects who were asked questions concerning the appearance of people in the painting—for example, questions about their ages—focused on the area around the face. Subjects who were asked questions concerning the theme of the painting focused on various points throughout the picture. Subjects asked to guess what the people were doing before the visitor arrived employed a different scan path from those asked to estimate how long it had been since the visitor was last seen by the family. In general, Yarbus showed, the scan varies systematically with the nature of the task.

The usual interpretation of this phenomenon is in terms of hypothesis formation and testing. A specific hypothesis is "planted" in the brain, and this leads to or directs the subject to focus on certain features. The eye brings the feature under the scope of foveation, sends a signal to the brain, and the brain analyzes the information in terms of the hypothesis. The process is repeated until enough information has been obtained to confirm or disconfirm the hypothesis.

There is nothing wrong with this explanation. But it is a little crude for our purposes. In particular, it slides over a crucial distinction between *task-driven* and *intention-driven* activity.

3   Task-driven versus Intention-driven Behavior

The types of eye movements at work in the phenomena elicited by Yarbus are, of course, *saccadic* movements. Studies consistently emphasize the role played by *attention* in controlling such movements. Saccadic movements, it seems likely, are always preceded by a shift of visual attention to the location where the shift terminates (Yantis 1996). The converse dependency does not hold: it is possible to shift visual attention without moving the eyes (Helmholtz 1909). Nonetheless, it is generally accepted that attention serves as a guide for saccadic eye movements.

However, in this context, the concept of attention is not a straightforward one, and vacillates between an intentional and nonintentional sense. As Yarbus has demonstrated, when viewing a piece of art, the visual scanning that takes place is not merely random jumping and pausing, but forms a clearly identifiable path that is related to the nature of the task at hand. Clearly intentions play a role in determining the trajectory of this path. One's eye movements will be directed toward specific features, based on what you are looking for. If you want to determine the ages of the people in the painting, then of course you will concentrate on the area of the face, since this is where most of the relevant information required to make this determination is contained. This focus on the face is intentional; it is performed with the intention of achieving a given goal. This behavior is a species of action in the strict and traditional sense identified in chapter 6. However, it is generally accepted that in conjunction with this intentional action, one's peripheral vision is constantly seeking out potentially interesting contextual features of the picture, similar to the way one might skip ahead a few lines in a book to get to the good part. The eye movements, that is, have the function of seeking regions or areas of the picture that are rich in information relevant to the task one is performing (Gould 1967; Loftus 1972).

This latter movement, it is important to realize, is *not* intention driven. This is for at least two reasons. First, the saccadic eye movements one is performing in this sort of search-and-locate mission can scarcely be intentional (i.e., performed with intention) since we have no idea what they are, the trajectory they are following, or the fact that we are performing them. One can scarcely intend to Φ if one has no idea what Φ is, and no idea that one is Φ-ing when one is in fact doing so. Second, although these exploratory saccadic movements are clearly related to one's intentional activity, and hence to one's intentions, these intentions are insufficient to individuate them as the movements they are. An array of exploratory saccadic movements can all serve, or help satisfy, the general antecedent intention of identifying information relevant to the task one is attempting to perform. The general antecedent intention is, accordingly, insufficient to discriminate between the distinct items in this array.

Therefore, the exploratory saccades involved in seeking out information relevant to the task one is (intentionally) attempting to accomplish cannot be regarded as actions in the strict sense. Although they are done for a reason, this reason is insufficient to individuate them. However, neither can such movements be plausibly relegated to the status of the subintentional act—akin to O'Shaughnessy's random tongue-moving. They are performed precisely because one has a certain task one *intends* to fulfill, and these movements help with this fulfilling.

The exploratory eye saccades, thus, conform to a picture that has, by now, become familiar. They are not intentional actions because there exists no intention that could serve to individuate them. But they are performed for a reason that the agent would endorse if he were to become aware of the acts and how they subserve his or her general antecedent intention to perform or accomplish a given task. The exploratory saccades are, in other words, preintentional acts. They are deeds. Rather than being intention driven, these deeds are *task driven*: the specific trajectory of the exploratory scan path is driven by the nature of the task at hand, and the type of information that must be accessed to accomplish that task. Thus, although attention clearly does play a crucial role in driving the particular scan path, it can do so only because the concept of attention is, in effect, ambiguous between an intention-driven and a task-driven phenomenon. In any act of search-and-locate activity involved in a visual task, the scan path is both intention driven and task driven. And the task-driven aspects of the scan path consist in deeds rather than actions. Thus, in the movements of the eye involved in accomplishing visual tasks, we find the same combination of intentional action and preintentional deeds that characterizes intelligent activity in general.

4 "Keep Your Eye on the Ball"

There is at least one sense in which the situations studied by Yarbus are artificial. Solving the Yarbus problems requires a level of intellectualization that is entirely absent from many—almost certainly most—of the visual tasks we commonly perform in day-to-day life. Identifying the ages of the people in the painting, guessing what the people had been doing prior to the arrival of the visitor, working out how long it had been since the people in the painting had last seen the visitor—these are all examples of highly intellectual activities. And as highly intellectual activities, intention plays a relatively prominent role in their genesis and explanation. Therefore, the result of undue focus on Yarbus-type cases, I think, is a tendency to overemphasize the extent to which visual, and visuomotor, tasks are intention driven.

As a useful antidote to this tendency let us return to our old friend—cricket. This time, however, our focus is not on how a fielder catches the ball, but on how a batsman hits it. Looking in the right place at the right time is, of course, crucial. But what, precisely, constitutes looking in the right place at the right time is less transparent than one might initially have thought. The old adage, found in just about every book on the subject, and passed down from countless coaches to their charges, is "keep your eye on the ball." However, as Land and Macleod (2000) have shown, in a seminal study, when facing fast bowlers, this adage is something that batsman neither *do* nor, indeed, *can* obey. Instead, they adopt a distinct eye-movement strategy; one that allows them to view the ball at crucial stages during its flight.

First, consider the visuomotor problem. The ball leaves the bowler's hand with a forward velocity v_0 and a downward velocity u_0. It hits the ground at distance x_1 from the batsman after time t_0. It then bounces upward, and reaches him at a height y at a time t_1 after the bounce. The values of y and t_1 are determined by the horizontal and vertical velocities of the ball after bouncing, v_1 and u_1, and by x_1. A fast bowler produces an x_1 between 0 and 10 meters, depending on the value of v_0 when he releases the ball. The corresponding values of y vary from 0 to 2 meters depending on the velocity of the ball, the hardness of the ball (they get softer as they get older), and the hardness of the ground. The estimation of y and t_1 from information provided by the approaching ball is a difficult problem for the batsman because of the required reaction time. Because of the weight of the bat, it takes around 200 ms for even an expert batsman to adjust his shot on the basis of novel visual information. Therefore, his judgment of y and t_1 must be essentially predictive, based on information available at least 200 ms before the ball reaches him. With a fairly average fast bowler, the ball takes around 600 ms to reach the batsman, and very quick bowlers such as Shoiab Akhtar and Brett Lee can reduce this window to not much more than 500 ms. So, the batsman must select an appropriate trajectory for his bat based on information from the first 300–400 ms of the ball's flight.

Traditionally, views on how the batsman acquired the necessary information were based on direct visual measurements such as image expansion and the rate of change of binocular disparity. But it is now generally accepted that such approaches do not work. To begin with, given the batsman's reaction time, judgments using such factors would have to be made when the ball's image and rate of expansion were very small, which would make the possibility of obtaining millisecond accuracy from such measurements very unlikely. Moreover, the precise determination of arrival time from image expansion requires that the object approach the eye directly, and at a constant velocity. Cricket balls, however, change speed when they bounce, decelerate as they approach the batsman, and travel in an arc rather than directly approaching the eye. So, it is unlikely that image expansion and the rate of binocular disparity can furnish the batsman with the information required to judge the ball-arrival time to within a few milliseconds. Most tellingly, as Land and Macleod have shown, even if the other factors were somehow satisfied, the batsman's eyes are not positioned in such a way that image expansion and binocular disparity could constitute significant factors.

Land and MacLeod measured, by way of a head-mounted camera, the eye movements of three batsmen as they faced balls delivered from a bowling machine at a velocity of 25 meters per second. The camera recorded the view from the batsman's left eye, as well as the direction of the fovea's gaze. The three batsmen were of varying levels of ability. Mark was a professional cricketer, Charlie an accomplished amateur, and Richard an enthusiastic but distinctly unaccomplished amateur. The following results emerged:

1. Contrary to the old adage about keeping one's eye on the ball, batsmen facing fast bowlers do not keep their eye on the ball throughout its flight. Instead, they view it at crucial moments during its flight. First, they fixate on it at the point of delivery—the moment it is released from the bowler's hand. The gaze is stationary for a period after delivery as the ball drops from the field of view. Second, they then saccade to, and fixate on, the anticipated point where the ball will bounce, and the gaze is focused on this point for a period of about 200 ms after the bounce. This profile was common to all three batsmen. However, there were also clear individual differences.

2. Mark, the most accomplished batsman, showed more pursuit-tracking than Charlie or Richard. In effect, the transition of his gaze from point of delivery to bounce point was accomplished by a combination of saccade and pursuit-tracking. Thus, for good length balls, the saccade accounted for only 48+/−11 percent of Mark's total prebounce gaze change, compared to 69+/− 8 percent for Charlie and 77+/−12 percent for Richard. The differences between Mark and Charlie were significant, but those between Charlie and Richard far less so.

3. Richard, the least skilled batsman, was slower to respond to the appearance of the ball, taking at least 200 ms to initiate the prebounce saccade. Thus, the times to the midpoints of his saccades were consistently greater than those of the other players. Comparing Richard's responses to very short balls with those of Mark or Charlie, it seems that Richard was not anticipating the movement of the ball, and was waiting until it completed a large portion of its flight to the bounce point before starting the saccade. This "catch-up" saccadic behavior is expected of someone who has not

played cricket. With the medium-paced deliveries used here, Richard's technique was adequate because he was (just) in a position to see the bounce on all deliveries. However, with a faster bowler, Richard's response would have been inadequate (in Richard's case, the speed of the ball had to be restricted for safety reasons). If a ball bounced 200 ms after delivery, Richard's saccade would have been too late to enable him to see it—either because he would not have started his saccade at this point, or because the bounce would have occurred at midsaccade, during which saccadic suppression would briefly suspend vision. By contrast, even with the very short balls (those that bounce soonest after delivery), Mark and Charlie reached the bounce point 100 ms before the ball.

The general picture that emerges, then, looks something like this. Batsmen pick up some trajectory information during the first 100–150 ms of the ball's flight, as demonstrated by the different latencies of the first saccade. However, this information is ambiguous, because, to the batsman, a slow and short delivery will have the same initial downward angular velocity as a fast and long delivery. The information acquired during the first 100–150 ms, therefore, is almost certainly used to get gaze direction to the bounce point, where unambiguous information is available.

Specifically, the information available at the bounce point looks something like this (Land and MacLeod 2000: 1344). At the bounce point, batsmen can make two straightforward measurements: the declination, ϕ, of the bounce point relative to the horizontal, and the timing of the bounce relative to the instant of delivery. These measurements are related to the physical variables that determine y and t_1 (the height and time at which the ball reaches the bat). Working backward from the contact point, y at t_1 are uniquely specified by v_1 and u_1 (the horizontal and vertical velocities of the ball after the bounce), by x_1 (the distance of the bounce point from the batsman), and by a pair of constants relating to the hardness of the pitch and of the ball. But x_1 is available to the batsman; it is given by $B/\tan\phi$, where B is the height of the batsman's eye. The batsman, of course, has no direct knowledge of the prebounce velocities, v_0 and u_0. However, the position and time of the bounce, x_0 and t_0, are uniquely related to v_0 and u_0 via H, the height at which the bowler releases the ball. Thus, the prebounce velocities are mapped onto x_0, t_0, and H. And these variables are all available to the batsman. The distance between the release point and the batsman (the length of pitch = 18.5 m) minus x_1 specifies x_0, the distance of the bounce from the batsman. Measurements from the time of delivery to the bounce specifies t_0, the time at which the ball will reach the batsman.

H can be estimated from the Batsman's height B plus Ltanθ, where θ is the angle of the delivery point from the batsman's eye level.

Thus, two variables that the batsman can obtain immediately after the bounce (ϕ and t_0) map onto the prebounce ball velocities. These convert the postbounce velocities via two constants (k_1 and k_2) that, with x_1 (again measured from ϕ) determine the time and height of bat–ball contact. Thus a mapping exists from ϕ and t_0 onto y and t_1. The constants, k_1 and k_2 (hardness of wicket, hardness of ball), are acquired during the course of the innings. Thus, on a wicket of unknown hardness, batsmen will typically play defensively for a number of deliveries while they "get their eye in." These shots do not require an accurate judgment of the time or height at which the ball will reach the bat. After a suitable period, they then attempt shots that do require accurate estimates of these values. Thus, the function of the initial "playing in" period is, in effect, to make appropriate adjustments to the mappings. Computationally, this means changing the values of k_1 and k_2. Roughly, this will amount to multiplying all the points on each surface by an appropriate constant. Getting these adjustments right is likely to be a high-order skill, as shown by the amount of practice that even a top-class batsman needs when playing in a country with a different climate, and hence, on wickets with different properties.

After the bounce, all three batsmen were found to track the ball for up to 200 ms. *Prima facie*, this might seem to be unnecessary on the scheme proposed by Land and MacLeod. However, this overlooks certain additional factors. First, the adjustment in the weighting of k_1 and k_2 just described requires an evaluation of the postbounce behavior of the ball, which can be obtained by observing the rate of change of ϕ after the bounce. Second, the ball can, in fact, move laterally in unpredictable ways when it bounces, especially if it lands on the seam or hits a crack in the wicket. Batsmen need to watch for this and switch to a defensive stroke if necessary.

There is no suggestion, of course, that batsmen calculate these sorts of mappings each time they face a bowler. Rather, the mappings are acquired through years of practice ("training up," if you like). That is, the mappings are embodied in connection weights in the batsman's brain, weights that are slowly set, and adjusted, on the basis of many years of trial and error.

5   Saccadic Deeds

The sorts of saccadic movements employed by the batsman in solving the problem of where and when the ball is going to reach him can scarcely be thought of as intentional actions. Popular wisdom imparted to each new generation of batsmen, to "keep your eye on the ball," is advice that not only *is* not followed but, when the ball reaches an appropriate velocity, *cannot* be followed. And this seems to show that batsmen have, essentially, no idea what their eyes are doing when they track a ball. Certainly, those exbatsmen who reflect on what they did as batsmen have no idea what they, in fact, did as batsmen—at least, not with regard to the saccadic eye movements they employed. The claim that batsmen have no clear idea what their eyes are doing when they track the trajectory of a ball is, of course, plausible on independent grounds. Typically, in a broad-brush way, we do have a general idea of what our eyes are doing—we know which way they are pointing, whether they are stationary or moving, and so on. But, at a more fine-grained level, such awareness dissipates. We have no idea of the fine-grained saccadic movements employed in accomplishing visual, or visuomotor, tasks. The case of the batsman provides merely a striking example of this more general point. Such saccadic movements occur beneath the level of intention.

On the other hand, it would be implausible to relegate them to the status of subintentional acts or doings. They are not at all akin to, for example, O'Shaughnessy's random tongue-waggling. They are clearly performed because of a goal that the agent wants, and intends, to accomplish. The batsman intends to hit the ball. The eye saccades he performs in the process of doing so are performed precisely because they help fulfill this general antecedent intention. So, they are done for a reason that the batsman does or would endorse if he were acquainted with them and made aware of the ways in which they help satisfy his general antecedent intention. Their *status* as something that the batsman does, rather than something that happens to him derives from this connection with his goals and intentions. However, their *identity* as the particular events they are cannot be explained by way of this connection. As we have seen, there are several, distinct, saccades that help with the satisfaction of the general antecedent intention to hit the ball. Therefore, these saccades cannot be individuated by way of this intention.

In short, the best way of understanding the saccades the batsman employs in the course of hitting the ball is as *deeds*: events whose status as something the batsman does depends on their connection with a general antecedent intention—they are done for a reason that the batsman does or would endorse—but which cannot be individuated by way of this intention.

The same is true of the exploratory saccades employed in Yarbus-type situations—and this is so despite the fact that the tasks involved are more intellectualized than those involved in hitting a cricket ball. In being asked to determine how long it has been since the people in the painting last saw the visitor, for example, one might intentionally direct one's attention to the areas around the faces of those people. Such directing of attention might derive both its status and identity from its connection with an associated intention to direct one's attention in this way. Nevertheless, at a more fine-grained level, the exploratory eye saccades one employs in seeking out the relevant information are ones that occur entirely beneath the level of intention. In general, we have no idea of the existence or nature of these fine-grained saccadic movements. And one cannot intend that p if one has no idea of the existence or nature of p. Nevertheless, it would be implausible to relegate such exploratory saccadic movements to the level of subintentional acts. They are not akin to random tongue-wagglings. Rather, they are performed precisely *because* of a general antecedent intention—to detect the information relevant to one's allotted task, for example. In this, they are unlike subintentional doings. However, this general antecedent intention is insufficient to individuate them. In this, they are unlike actions. Once again, the exploratory saccades employed in Yarbus-style situations are best thought of as deeds. The key, of course, is understanding the *because* in the claim that these deeds are performed *because* of a general antecedent intention. This is where the thesis of representation in action can help.

If the saccades employed by the batsman, or by agents performing more intellectual visual tasks, are deeds, rather than actions or doings, then they cannot acquire whatever representational status they possess from the general antecedent intention. Therefore, *if* these saccades were to possess representational status, then it is not a status that they could have acquired from other representational states. They would have representational status independently of their connection to other representational states. The goal of the rest of this chapter is to argue that they do, in fact, possess representational status.

6   Saccadic Representation

To qualify as deeds, the saccades agents perform in accomplishing, or attempting to accomplish, visual or visuomotor tasks would have to satisfy the criteria of representation identified and discussed in previous chapters. I shall argue that they do satisfy these criteria, and thereby count as representational. In line with the qualifications introduced earlier this does not mean that I shall claim that they are *representations* as such. Rather the claim is that (i) they play a role in the overall process of representing the world, and (ii) this role is itself a representational one. That is, the role is not merely one of *facilitating* a genuinely representational process, even if this facilitation is essential. The claim is that this role is itself genuinely representational. Or, if you do not like the word "genuine" in this context, then it is as representational as any other part of the process. This is *not* to say, of course, that the process of visually representing the world is occurring *only* in the eye movements. No one, presumably, would want to claim that. Rather, it is to claim that *some* of this process is. Clearly, what is going on inside the perceiving subject is part of the process of representing the relevant features of the world—but so, I shall argue, is what is going on outside. The process of representing the world straddles both internal and external processes. Visual representation is representational *all the way out*.

7 The Informational Constraint

Part of the problem, of course, in considering the representational status of saccades is that they are such small, rapid, and ephemeral episodes. To find something more concrete, and obvious, upon which to base our thinking, we can imagine a Yarbus case *writ large*. The basic idea is that, in certain situations, saccadic eye movements have to be accompanied, or even replaced, by gross compensatory movements of the entire head or body. There are two different contexts in which these might become necessary. One type of case is provided by creatures that are unable to perform saccadic eye movements in the same way as us—where some of the role played by our eye movements has to be taken over by compensatory movements of the head or body. These are not imaginary creatures. For example, humans, like other predatory animals, have eyes in the front of their head. Many prey animals, on the other hand, have eyes at the side of their head, to facilitate wider surveillance of the surrounding environment. As a result of this, there are certain things that they must do—things that we don't have to do—in order to see things placed in front of them. Most obviously, they have to turn their head so that the side of it—and hence an eye—is facing the object. We, of course, have to perform the corresponding movements to survey the visual scene that lies outside our peripheral vision.

The other type of case, and the one with which I am going to work, involves truncating the human visual system. As a result, information that is normally obtained by way of exploratory saccadic movements must now be obtained by way of gross movements of the head or body. For example, there is a type of goggles sometimes employed by societies such as the

Royal National Institute for the Blind as a pedagogical device. The goggles simulate a form of visual impairment by narrowing down the field of vision to a narrow tunnel. The size of this tunnel depends on the goggles, but we shall imagine an extreme version that narrows the field of vision to nothing more than foveal vision—that is, an arc that subtends approximately 3–5° of the normal human visual field.

Our visually impaired subject is, a là Yarbus, asked to perform a number of visual tasks, and then presented with a visual scene. Suppose, at least initially, this visual scene is much simpler than that employed by Yarbus. Suppose it is simply a red square on a white background. The square, however, subtends far more of the visual scene than that encompassed in foveal vision. Suppose the scene in its entirety would encompass 100 percent of the normal human visual field, and the square in the foreground would encompass 60 percent of this field. Prior to the presentation of the scene, the subject is presented with one simple question:

What *shape* is the object in the foreground?

Given his or her current impairment, the subject, to answer the question, is going to have to employ scan paths that involve moving the entire head, rather than simply saccadic movements of the eyes. Think of the movement the head will have to undergo in answering the first question. In all essentials, the movements are going to have to be such that they trace a substantial portion of the outline of the shape of the object. Indeed, to a substantial extent, the head is going to have to move in a way akin to that shape. It may not do this initially, since the subject may be testing other hypotheses about the shape. But a stable solution to the problem will involve the head tracing out a path substantially similar to the shape of the object.

The salient point is not, of course, that the scan path *resembles* the shape of the object, although it almost certainly does. The idea that representation consists in resemblance, of course, is one that has been thoroughly discredited, and rightly so. Rather, the point is that the scan path is related to the shape in such a way that it carries information about that shape. Specifically, to establish whether a shape of a given type is present, one must perform head movements of a certain type. To establish whether a square, rather than any other shape, is present in the foreground of the visual scene, then, given the truncated visual apparatus available, one must perform movements of a certain character.

We might divide the overall process into a *testing* phase, where the subject tries out various hypotheses concerning the shape of the object in the foreground, and a *determining* phase, where the subject establishes the specific character of that shape. In the testing phase, the head movements are not, of course, related to the shape of the object in any systematic or reliable way. But in the determining phase, they are related to the shape of the object in this way. And it is in the determining phase that the head movements can carry information about the shape of the object.

As we have seen, there are two distinct concepts of information that might be thought to underpin representation. The first sees informational relations as consisting in a simple increase in conditional probability. One item, X, carries information about another item, Y, when the occurrence of X increases the probability of the occurrence of Y. The second, more restricted, concept of information insists that this increase in conditional probability must be to the value of 1. That is, X carries information about Y if and only if the probability of Y given X is 1.

Consider the first concept of information. During the determining phase of the process, where the subject settles on a stable solution to the problem of what shape is present in the foreground of the visual scene, the head movements clearly carry information about this shape. Or, at least, they carry such information if we assume that subjects usually get the right answer to this problem. To conclusively establish whether one type of shape, rather than another, is present, we must perform head movements of a certain type. The presence of such movements in the determining phase of the process, therefore, raises the probability that a shape of a given type is present in the foreground of the visual scene. Therefore, given the first concept of information, the movements carry information about that shape.

Of course, subjects are not infallible. And the possibility of their being mistaken about the shape entails that this increase in conditional probability is not to the value of 1. The presence of head movements of a certain character in the determining phase of the process may increase the probability of a shape of a given type in the foreground of the visual scene, but it does not make the presence of this shape certain. However, as we have seen earlier, this fact undermines the representational status of these movements no more than it does that of internal representations, traditionally construed. The presence of an internal representation of a given type of shape would, obviously, not raise the conditional probability of the environment containing a shape of that type. And this is for precisely the same reason: the fallibility of the subject. So, to the extent that the concept of information is to play a role in explicating the concept of representation, we must be able to make sense of the idea of information obtaining in the absence of nomic correlation. Conversely, to the extent that we want to hold onto the strict sense of information as consisting in a conditional probability of 1, this undermines the representational status of the relevant deeds no more than it does that of internal representations, traditionally construed.

The experiments can be varied along at least three dimensions: (i) variations in impairment, (ii) variations in questions, and (iii) variations in scene. But the same general point emerges. Often—not necessarily, not even always, but often—the presence of a visual feature of a given type can only be established if certain head movements are performed by the subject. The occurrence of such movements in the determining phase of the process, therefore, raises the probability of the presence of a feature of a given type in the visual scene. Such movements carry information about that scene to no lesser, and no greater, extent than internal representations, traditionally construed.

The same is true of saccadic eye movements. Indeed, the preceding scenario has been designed so that head movements play precisely the same functional role as that normally played by saccades in establishing the presence of certain visual features in the environment. Thus, in the determining phase of the process of establishing the presence, or otherwise, of a shape of a certain type, the specific saccadic scan path traced raises the probability of the presence of a feature of a given type. Given the fallibility of the subject, of course, this increase in conditional probability is not to the value of 1. But, as we have seen, this undermines the representational status of the saccadic path no more than it does that of internal representations, traditionally construed.

The same sort of picture emerges when we switch from neo-Yarbus cases to cricket. In the case of competent batsmen, such as Mark and Charlie, the eyes will saccade, within 100 ms of the moment of delivery (i.e., time of release from the bowler's hand), to the anticipated bounce point. A saccade to, and resulting foveation on, a particular point thus raises the probability of the ball bouncing at that point. Thus, in the first, looser, sense of information, foveation on that point carries information about the bounce point of the ball. Batsmen are, of course, fallible, and some are more fallible than others, and so saccading to, and foveating on, a particular point does not raise the probability of a ball's having that precise bounce point to a value of 1. But, as we have seen, this compromises the representational status of the saccade and resulting foveation no more than it does that of internal representations, traditionally construed.

Therefore, it seems, in the determining if not testing phase of the process, saccadic eye movements can carry information about features of the environment to no lesser extent than internal representations traditionally construed. More precisely, whatever reasons we have for thinking that internal representations carry information applies also to the sorts of saccadic eye movements discussed above. And whatever reasons we have for thinking that such movements do not carry information applies also to internal representations. Therefore, with regard to the informational constraint, saccadic eye movements are no worse off than internal representations.

8   The Teleological Constraint

To satisfy the teleological constraint, the sorts of saccadic eye movements we have examined above would not only have to track environmental features, they would have to possess a proper *function*. Earlier, we distinguished two different forms this function might take, depending on whether one leaned toward a stimulus- or a benefit-based version of teleosemantics. We also noted that these two functions were not, necessarily, incompatible, and could be reconciled by way of the distinction between *personal* and *subpersonal* proper functions: distinct proper functions that, although belonging to the same mechanism, licensed the attribution of content to distinct items. Putting these subtleties temporarily aside, however, what will, in all cases, license the attribution of function is *history*. The first question to address, therefore, is whether the saccadic eye movements we are discussing possess the sort of history that might give them a function.

The general reasons for thinking that they do possess a history, of course, turn on the phenomenon of *perceptual learning*, a phenomenon that is well documented in a variety of domains. Perceptual learning is the specific and relatively permanent modification of perception and behavior following sensory experience. Crucially, for our purposes, the learning process involved is quite distinct from, and independent of, conscious and intentional forms of learning and involve structural and/or functional changes in primary sensory cortices.

The key for our purposes, of course, is not structural and functional changes in primary sensory cortices but differences over time in saccadic eye movements and whether these differences can be explained in terms of learning and, therefore, history. Recall Land and MacLeod's investigation of the eye movements involved in hitting a cricket ball. The investigation revealed, first, a broad similarity between the eye-movement strategies employed by three batsmen, Mark, Charlie, and Richard. All three batsmen fixate on the ball at the point of delivery (the moment it is released from the bowler's hand) and their gaze is stationary for a short period after delivery. Then they saccade to, and fixate on, the anticipated point where the ball will bounce, and gaze is focused on this point for a period of about 200ms after the bounce.

Within this general framework, however, there are clear individual differences, and these are related to the skill level of the batsmen. Two types of difference were particularly evident. First, Mark—the most accomplished of the batsmen—exhibited more pursuit-tracking than Charlie or Richard. That is, the size of his saccade from point of delivery to point of bounce was considerably smaller than that of Charlie or Richard. The remainder of the movement consisted in pursuit tracking of the ball. Second, Richard, the least skilled batsman, was far slower to initiate his prebounce saccade, taking at least 200 ms to initiate it. And this was so despite the fact that the size of his prebounce saccade was larger. This deficit, as Land and MacLeod point out, would place Richard in a difficult situation if the speed of the ball were to be increased. The ball would reach its bounce point before Richard had succeeded in saccading to that spot, and Richard would, in essence, fail to see the ball. In contrast, even on short-pitched deliveries, Mark and Charlie routinely reached the bounce point 100 ms before the ball.

The ability of an individual batsman to track the ball, then, involves both a general framework—fixate on delivery point then saccade to bounce point—and individual differences within that framework: size of saccade, time of initiation of saccade, and so forth. Both the framework and the individual differences are the result of trial-and-error learning.

Consider, first, the general framework—fixate on delivery point then saccade to bounce point. The key point, of course, is not that the ball is moving, but that it is moving in a specific way—in an arc relative to the batsman, and with a velocity that makes it inevitable that it will move outside the batsman's field of view. Because of this, visual factors such as image expansion and the rate of binocular disparity—factors that in other contexts might prove important—cannot be applied. Therefore, a distinct strategy has to be employed, and this is what results in the general framework of fixation plus saccade adopted by all three batsmen. It is clear that this strategy is something that can be identified only through trial-and-error learning.

This learning provides the strategy with a *history*. Those who fail to identify the strategy will fail to track the ball. Moreover, grossly oversimplifying, you employ the strategy on a given occasion t_3 because on earlier occasions t_1 when you did not employ the strategy you failed to track the ball, and on other occasions t_2 when you did employ the strategy you succeeded in tracking the ball. The framework—fixate on delivery point then saccade to bounce point—is employed by an individual on a given occasion because it has worked in the past for that person. And it has worked in the past for that person because it is the only strategy that provides a viable solution to the problem of tracking a moving object traveling in a given type of arc with a given type of velocity. And it provides a viable solution to this problem because of certain features of the framework, features that allow it to provide such a solution. Thus, the employment of the strategy on a given occasion is the result of certain *reproduced* features of the involved framework. And for this reason, the strategy, and the framework, has a *history*.

It is because the strategy possesses a history that it possesses a proper function. In line with earlier discussion, we can identify at least two distinct proper functions possessed by the strategy, one personal the other subpersonal. The subpersonal function of the strategy is to track the trajectory of the ball. The personal proper function is to enable the batsman to hit the ball. These functions are, of course, not incompatible.

The same claims about the history and the function of the strategy can be developed in terms not of the general framework itself, but of the individual differences within this framework. The individual differences, that is, point to the role played by learning in the development of the strategy. In this sense, they are the visible traces of the historical character of the strategy. The strategy is employed because it is the only one capable of allowing a batsman—with a human visual system at any rate—to successfully track the path of a ball moving in the sort of arc and with the sort of velocity in which cricket balls typically move. However, the strategy can be implemented more or less perfectly. Richard's "catch-up" saccadic behavior is an imperfect implementation, because although it will work for deliveries whose velocity is low, it will fail when that velocity increases above a certain threshold. When a batsman is provided with suitable exposure to deliveries above this threshold, the usual result is that he or she adapts, and the time taken to initiate the prebounce saccade is reduced. How long it takes for this adaptation to take place is usually a good indicator of the natural ability of the batsman. As Land and Macleod note, it seems that Richard is not able to anticipate the movement of the ball, and was waiting until it completed a large portion of its flight to the bounce point before starting the saccade. The perceptual learning involved here, then, consists in the ability to more rapidly identify the information, contained at the point of delivery, that is specific (in Gibson's sense) to the ball's bounce point.

The additional pursuit-tracking of the ball, exhibited by Mark but not by Charlie or Richard, after the point of delivery and before initiation of the prebounce saccade is also evidence of refinement of the technique. During this period, additional information concerning the likely bounce point can be acquired and this will allow the batsman to make a more precise determination of the bounce point. Its presence in only the professional cricketer, Mark, suggests that the ability to pursuit-track to this additional, but small, degree is an ability whose acquisition is extremely difficult and acquired only through many years of practice.

To sum up: the strategy employed by batsmen to track the flight of a cricket ball is one that results from individual, trial-and-error, *learning*. It works because it possesses certain features—pertaining to the relation between the limits of the human visual system and the trajectory and velocity of the tracked moving object—that this individual, trial-and-error learning allows one to *reproduce* from one occasion to the next. Because of this, the employment of the strategy on each new occasion has a *history*, the visible traces of which are written on it in the form of the differences in the way the strategy is implemented by batsman of differing ranges of ability. And because of this history the strategy has a proper function: to track the trajectory of the ball (subpersonal) and to enable the batsman to hit the ball (personal). The eye movements employed by batsmen in solving the problem of how to hit a cricket ball, therefore, satisfy the teleological constraint.

9   The Misrepresentation Constraint

There are at least two different ways in which the strategy employed by the batsman can misrepresent the trajectory of the ball. The first type of misrepresentation consists in failures that stem from the limits of the *batsman*. Most commonly, this will simply consist in cases where the batsman *gets it wrong*. As we have seen, the possibility of deeds misrepresenting lies in the possibility of divergence between what a deed is supposed to do, and what it in fact does; equivalently, in the possibility of divergence between the eliciting stimulus to which the deed should be a response and the eliciting stimulus to which it is in fact a response.

Thus, moving from general to particular, on the basis of information appropriated during the foveation on point of delivery, the batsman saccades to anticipated bounce point x_1, but the ball has in fact bounced at point x_2. Thus, the batsman "plays down the wrong line," or "plays off the front foot when he should have played off the back." In this case, the saccade to bounce point x_1 has the (subpersonal) proper function of indicating the ball as bouncing at that point; it is just that the ball does not, in fact, bounce there. The movement—or deed—has a proper function that enables it to be typed independently of its effects; it is just that, in this instance, it fails to fulfill this proper function. In virtue of this, the saccade to anticipated bounce point x_1 misrepresents the bounce point of the ball. This is an entirely run-of-the-mill failure of the sort akin to believing that *p* when *not-p* is the case. If we can tell a teleological story of misrepresentation for inner representational states, then we can also tell such a tale for deeds. In both cases, it is the combination of the possession of a proper function and the failure to fulfill this function that is the basis for the claim of misrepresentation. Whether the item with the proper function that it fails to fulfill is "inner" or "outer" is irrelevant to this story.

There is, however, another type of possible failure, one that pertains not to the limits of the batsman but to the limits of the *strategy* itself. Part of the allure of the great game of cricket is that the strategy employed by the batsman in tracking the ball is susceptible to subversion, sometimes fatally so, by the bowler. As we have seen, to saccade from delivery to bounce point, the batsman needs access to Φ, the declination of the bounce point relative to the horizontal. However, to access this information, the batsman needs to be able to "see over" the ball. That is, Φ becomes available to the batsman only after the ball has passed below the level of his eyes. Because of this, various circumstances can conspire to render the necessary information problematic.

There is a type of delivery known as a *beamer*. It is not generally bowled in polite games, and if it is, it is usually the result of an accident (or sometimes "accident") on the part of the bowler. With a beamer, the ball does not bounce at all. Instead, it just travels straight toward the batsman at head height (that it is at or near head height and not lower distinguishes it from the far more amenable "full toss"). Beamers do not generally dismiss batsmen. They are avoided by simply ducking or swaying out of the way. However, the problem is that, in the case of a fast beamer, the information available to the batsman at the point of delivery and soon thereafter is almost indistinguishable from the information that will be present in the case of a quite different ball; a slow *yorker*. A yorker is a ball that is designed to hit the ground at the same time as it reaches the batsman. Ideally, it will squeeze in beneath the bat and hit the stumps. In the present context, the problem is that a slow yorker can often exhibit, to the batsman at the point of delivery, the same informational profile as a fast beamer. The result is that one will sometimes find batsmen attempting to duck or sway out of the way of balls that are, in fact, directed toward their stumps, which is one of the most embarrassing things that can happen to a batsman.

The limits of the strategy can also sometimes be challenged by the simple physical dimensions of the bowler. Joel Garner, the great West Indian fast bowler, stood 6'8", and so propelled toward the batsman from a height of well over 8'. This increased the length of time required before a batsman was able to acquire the necessary information about the bounce point, and thus saccade to that point. And this often made it difficult to saccade to the bounce point in time. The result was that Garner's deliveries were sometimes very "difficult to see."

In both cases, the resulting inability to track the ball can result not from failings of the batsman as such, but from failings of the strategy. And since this is the only strategy available to the batsman, such failings are as unfortunate as they are unavoidable. In such cases, we also find examples of misrepresentation. However, these are systemic rather than individual failings. They are not akin to believing that *p* when *not-p* is the case. Rather, they are far more akin to the sort of misrepresentation involved in, say, the Müller–Lyer illusion. The visual representation of the lines as unequal is a case of misrepresentation, but it is one that stems from failings in the visual apparatus—and the various *assumptions* programmed into it—rather than failings on the part of the individual perceiver.

In the case of the ball-tracking strategy employed by the batsman, then, we can make sense of both individual and systemic types of misrepresentation. The saccadic deeds employed by the batsman can misrepresent the world both because they fail to fulfill their proper function, and because this proper function is simply not up to the exigencies of the environment.

10   The Decouplability Constraint

I have argued that—in the case of perceptual representation, though not necessarily in the case of other forms of representation—the decouplability constraint is parasitic on the teleological constraint. That is, in the case of perceptual representation, we need as much, and only as much, decouplability of representation and represented as is necessary to satisfy the teleological constraint. Therefore, since the visual scan path employed by the batsman does, in fact, satisfy the teleological constraint, we should have every reason to expect it to satisfy the decouplability constraint also.

To satisfy the teleological constraint, it must be possible for a representation of a given type to be tokened incorrectly. That is, it must be possible for a representation of type Φ to occur even if the immediate environment is not, in fact, Φ. And for this to be possible, it must be the case that the type to which a representation-token belongs does not, in general, essentially depend on the character of its immediate environment. In satisfying the teleological constraint, deeds possess a function that provides for their being typed independently of the specific nature of their *immediate* environment, though not, of course, of their *historical* environment, or their environment *in general*. So, to the extent that deeds have a function, we should expect them to satisfy the relevant form of the decouplability requirement.

The scan path employed by the batsman clearly satisfies the decouplability constraint in this requisite sense. The scan path can vary independently of the trajectory of the ball, and vice versa. Obviously, the scan path employed by the batsman makes not the slightest difference to the flight of the ball. And, as the previously defended possibility of misrepresentation makes clear, the scan path can be wholly inappropriate to the flight of the ball. So, obviously, the scan path and ball trajectory do not physically constrain each other (in the manner of the relation between arm angle and engine speed in the Watt governor). More subtly, but equally significantly, the proper function of the scan path affords its being typed independently of the trajectory the ball follows. So, the scan path and ball trajectory do not logically constrain each other (in the manner of a naïve causal theory of representation). There is no necessary individuative relationship between scan path and ball trajectory, or vice versa. If we combine these claims, we arrive at all the decouplabilty one can reasonably require for a case of visual representation. The saccadic deeds employed by the batsman in tracking the ball can satisfy the decouplability constraint, just as much as can the supposed internal visual representations of that batsman.

11   The Combinatorial Constraint

That scan paths should possess iconic, but not, of course, semantic, structure is most obvious in neo-Yarbus cases of the sort described above. In our imagined case, the subject with the tunnel-vision goggles must, to answer the question, employ scan paths facilitated by movement of the entire head. Thus, to answer the question, "what shape is the object in the foreground?" the subject's head movements will have to trace a substantial portion of the outline of the shape of the object. This may not be true of the testing phase, where the subject is trying out various hypotheses concerning the shape, but it will be true of the determining phase of the process where a stable solution to this problem is reached.

As I pointed out earlier, whether or not the scan path employed by the subject in the determining phase resembles the shape of the object is not crucial to whether this path counts as representational. Resemblance is neither necessary nor sufficient for representation. However, the fact that the scan path does, to a considerable and discernible extent, resemble the shape of the object should remove any principled reluctance to allowing that the scan path is structured iconically. Crucially, it is not simply that the scan path carries information about the shape of the object, and has the function of tracking objects of this shape, but also that the scan path is decomposable into aspects or vectors, and these carry information about aspects of the shape of the object, and, indeed, have the function of tracking aspects of this sort. In other words, the scan path, in the determining phase, has a structure that mirrors the spatial structure of the object. The structure of the scan path is, admittedly, a simple one, but this is because the object with which it coordinates is a simple one. In this sense, the scan path possesses iconic structure—a structure that maps onto the structure of the object, or rather, to that aspect of the object's structure that is pertinent to the problem being solved (in this case, the shape).

A similar, if somewhat more complex picture, emerges with respect to the scan path adopted by the batsman. Here, the problem is quite different: working out where and when the ball will reach the batsman. There is information embodied in the trajectory of the ball that is sufficient to specify this spatiotemporal location. However, given the trajectory, and the limitations of the batsman's visual system, this information becomes accessible to the batsman only at certain points in the ball's flight. The key, then, is to make sure the eyes are positioned to be able to access this information when it becomes accessible. And this is why the batsman adopts the type of scan path he or she, in fact, adopts.

In this case also, the scan path possesses an iconic structure that maps onto certain aspects of the object's structure. In this case, however, the object is the ball trajectory, and the relevant aspects of its structure consist in those accessible quantities of information that will afford the solution to the problem of where and when the ball will reach the batsman. That is, in this case, accessible, relevant information is the analogue of shape in our imagined neo-Yarbus case. The structure of the scan path is, thus, correlated with the ball trajectory, where this is structured according to the relevant, accessible, information it contains—relevant to the solution of the problem of when and where the ball will reach the batsman, and accessible given the limitations of the batsman's visual apparatus.[1]

Thus, the scan path breaks down into a certain order and it must, of course, be performed in this order if it is to succeed. Fixation on the point of delivery must precede the saccade to bounce-point. The saccade to bounce-point must precede the subsequent 100–200 ms of pursuit-tracking. Within each component of this structure, various degrees of freedom are permitted. How much of the scan path from point of delivery to bounce-point is composed of saccade and how much of pursuit-tracking is negotiable, within the limits imposed by the abilities of the batsman. But, these degrees of freedom are strictly limited. And beyond those limits the scan path can be divided up into a clear, nonnegotiable, structure. In this sense, the scan path is iconically structured. And it is structured in this way for a simple reason. Its structure reflects, or is coordinated with, a certain quantity present in the trajectory of the ball: relevant, accessible, information. The scan path is structured in the way it is because the relevant, accessible, information contained in the scan path exists only at certain points. The scan path is, thus, an iconic reflection of these points.

12   In the Beginning Was Also the Deed

Perhaps the defining tendency of modern thought is to suppose that our primary epistemic grip on the world comes from the *inside out*. Our grip on the world derives from our having representations of it, and, whatever else they may be, these are things that belong to the inside of us. If these representations are true, or reliable, then our grip on the world is an adequate one; if not, our grip is accordingly inadequate. The persistent anxieties of modern thought turn on understanding how a representation could reach out and "grasp" its object. Our ability to act on the world might admittedly help, but this help is strictly limited. For actions are also structured from the inside out: both their status and identity depends on their relation to what is on the inside. Understood in this way, the role of action is, at best, pragmatic. It can put us in a position to have new, perhaps more sophisticated, representations. But it can play no constitutive role in representation itself.

The burden of this book has been to try and argue against this picture. Our epistemic grip on the world does not come from the inside out. We are already out in the world in the form of our deeds. The deeds we employ in representing the world are *themselves* representational. These deeds do not function merely to facilitate the *real* process of representation that exists in the relation between an inner representing item and an outer represented item. We cannot even notionally separate the role played by representation and the role played by deeds in our ability to represent the world. For the role played by our deeds is itself a representational one. The vehicles of representation do not stop at the skin; they extend all the way out into the world. How do representations reach out and grasp their objects? How do I reach out and grasp my objects? I am already out there with the objects, and so too is my representing of them. Representation is representational all the way out. And in the beginning was not just the word, but also the deed.

Notes

Chapter 1

1. Davidson's classic example: sunburn. The property of being sunburnt is externally individuated in the sense that it is individuation dependent on external factors such as the presence of solar radiation. This does not entail, however, that a token instance of sunburn is located outside the skin: clearly it is not. See Davidson 1987.

2. Of course, not all models of representation will see things this way. Neural network models will typically regard the representation as something constructed on the fly. In which case, both representation and *a* representation will possess genuine duration.

3. Thanks to Larry Shapiro for this point.

Chapter 2

1. For reasons that will become clear later, I have modified McGinn's version of (iii): "the essence of *Fs* is (partly) constituted by that of *Gs*."

Chapter 3

1. The expression "the extended mind" derives from Clark and Chalmers (1998), as does the expression "active externalism." "Environmentalism" is employed by Rowlands (1999). The expression "vehicle externalism" is employed by Hurley (1998), and I am going to use that expression, given the qualifications and clarifications to follow in section 2, in a way that is recognizably akin to the use made of it by Hurley.

2. I am working here specifically with Millikan's version of teleosemantics. See chap. 8 for a detailed discussion.

3. See chap. 7 for a detailed discussion of this idea.

4. This may sound unacceptably vague. But these are early days, and the purpose of this book, in effect, is to find out just how broad this sense can be.

5. Recognizable forms of this view have been defended by Donald (1991), Hutchins (1995), Wilson (1995, 2004), Clark (1997), Clark and Chalmers (1998), Hurley (1998), Rowlands (1999, 2003), O'Regan and Noë (2001, 2002), and Noë (2004). Arguably, the daddy of them all, however, is James Gibson (1966, 1979).

6. My account differs from some other versions of the extended-mind idea by according a larger role to the notion of representation. This idiosyncrasy will be discussed at length, and defended at even greater length, later.

7. See chap. 7 for a detailed discussion.

8. This is not, of course, to say that it will in fact be utilized in further processing. Availability for utilization is one thing, actual utilization quite another.

9. See Donald 1991, Hutchins 1995, Wilson 1995, Clark 1997, 2001, Clark and Chalmers 1998, Hurley 1998, and Rowlands 1999, 2003.

10. For a discussion of the importance of our response to nonnomic properties in motivating the belief in mental representations, see Fodor 1986: 9.

11. For a balanced discussion, albeit one that leans toward the eliminativist option, see Keijzer 1998.

Chapter 4

1. Cf. Kripke 1984.

2. See chap. 6 for a detailed discussion.

3. Thanks to Andy Clark for the *infusion* metaphor.

4. See chap. 6 for a discussion and defense of this point.

Chapter 5

1. In particular, Shimojo et al. (2001) have shown that amodally filled-in figures generate afterimages, and it would be difficult to explain this in the absence of filling-in operations of some sort.

2. This is all surmise on my part, since, sadly, UK university professors' salaries don't run to Porsches.

Chapter 7

1. The reliance of informational accounts in particular on facts or states of affairs has been explicitly recognized by Israel and Perry (1990). In addition, note that I

propose to use *facts* and *states of affairs* interchangeably, and use the abridged *state* as an equivalent to *state of affairs*.

2. See Dretske 1981: 38–93 for some problems with the necessity claim.

Chapter 8

1. This definition is taken from Millikan, "Compare and Contrast Dretske, Fodor, and Millikan on Teleosemantics," in her 1993: 123.

2. Actually, unless the chameleon in question is extremely artistically gifted, the mechanism is, presumably, not sophisticated enough to replicate a Jackson Pollock *Number 4*. But, for the purposes of illustration, just suppose it is.

3. I am going to ignore Millikan's distinction between *adapted derived proper functions* and *invariant derived proper functions*. Although extremely important in some contexts, the distinction will play no role in this book.

4. Here the content of the *personal* is given simply by its opposition to the concept of the subpersonal. So, there is no claim that bees, or even beavers, are persons. If you don't like the terminology, feel free to replace the personal with the organismic (a terminology I employed in earlier work).

5. I think "food" or "eatability" provides the most plausible interpretation of the benefit, rather than "mouse," "rodent," or "mammal." The benefit is the same to the snake whether it eats a mouse, vole, or shrew (hence ruling out "mouse"), and is also the same whether it eats a mammal or an amphibian (hence ruling out "rodent" or "mammal"). In other words, the benefit to the snake cuts across all these latter interpretations.

6. This is not to say that people have not worried about indeterminacy of biological function. However, nothing in the debate between stimulus- and benefit-based versions of teleosemantics suggests that this worry is operative here. In this debate, we do find multiplicity of biological function, but there is nothing to suggest that we have to interpret this as indeterminacy of biological function.

Chapter 9

1. See Rubin 1995. I discuss Rubin's account in more detail in my 1999, chap. 6.

2. See chap. 3.

3. Actually, one presumably can do so. The property of being a horse is a composite one, and can therefore be entertained in any world where the requisite simpler properties that compose it are instantiated, as long as the subject is able to combine these properties in the requisite way. Cf. McGinn 1989, chap. 1. This wrinkle is irrelevant to the argument developed above, and I propose to henceforth ignore it.

Chapter 10

1. For the existence and importance of mental models, see Johnson-Laird 1983 and Gallistel 1993.

2. See, for example, McGinn 1989: 188.

Chapter 11

1. In the previous chapter, we witnessed a similar pattern with the structure of the gorilla's nettle-processing behavior: this structure derives from the exigencies of the task the gorilla is required to perform coupled with the limitations of the gorilla's manual apparatus.

References

Akins, C., E. Klein, and T. Zentall (2002). "Imitative learning in Japanese quail (*Conturnix japonica*) using the bidirectional control procedure." *Animal Learning and Behavior* 30, 275–281.

Akins, C., and T. Zentall (1996). "Imitative learning in male Japanese quail (*Conturnix japonica*) using the two-action method." *Journal of Comparative Psychology* 110, 316–320.

Akins, C., and T. Zentall (1998). "Imitation in Japanese quail: The role of reinforcement of demonstrator responding." *Psychonomic Bulletin and Review* 5, 694–697.

Baker, G. and P. Hacker (1984). *Scepticism, Rules, and Language*. Oxford: Blackwell.

Bargh, J., and T. Chartrand (1999). "The unbearable automaticity of being." *American Psychologist* 54, 462–479.

Bargh, J., M. Chen, and L. Burrows (1996). "Automaticity of social behaviour: Direct effects of trait construct and stereotype activation on action." *Journal of Personality and Social Psychology* 1, 230–244.

Bateson, G. (1972). *Steps to an Ecology of Mind*. New York: Ballantine.

Baumeister, R., E. Bratslavsky, M. Muraven, and D. Tice (1998). "Ego depletion: Is the active self a limited resource?" *Journal of Personality and Social Psychology* 74, 1252–1265.

Berkowitz, L. (1984). "Some effects of thoughts on anti- and prosocial influences of media events: A cognitive neo-association analysis." *Psychological Bulletin* 95, 410–427.

Berkowitz, L. (1997). "Some thoughts extending Bargh's argument." In R. Wyer, ed., *Advances in Social Cognition* 10, 83–94. Hillsdale, N.J.: Lawrence Erlbaum.

Blackmore, S., G. Brelstaff, K. Nelson, and T. Troscianko (1995). "Is the richness of our visual world an illusion? Transsaccadic memory for complex scenes." *Perception* 24, 1075–1081.

Byrne, R. (2002). "Seeing actions as hierarchically organized structures: Great ape manual skills." In A. Meltzoff and W. Prinz., eds., *The Imitative Mind: Development, Evolution, and Brain Bases*, 122–140. Cambridge: Cambridge University Press.

Byrne, R. (2003). "Imitation as behaviour parsing." *Philosphical Transactions, Royal Society of London B* 358, 529–536.

Byrne, R. (2005). "Detecting, understanding, and explaining animal imitation." In S. Hurley and N. Chater, eds., *Perspectives on Imitation: From Neuroscience to Social Science*, vol. 1. Cambridge, Mass.: MIT Press.

Byrne, R., and A. Russon (1998). "Learning by imitation: A hierarchical approach." *Behavioral and Brain Sciences* 21, 667–721.

Byrne, R., and E. Stokes (2002). "Effects of manual disability or feeding skills in gorillas and chimpanzees." *International Journal of Primatology* 23, 539–554.

Carver, C., R. Ganellen, W. Froming, and W. Chambers (1983). "Modeling: An analysis in terms of category accessibility." *Journal of Experimental Social Psychology* 66, 840–856.

Chambers, D., and D. Reisberg (1985). "Can mental images be ambiguous?" *Journal of Experimental Psychology: Human Perception and Performance* 2, 317–328.

Chartrand, T., and J. Bargh (1999). "The Chameleon effect: The perception-behavior link and social interaction." *Journal of Personality and Social Psychology*, 76, 893–910.

Chomsky, N. (1957). *Syntactic Structures*. The Hague: Mouton.

Clark, A. (1997). *Being There: Putting Brain, Body, and World Back Together Again*. Cambridge, Mass.: MIT Press.

Clark, A. (2001). *Mindware*. Oxford: Oxford University Press.

Clark, A., and D. Chalmers (1998). "The extended mind." *Analysis* 58, 7–19.

Clark, A., and J. Toribio (1994). "Doing without representing?" *Synthese* 101, 401–431.

Davidson, D. (1984). *Inquiries into Truth and Interpretation*. Oxford: Oxford University Press.

Davidson, D. (1987). "Knowing one's own mind." *Proceedings of the American Philosophical Association* 60, 441–458.

Dawkins, R. (1976). "Hierarchical organization: A candidate principle for ethology." In P. Bateson and R. Hinde, eds., *Growing Points in Ethology*, 7–54. Cambridge: Cambridge University Press.

Dennett, D. (1991). *Consciousness Explained*. Boston: Little, Brown.

Dijksterhuis, A. (2004). "Why we are social animals: The high road to imitation as social glue." In S. Hurley and N. Chater, eds., *Perspectives on Imitation: From Neuroscience to Social Science*, vol. 2. Cambridge, Mass.: MIT Press.

Dijksterhuis, A., J. Bargh, and J. Miedema (2000). "Of men and mackerels: Attention and automatic behavior." In H. Bless and J. Forgas, eds., *Subjective Experience in Social Cognition and Behavior*. Philadelphia: Psychology Press.

Dijksterhuis, A., and A. van Knippenburg (1998). "The relation between perception and behaviour or how to win a game of Trivial Pursuit." *Journal of Personality and Social Psychology* 74, 865–877.

Donald, M. (1991). *Origins of the Modern Mind*. Cambridge, Mass.: Harvard University Press.

Dretske, F. (1981). *Knowledge and the Flow of Information*. Oxford: Blackwell.

Dretske, F. (1986). "Misrepresentation." In R. Bogdan, ed., *Belief*. Oxford: Oxford University Press.

Dretske, F. (1990). "Reply to reviewers." *Philosophy and Phenomenological Research* 1 (4), 819–839.

Fisher, E., R. Haines, and T. Price (1980). "Head-up transition behavior of pilots with and without head-up display in simulated low visibility approaches." NASA technical paper (F1, aJKO).

Fodor, J. (1986). *Psychosemantics*. Cambridge, Mass.: MIT Press.

Fodor, J. (1990). *A Theory of Content and Other Essays*. Cambridge, Mass.: MIT Press.

Fodor, J., and Z. Pylyshyn (1988). "Connectionism and cognitive architecture: A critical analysis." *Cognition* 28, 3–71.

Foley, J. (1990). *Traditional Oral Epic: The Odyssey, Beowulf, and the Serbo-Croatian Return Song*. Berkeley: University of California Press.

Gallese, V. (2004). "'Being like me': Self–other identity, mirror neurons, and empathy." In S. Hurley and N. Chater, eds., *Perspectives on Imitation: From Neuroscience to Social Science*, vol. 1. Cambridge, Mass.: MIT Press.

Gallese, V., L. Fadiga, L. Fogassi, and G. Rizzolatti (1996). "Action recognition in the premotor cortex." *Brain* 119, 593–609.

Gallistel, C. (1993). *The Organization of Learning*. Cambridge, Mass.: MIT Press.

Gibson, J. (1966). *The Senses Considered as Perceptual Systems*. New York: Houghton-Mifflin.

Gibson, J. (1979). *The Ecological Approach to Visual Perception*. New York: Houghton-Mifflin.

Gould, D. (1967). "Pattern recognition and eye movement parameters." *Perception and Psychophysics* 2, 399–407.

Haines, R. (1991). "A breakdown in simultaneous information processing." In E. Obrecht and L. Stark, eds., *Presbyopia Research: From Molecular Biology to Visual Adaptation*. New York: Plenum Press.

Haugeland, J. (1991). "Representational genera." In W. Ramsey, S. Stich, and J. Garron, eds., *Philosophy and Connectionist Theory*. Hillsdale, N.J.: Lawrence Erlbaum.

Helmholtz, H. von (1909). *Physiological Optics*, 3 vols. Trans. J. Southall. New York: Optical Society of America.

Herman, L. (2002). "Vocal, social, and self-imitation by bottle-nosed dolphins." In K. Dautenhahn and C.Nehaniv, eds., *Imitation in Animals and Artifacts*. Cambridge, Mass.: MIT Press.

Hunt, G., and R. Gray (2003). "Diversification and cumulative evolution in New Caledonian crow tool manufacture." *Proceedings of the Royal Society London B*, 270, 867–874.

Hurley, S. (1998). *Consciousness in Action*. Cambridge, Mass.: Harvard University Press.

Hurley, S., and N. Chater, eds. (2004). *Perspectives on Imitation: From Neuroscience to Social Science*, 2 vols. Cambridge, Mass.: MIT Press.

Hutchins, E. (1995). *Cognition in the Wild*. Cambridge, Mass.: MIT Press.

Iacaboni, M. (2004). "Understanding others: Imitation, language, empathy." In S. Hurley and N. Chater, eds., *Perspectives on Imitation: From Neuroscience to Social Science*, vol. 1. Cambridge, Mass.: MIT Press.

Israel, D., and J. Perry (1990). "What is information?" In P. Hanson, ed., *Information, Language, and Cognition*. Oxford: Oxford University Press.

Johnson-Laird, P. (1983). *Mental Models: Towards a Cognitive Science of Language Inference, and Consciousness*. Cambridge: Cambridge University Press.

Keijzer, F. (1998). "Doing without representations which specify what to do." *Philosophical Psychology* 9, 323–346.

Kripke, S. (1980). *Naming and Necessity*. Oxford: Blackwell.

Kripke, S. (1984). *Wittgenstein on Rules and Private Language*. Cambridge, Mass.: Harvard University Press.

Land, M., and P. MacLeod (2000). "From eye movements to actions: How batsmen hit the ball." *Nature Neuroscience* 3, 1340–1345.

Lashley, K. (1951). "The problem of serial order in behaviour." In L. Jefress, ed., *Cerebral Mechanisms in Behaviour: The Hixon Symposium*, 112–136. New York: Wiley.

Lloyd, D. (1989). *Simple Minds*. Cambridge, Mass.: MIT Press.

Loftus, G. (1972). "Eye fixations and recognition memory for pictures." *Cognitive Psychology* 3, 525–551.

Mack, A., and I. Rock (1998). *Inattentional Blindness*. Cambridge, Mass.: MIT Press.

Mackay, D. (1967). "Ways of looking at perception." In W. Watthen-Dunn, ed., *Models for the Perception of Speech and Visual Form*. Cambridge, Mass.: MIT Press.

Marr, D. (1982). *Vision*. San Francisco: W. H. Freeman.

Maturana, H., and F. Varela (1980). *Autopoiesis and Cognition*. Dordrecht: Reidel.

McCullough, G. (1994). *The Mind and Its World*. London: Routledge.

McDowell, J. (1986). "Singular thought and the extent of inner space." In P. Pettit and J. McDowell, eds., *Subject, Thought, and Context*, 136–169. Oxford: Oxford University Press.

McDowell, J. (1993). "Wittgenstein on following a rule." In A. Moore, ed., *Meaning and Reference*, 257–293. Oxford: Oxford University Press.

McDowell, J. (1994). *Mind and World*. Cambridge, Mass.: Harvard University Press.

McDowell, J. (1998). "Meaning and intentionality in Wittgenstein's later philosophy." In his *Mind, Value, and Reality*. Cambridge, Mass.: Harvard University Press. Originally published in *Midwest Studies in Philosophy* 17 (1992), 30–42.

McGinn, C. (1982). "The structure of content." In A. Woodfield, ed., *Thought and Object*, 207–258. Oxford: Oxford University Press.

McGinn, C. (1989). *Mental Content*. Oxford: Blackwell.

Miller, G., E. Galanter, and K. Pribram (1960). *Plans and the Structure of Behavior*. New York: Holt.

Millikan, R. (1984). *Language, Thought, and Other Biological Categories*. Cambridge, Mass.: MIT Press.

Millikan, R. (1989). "Biosemantics." In Millikan 1993: 83–101.

Millikan, R. (1993). *White Queen Psychology, and Other Essays for Alice*. Cambridge, Mass.: MIT Press.

Milner, A., and M. Goodale (1995). *The Visual Brain in Action*. Oxford: Oxford University Press.

Muraven, M., D. Tice, and R. Baumeister (1998). "Self-control as limited resource: Regulatory depletion patterns." *Journal of Personality and Social Psychology* 74, 774–789.

Neander, K. (1995). "Misrepresenting and malfunctioning." *Philosophical Studies* 79.

Neisser, U. (1979). "The control of information pickup in selective looking." In A. Pick, ed., *Perception and Its Development*. Hillfield, N.J.: Lawrence Erlbaum.

Newell, A., J. Shaw, and H. Simon (1958). "Elements of a theory of human problem solving." *Psychological Review* 65, 151–166.

Newell, A., and H. Simon (1972). *Human Problem Solving*. New York: Prentice Hall.

Noë, A., ed. (2002a). *Is the Visual World a Grand Illusion?* Special edition of *Journal of Consciousness Studies* 9, 5–6.

Noë, A. (2002b). "Is the visual world a grand illusion?" In Noë 2002a: 1–12.

Noë, A. (2004). *Action in Perception*. Cambridge, Mass.: MIT Press.

Nørretranders, T. (1998). *The User Illusion*. New York: Viking.

O'Regan, K. (1992). "Solving the 'real' mysteries of visual perception: The world as an outside memory." *Canadian Journal of Psychology* 46, 461–488.

O'Regan, K., H. Deubel, J. Clark, and R. Rensink (2000). "Picture changes during blinks: Looking without seeing and seeing without looking." *Visual Cognition* 7, 191–212.

O'Regan, K., and A. Noë (2001). "A sensorimotor account of vision and visual consciousness." *Behavioral and Brain Sciences* 23, 939–973.

O'Regan, K. and A. Noë (2002). "What it is like to see: A sensorimotor theory of perceptual experience." *Synthese* 79, 79–103.

O'Regan, K., R. Rensink, and J. Clark (1996). "'Mud splashes' render picture changes invisible." *Investigations of Opthalmological Vision Science* 37, S213.

O'Shaughnessy, B. (1980). *The Will*, 2 volumes. Cambridge: Cambridge University Press.

Papineau, D. (2003). "Is representation rife?" *Ratio*, 16, 2, 107–123.

Pepperburg, I. (1999). *The Alex Studies: Cognitive and Communicative Studies on Grey Parrots*. Cambridge, Mass.: Harvard University Press.

Pepperburg, I. (2002). "Allospecific referential speech acquisition in Grey parrots (*psittacus erithacus*): Evidence for multiple levels of avian vocal imitation." In K. Dautenhahn and C. Nehaniv, eds., *Imitation in Animals and Artifacts*. Cambridge, Mass.: MIT Press.

Pepperburg, I. (2004). "Insights into vocal imitation in Grey parrots (*psittacus eritha-cus*)." In S. Hurley and N. Chater, eds., *Perspectives on Imitation: From Neuroscience to Social Science*, vol. 1. Cambridge, Mass.: MIT Press.

Putnam, H. (1975). "The meaning of 'meaning.'" In K. Gunderson ed., *Language, Mind, and Knowledge*: *Minnesota Studies in the Philosophy of Science*, 7, 131–193. Minneapolis: University of Minnesota Press.

Rensink, R. (2000). "Seeing, sensing, and scrutinizing." *Vision Research*, 40, 1469–1487.

Rensink, R., K. O'Regan, and J. Clark (1997). "To see or not to see: The need for attention to perceive changes in scenes." *Psychological Science* 8, 368–373.

Rizzolatti, G., L. Fadiga, and V. Gallese (2002). "From mirror neurons to imitatory facts and speculations." In A. Meltzoff and W. Prinz, eds., *The Imitative Mind: Development, Evolution, and Brain Bases*, 247–266. Cambridge: Cambridge University Press.

Rowlands, M. (1997). "Teleological semantics." *Mind* 106, 279–303.

Rowlands, M. (1999). *The Body in Mind: Understanding Cognitive Processes*. Cambridge: Cambridge University Press.

Rowlands, M. (2001). *The Nature of Consciousness*. Cambridge: Cambridge University Press.

Rowlands, M. (2002). "Two dogmas of consciousness." In Noë 2002a: 158–180.

Rowlands, M. (2003). *Externalism: Putting Mind and World Back Together Again*. London: Acumen.

Rubin, D. (1995). *Remembering in Oral Traditions*. Oxford: Oxford University Press.

Saffran, J., R. Aslin, and E. Newport (1996). "Statistical learning by 8-month-old infants." *Science* 274, 1926–1928.

Shimojo, S., Y. Kamitani, and S. Nishida (2001). "Afterimage of perceptually filled-in surface." *Science* 293, 1677.

Simons, D. (2000). "Attentional capture and inattentional blindness." *Trends in Cognitive Sciences* 4, 147–155.

Simons, D., and C. Chabris (1999). "Gorillas in our midst: Sustained inattentional blindness for dynamic events." *Perception* 28, 1059–1074.

Simons, D., and D. Levin (1997). "Change blindness." *Trends in Cognitive Sciences* 1, 261–267.

Skarda, C., and W. Freeman (1987). "How brains make chaos in order to make sense of the world." *Behavioral and Brain Sciences* 10, 161–195.

Smithers, T. (1994). "Why better robots make it harder." In D. Cliff, P. Husbands, J. Meyer, and S. Wilson, eds., *From Animals to Animats*, vol. 3, 64–72. Cambridge, Mass.: MIT Press.

Stokes, E., and R. Byrne (2001). "Cognitive capacities for behavioral flexibility in wild chimpanzees: The effect of snare injury on complex manual food processing." *Animal Cognition*, 4, 11–28.

Strawson, P. (1959). *Individuals: An Essay in Descriptive Metaphysics*. London: Methuen.

Thelen, E., and L. Smith (1994). *A Dynamic Systems Approach to the Development of Cognition and Action*. Cambridge, Mass.: MIT Press.

Thorndike, E. (1898). "Animal intelligence: An experimental study of the associative process in animals." *Psychology Review Monographs* 2, 551–553.

Tomasello, M. (1990). "Cultural transmission in the tool use and communicatory signalling of chimpanzees." In S. Parker and K. Gibson, eds., *"Language" and Intelligence in Monkeys and Apes*. Cambridge: Cambridge University Press.

Tomasello, M., A. Kruger, and H. Ratner (1993). "Cultural learning." *Behavioral and Brain Sciences* 16, 495–552.

van Gelder, T. (1995). "What might cognition be, if not computation?" *Journal of Philosophy* 92, 345–381.

Webb, B. (1994). "Robotic experiments in cricket phonotaxis." In D. Cliff, P. Husbands, J. Meyer, and S. Wilson, eds., *From Animals to Animats*, vol. 3. Cambridge, Mass.: MIT Press.

Wheeler, M. (1994). "From activation to activity." *Artificial Intelligence and the Simulation of Behaviour (AISB) Quarterly* 87, 36–42.

Whitehead, A. (1911). *An Introduction to Mathematics*. New York: Holt.

Whiten, A., V. Horner, C. Litchfield, and S. Marshall-Pescini (2004). "How do apes ape?" *Learning and Behaviour*, 32, 36–52.

Wilson, R. (1995). *Cartesian Psychology and Physical Minds: Individualism and the Sciences of the Mind*. New York: Cambridge University Press.

Wilson, R. (2004). *Boundaries of the Mind: The Individual in the Fragile Sciences*. New York: Cambridge University Press.

Wittgenstein, L. (1953). *Philosophical Investigations*. Trans. E. Anscombe; ed. E. Anscombe, R. Rhees, and G. von Wright. Oxford: Blackwell.

Yantis, S. (1996). "Attentional capture in vision." In A. Kramer, M. Coles, and G. Logan, eds., *Converging Operations in the Study of Selective Visual Attention*, 45–76. Washington, D.C.: American Psychological Association.

Yarbus, A. (1967). *Eye Movements and Vision*. New York: Plenum Press.

Index